ETHAN CROSS

"Francis Ackerman is a
manipulative monster with a corrupt conscience."
The Times

"The surprises are fast and furious
and will leave you breathless to read more."
Gardner, #1 *New York Times* **bestselling author of** *Find Her*

"A fast paced, all too real thriller with
a villain right out of James Patterson and *Criminal Minds*."
Andrew Gross, #1 *New York Times* **bestselling author of** *Reckless*

"*Silence of the Lambs* meets *The Bourne Identity*."
Brian S. Wheeler, author of *Mr. Hancock's Signature*

"An intense novel that will have you locking your
windows and doors, installing a safe room and taking
Ambien so you can sleep through the night after finishing."
Jeremy Robinson, author of *Pulse* **and** *Instinct*

"A superbly crafted thriller skillfully delving into
the twisted mind of a psychopath and the tormented soul
of the man destined to bring him down."
D.B. Henson, bestselling author of *Deed to Death*

"A taut, violent and relentless nightmare."
A.J. Hartley, bestselling author of *What Time Devours*

"A great mix of gruesome murders,
a psychotic killer, revenge and great writing."
CrimeSquad

By Ethan Cross

THE ACKERMAN THRILLERS

I Am the Night
I Am Fear
I Am Pain
I Am Wrath
I Am Hate
I Am Vengeance

I
AM
VENGEANCE

ETHAN CROSS

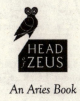

An Aries Book

I Am Vengeance
was previously published as
The Taker

First published as *The Taker* in the United States
in 2020 by Fiction Studio Books
The Story Plant, The Aronica-Miller Publishing Project, LLC

This edition first published in the United Kingdom by Head of Zeus in 2021
An Aries book

9 7 5 3 1 2 4 6 8

A CIP catalogue record for this book is available
from the British Library.

ISBN (PBO): 9781838931049
ISBN (E): 9781838931032

Printed and bound by CPI Group (UK) Ltd, Croydon, CR0 4YY

Aries
5–8 Hardwick Street
London EC1R 4RG
WWW.HEADOFZEUS.COM

To my dad, Leroy, for being a better father than
any of those found in these stories...

PART 1

1

Maggie Carlisle awoke atop a sea of bones. Some were brittle as kindling and crunched beneath her weight, sending clouds of dust and spores into her face. Rolling over, she discovered that when her captor had dropped her into this pit, she had landed atop a set of remains no older than a couple of years. She dry-heaved from the rancid smell of the pit, which caused starbursts of pain to explode out from a wound in her side. Pulling up her shirt, she found that a shard from a rib bone had punctured her abdomen. As she debated on whether it would be best to pull the bone or leave it in place, the realization struck that she could currently see inside the pit, although it had been pitch black when the Taker had pulled back the sheet of metal covered with sand, which hid the twenty-five foot drop into his personal den of horror, and threw her into the darkness below.

Searching for the source of the illumination and crawling toward the faint glow, she discovered a flashlight with a crank mounted to its side. It was the kind that didn't require external batteries and was instead powered by the wielder manually charging the device by spinning the crank. The flashlight's beam was already growing dim. Without the light, she knew that darkness inside the burial pit would be absolute, but she wondered if that would be for the best.

Although, she supposed she still wouldn't be able to escape the smells of the fresher victims.

The entire floor of the teardrop-shaped pit was covered with bones. Some old and white and free of flesh. Others appeared almost ancient, like something from a museum exhibit. But many of the remains were still bloody and stinking of decay. She noticed some kind of black bugs swarming the fresher corpses, slowly devouring the dead flesh. Perhaps, it would be a small blessing to allow the darkness to take her and escape watching the feast for long. Although, she would still see the gore in her mind's eye, and imagining those same black bugs burrowing under her skin for their next meal was not a comforting thought. In fact, the idea caused tears to flow down her cheeks and every muscle in her body to tremble, which caused her even greater pain.

Having decided to leave the bone in place—fearing blood loss and dehydration more than infection—she allowed the light to go out for a moment while she tried to bring her body under control and regain some of her strength. Pushing aside thoughts of her impending death, she instead concentrated on happier times and tried to ignore all the pain and death surrounding her at the moment.

In the darkness, her mind focused in on her baby brother, Tommy. She had always loved playing hide and seek. She and her brother would spend hours playing the game. Each aspiring to be the one to stay hidden the longest. She remembered climbing up into the rafters of the barn at her grandparents' farm, and her brother finally giving up and enduring the shameful process of announcing his defeat and conceding to her superior skills.

But then her brother was taken, and she learned that her hiding and seeking abilities were not nearly as astute as she believed.

After twenty years of banging her head against the wall with little to no progress in the case, help had come from two of the most unlikely of sources: Francis Ackerman Jr.— an infamous serial killer turned government consultant— and a random photograph her mother had received in the mail.

Ackerman had glanced over the same papers that she had spent years of her life studying and had pulled out several new threads for the investigation. During his time as a consultant for the Shepherd Organization, she had witnessed Ackerman save literally hundreds of lives, including her own. Despite all that, and the fact that she had accepted his help as a necessary evil, she couldn't allow herself to forgive the killer for his crimes, which included the murder of one of her closest friends.

She didn't deny that he was a different man than he was during what he referred to as "The Dark Years," and she supposed that a more enlightened person would be able to move forward and start anew. But that was something that she couldn't do. Maggie was amazed by a women like Emily Morgan, who had gone from one of Ackerman's victims to his counselor and friend.

Despite any good he'd done or atonement he'd achieved, she hated him. A part of her felt guilty that she couldn't release those negative emotions. Ackerman had proven himself time and time again. He had been the one who opened the door and sent her on this journey, one she hoped would finally complete the game of hide and seek that she and her brother had been playing for the past twenty years.

Regardless of her feelings, as Special Agent Maggie Carlisle sat in the dark, atop a sea of bones, her only comfort was that she knew Ackerman would find her and kill the man who had stolen her brother—an unsub whom law enforcement had dubbed the Taker.

She knew Ackerman would kill the Taker because that was what he did. He was a hunter, a predator. She simply needed to give him a target and motivation, and her becoming the Taker's next victim would provide both. Her bones were about to join the mass grave of countless others, and when Ackerman found her body, she knew that he would make the Taker pay dearly for his crimes.

And even if Ackerman didn't, she knew that the man she loved would finish the job.

Special Agent Marcus Williams was Ackerman's brother and a hard and dangerous man in his own right, but she had known him in ways that she suspected no one else ever had, even the mother of his son. Marcus was gruff, stubborn, and never passed up the opportunity to make a smartass comment, and yet, he was also kind, funny, and loyal to the point that she had no doubt he would die for her without even the slightest hesitation. The pain of her guilt nearly overshadowed the pain from her wounds, but this had been the only path she could imagine to flush out the man who had taken her brother.

Certain that Marcus and Ackerman would be coming for the Taker hard and fast, she realized that the game was already won, the case all but closed. Like a sacrificial pawn, her demise would pave the way for justice to finally be done. Thinking of all the bones that now surrounded her, all the lives this man had stolen, she supposed that her own life was a small price to pay to ensure that no other families, no other sisters, would be torn apart by the perversions of the Taker's twisted mind and blackened heart.

2

When Liana Nakai was eight years old—after having seen *Annie* for the first time—she had prayed to the Great Spirit to take her away to live with a rich white man like the little girl in the movie. Upon waking the next morning, she had found her hogan empty and had feared the worst. She had imagined herself being used as a lesson for her people. The story of the girl who wished away the world. Her mother had been out tending to the blue corn that her family used to grow when they lived in the valley. Even though the fear had been nothing more than a shadow, the incident had given the eight-year-old Liana Nakai nightmares for months to come.

She had thought the lesson learned, but apparently, she had a bad habit of not being careful with her wishes. Right before the man calling himself Frank walked into the Roanhorse Police Outpost covered in blood, Liana had wished for a strong man to save her from the monotony of her dead-end life in this dead-end place.

She had been assigned desk duty on the slowest night of the week during the slowest shift of the week. The other three officers in her tiny department treated her like a child in need of protection, clinging to their people's traditions of the proud male warriors protecting the feeble females.

Liana resented them tremendously for underestimating her. She could hold her own with any of her male counterparts physically, and she trumped them all in brains and schooling. Having received a degree in criminal justice, she often wondered how she ended up right back on the Rez, working as a tribal police officer and making a quarter of what she could have been making as a paralegal in one of the belegana cities.

But she supposed it was no mystery why she had come back. Grandmother was sick and refused to leave the only home she had ever known. Liana couldn't really blame the old woman. At first, even she had been intimidated by the idea of living among the whites. There hadn't been much of a choice. She couldn't abandon Grandmother, and the fading matriarch refused to budge. So, for the foreseeable future, she was still confined to the cage she had been fighting to escape her whole life.

Liana had been expecting an uneventful night pretending to fill out reports while listening to an audiobook. Instead, only an hour into her shift, the door to the small station house burst open, and the most handsome man she had ever seen stepped inside. He wore a pair of blue jeans and no shirt. His exposed torso was all muscle and sinew, and fresh blood covered his whole body.

Her initial thought was that there had been an accident of some kind, but then she noticed the man's demeanor. He wasn't frantic or afraid. He seemed to be without a care in the world. A man without fear. Her police training told her that he must have been in shock.

"Sir, I need you to remain calm and tell me what happened. Were you in some sort of an accident?"

"Why do you ask? Oh yes, the blood. No, it's not mine."

"Then whose blood is it," she said. Liana's hand had been inching ever closer to the Glock pistol mounted on her hip. Placing her palm over the butt of the weapon, she added, "Sir, I'm going to need to see your hands."

"How many officers are on duty right now? Are you the only one here?"

"Hands. Now," Liana said as she pulled her pistol and trained it on the newcomer.

"If I wanted to report a crime, is there some sort of form I need to fill out?"

Liana took aim at a spot in the middle of the terrifying interloper's chest. Keying the radio attached to her shoulder, she said, "Officer Nakai at the station. I need immediate backup."

A voice she recognized as belonging to Officer Pitka replied, "Pitka, two minutes out. What's the situation?"

"Possible homicide," Liana said, her voice cracking.

The blood-covered belegana merely looked around the tiny station house as if he were there on some kind of routine business, just some guy filing a noise complaint or reporting the theft of a lawnmower.

"Sir, I'm not going to ask you again. Raise your hands slowly. No sudden movements."

With a roll of his eyes, the man finally complied and raised his hands over his head. As he did, she noticed that he held two cylindrical objects in his hands. "What are you holding? Drop whatever it is right now, or I will have no choice but to fire."

"I'm afraid that may be a bit of a problem. You see, these are glued into my palms. I couldn't drop them if I wanted to."

"Who would do something like that?" Liana said before she had even realized she had spoken aloud. There was nothing in the handbook, no training at the academy on how to handle a situation like this. Despite her degree and knowledge, her mind was a blank. All she could think to do was to keep her gun on the target and wait for the others to arrive.

The bloody man said, "Actually, I glued them there myself."

"Why would you do that? And whose blood is all over you?"

"Yes, well, about that. I'm here to report a murder. Well, more precisely, several murders."

3

Francis Ackerman Jr. liked the young Navajo Nation Police officer from the moment he had laid eyes upon her. She reminded him slightly of the Mayan girl who had taken his virginity, but there was more to it than that. She had something that so many lacked, a spark in her eyes, a transcendent fire just waiting to burst forth.

The average normal would have likely admired her spunk and would have elected to take it easy on her during the coming altercation. The old Ackerman would have enjoyed extinguishing such a fire slowly through pain and blood. The present version of himself, which he had come to view as Ackerman 2.0, felt a strange stirring to show dominance over her, but he had also been given a holy mission, the nature of which endowed him with a level of self-control he had never experienced before.

He was about to cause bodily harm to the young officer, but only because it was part of the plan. Not because he was going to enjoy it. Of course, that wasn't to say that he wouldn't thoroughly enjoy the rush of battle, but he wasn't rushing to battle for enjoyment's sake. And he felt that to be a definite step in the right direction.

The backup officer whom Officer Nakai had radioed, responded in a shaky, breathless voice that said he was already rushing to her aid. Ackerman had no intelligence about the officers on duty and wasn't sure whether the quick response was merely a superb dedication to the job or if there were certain undertones of affection between the young female officer and her partner. Just one of a million facts he filed away for possible exploitation.

Ackerman knew that many would find his methods and machinations distasteful, but as always, he maintained that the shortest distance between two points is a straight line. And when someone he cared about was missing, Ackerman wouldn't hesitate to steamroll anyone who got in the way of his straight line.

Unfortunately, by no fault of her own, Officer Nakai had found herself in his path.

He had hoped she would wait for backup before approaching, that would make it easier on her. Since he wouldn't have to render her temporarily unconscious while he waited for her friends to arrive. In an effort to be as responsible as the circumstance allowed, he preferred to limit himself to one performance of higher difficulty rather than several small showings.

The door to the tiny substation of the Navajo police flew open and a wild-eyed American Indian youth stormed in with his weapon drawn and its hammer cocked. The newcomer was a squat but muscular young man wearing the earth-toned uniform of the Navajo Tribal Police. Waving his Glock 22 like it was a cross warding off evil spirits, the male officer caught sight of him and immediately shouted, "Get down on the ground!"

Officer Nakai had taken the opportunity to round the desk and move into position to assist. She said, "Place your hands behind your back and get down on the ground."

"I don't think so," he replied.

"Get down or we will be forced to taze you."

Ackerman laughed. "I enjoy a good jolt as much as the next guy, but I'm afraid that I will have to respectfully decline. Are there more officers coming or are you my only two playmates this evening?"

The male officer ignored him completely and shouted his instructions again. "Get do—"

Before the last word had left the officers mouth, Ackerman sprung into action. With a jerk of his arms and a flick of his wrist, he extended the collapsible batons he held in each hand. The weapons were a standard for most police officer's utility belts, and when they were extended to their full length of nearly three feet, they increased Ackerman's effective reach enough that the distance the officers had placed between themselves and their blood-covered interloper had been completely mitigated.

Dropping low and spinning on his heels, Ackerman took the two officers completely by surprise.He heard the sound of the Taser discharging and the air rushing past his right shoulder as the barbed prongs of the device embedded themselves in the wooden paneling that covered the walls of the station.

Ackerman had no fear that he would fail in his task of overwhelming both officers. First of all, he was well-versed in several martial arts disciplines and had honed those skills on countless opponents over the years. Second, due to the neurosurgical experimentation of his deranged father, Francis Ackerman Jr. was incapable of feeling fear. He was once bitter about the years of torture he had endured at the hands of his progenitor. Anger at the world had fueled a man who had been designed from the ground up to be the perfect killing machine. But then Ackerman had connected with a brother he didn't even know he had and discovered that destiny had merely been grooming him for the great works to come.

He had also learned that his lack of fear gave him a split second advantage in nearly every circumstance. While others experienced a moment of doubt and indecision, he merely analyzed the situation and reacted.

For the current encounter, that reaction took the form of a roll to the ground and a hard swipe of one of the collapsible batons directed at the achilles tendon of the male officer. Then, as the man left his feet, Ackerman brought the other baton down on the officer's chest, driving the air from the man's lungs and momentarily taking him out of the fight.

Officer Nakai squeezed off a shot that sailed wide, and Ackerman hurled one of the batons in her direction. The metal weapon struck her in the chest, doubling her over.

Before the baton fell to the ground, he rushed forward caught the weapon and brought it down on Officer Nakai's arm, causing her to release a shrill cry of pain and drop her gun. With a reaction time that spoke of skill and training, the young woman ignored the pain in her right arm and pulled a can of pepper spray with her left. Ackerman merely disarmed her again and then brought the full force of one of the batons to bear on the back of her thigh, bringing her down to the speckled linoleum.

The male backup officer was starting to recover and acquiring a target with his Glock 22, but Ackerman easily disarmed him with a few well-placed blows designed to demonstrate exactly who was in charge.

With both officers rolling on the ground, clutching

wounded limbs, Ackerman retrieved their sidearms, ejected the magazines and the chambered rounds and then disengaged the locking mechanism of the top slide and pulled it free from the lower assembly, rendering the weapons inert. The male officer was still trying to stand and required a bit more negative reinforcement. Once that was done, Ackerman—whistling the "Heigh-Ho!" song of Disney's seven dwarves—retrieved the Tasers and removed the batteries from those weapons.

Then he pulled over a metal folding chair between the two tribal officers and waited while the young ones tried to reconcile their defeat.

The woman asked, "Who are you?"

With a small smile spreading across his face, Ackerman said, "You've heard of Pandora's box, I assume. I'm kind of like that. If you poured all of the darkness in the world, the pain, the death, all the depravity of which man is capable, and dumped that into the life of a child—that would be me. I am the amalgamation of all the world's worst monsters. I am the night, imbued by a darkness that few have witnessed but all men fear on a primal level."

She looked at him as if he had just declared himself to be the re-incarnated spirit of Elvis. She said, "What do you want?"

In response, he held out both wrists to her in surrender and said, "I'm here to turn myself in."

4

Due to budgetary constraints, only the larger tribal police substations held actually jail cells, the closest being the headquarters at Shiprock, which was over a two hours' drive. The prospect of riding over a hundred miles with a clearly insane white man in her back seat terrified Officer Liana Nakai. She hoped that when the captain arrived those wouldn't be his orders.

They had placed the now compliant assailant into the small barred cell that filled one of the substation's corners. It was really nothing more than a fenced off six-by-six square with a cot along the back wall. It wasn't actually a proper jail cell and was never supposed to be used for real criminals. The officers of Roanhorse had simply gotten tired of driving two hours to throw someone in the drunk tank, especially when their most frequent customer had a tendency to urinate and defecate on himself. They had all taken a turn driving a stench-filled squad car to Shiprock. Still, Liana would have picked a feces covered drunk over a blood covered madman any day of the week.

The stranger now sat ramrod straight on the cot, staring out at her and Ernie Pitka, the officer who had rushed to her aid. She tried to identify the expression on the stranger's face. After a moment, she settled on "whimsical curiosity."

Liana said, "Where did all the blood come from? Is someone hurt? Did you attack someone?"

"I've done many terrible things to people over the years, far worse than the damage I've caused tonight. But yes, certain people from your town are definitely experiencing an evening of unsettling ramifications. And this is only the beginning."

"Who? Where?"

"All good questions, but I'm afraid that I can only provide that information to the man in charge of your little town."

"Captain Yazzie is on his way, but if you—"

"I wasn't referring to your commanding officer. I'm waiting for the man who pulls your superior's strings."

Upon considering the statement, Liana surmised that there was only one man in town fitting that description, the business man who had founded the town and employed nearly all of the residents at his ranch. John Canyon had inherited a small sheep farm from his father and had turned it into one of the largest Basque-style sheep and cattle operations in the Southwest. But everyone in town also quietly accepted that John Canyon traded in much more than sheep and not all of his business endeavors were strictly legal.

Liana wondered what connection the stranger had to Canyon and whatever illicit dealings Canyon was caught up in, but if their benevolent benefactor was involved, then Captain Yazzie would want to handle this situation personally. He had informed her on her first day as to the policy involving Mr. Canyon and the ranch. The man was loved by most everyone in the county and had powerful connections on both the tribal council and the government beyond the reservation. Captain Yazzie had told her that any complaints or problems involving John Canyon should come directly to him, and his tone had more than implied that Canyon was beyond reproach and, at least in this valley, immune from the long arm of the law.

She didn't necessarily have a problem with Canyon and had even gone on a few dates with his son, Tobias. It was the way of the world for people with money and power to control and manipulate others in order to gain more money and power. Or, at least, that was the way of the belegana world. She had accepted the Canyon situation as a necessary evil, especially considering that the man had done more than any cop could ever hope to accomplish in way of taming illicit dealings within the county.

Still, Liana had always kept it in the back of her mind that someday the deal that the town of Roanhorse had made with the devil would burn them all. As she stared into the drunk tank at the stranger, trying to get a handle on what game the man was playing, she wondered if today would be that day of reckoning.

When the station's back door opened and Captain Yazzie stomped his way inside, she felt like a weight had been lifted from her shoulders. She had never been so happy to see her boss as she was at that moment. In fact, most of the time, she cringed when he entered a room.

The tan uniform of the Navajo Nation Tribal police hugged Yazzie's five foot nine frame snuggly. Although the captain wore an official uniform from the neck down, above that was hardly within regulations. He wore his typical buffalo skin revenger-style Stetson wrapped by a band made from the skin of a Copperhead. A pair of small spectacles— which adjusted to the light so that he could wear them day or night, outside or in—always seemed to hide his eyes. The glasses reminded her of those worn by John Lennon, only more sophisticated in order to accommodate the captain's sensitivity to light.

Moving to her first, the captain rubbed Liana's shoulder and said, "Are you okay?"

"We're fine, sir."

"It's a damn good thing Pitka was nearby."

Ernie Pitka whispered, "I can't say that I was much help, sir. He pretty much kicked our asses. He's only in that cell because he wants to be and the prospect of that scares the hell out of me."

Yazzie said, "Calm down, officer. We don't even know what's going on yet."

Liana felt like she should offer something to the conversation. She had drawn a hundred insights from watching the prisoner and imagined a thousand possible scenarios to explain the blood. But in the moment, her mind went blank, and all she could think to say was, "The stranger claims that he will only speak to John Canyon."

Yazzie's face went cold and the sternness in his eyes showed his annoyance at not being notified of this earlier. He said, "This guy asked for Mr. Canyon by name?"

Liana's stomach flipped like an old biplane when she realized her mistake. Had the prisoner actually mentioned Canyon or had that merely been her own inference? Trying to recall the conversation, she replied, "He said something about wanting to talk to the puppet master or something."

"'Or something?' That the kind of terminology they teach you at that fancy belegana school? What did he say precisely?"

She felt the blood rush to her cheeks and she fought for words. She looked to Ernie Pitka—who had been crushing on her since junior high—for assistance again. Ernie's eyes went wide, and he offered, "The prisoner said that he was waiting for the man who pulled our superior's strings."

The captain said, "So...Officer Nakai...Our prisoner mentions the person who pulls my strings and you instantly assumed he was referring to John Canyon. That's an interesting assertion, officer."

"I'm sorry, sir," Liana whispered, her head bowed in deference, "I didn't mean to imply that—"

Yazzie raised a hand to stop her. "You've said enough. It's fine. You've been attacked and aren't thinking clearly. I shouldn't have pushed you. Either way, perhaps it's time that I hear it from the horse's mouth."

5

Ackerman smiled a warm greeting as the wannabe-cowboy police captain approached the bars. He said, "I would extend a handshake, but your officers insisted on securing my arms behind my back."

The captain said nothing. He merely observed with a stone face and eyes unreadable behind round wire-framed glasses. Ackerman had immediately noted the captain's choice of weapons—two Colt Peacemakers, one on each hip.

Ackerman said, "I like your old wheel guns. A couple of famous pieces of Americana. Known as 'The Gun That Won the West'"

The captain said nothing.

"You remind me of another little piggy I met on the road to Cancun. Actually, I believe that was the last occasion I was in a foreign nation, and I have to say that I find the Diné people to be significantly more hospitable than your Mexican neighbors. That now-deceased police captain underestimated my fortitude and the bloody lengths to which I would go for revenge. I only mention it because I see some parallels between your current predicament and the unfortunate deaths of a great many people south of the border. You see, that dead Mexican captain took someone dear to me. Just as your friend, John Canyon, has taken someone very close to me now. Would you like to know the ultimate fate of your Southern counterpart?"

The cowboy captain's lip curled back. Ignoring Ackerman's question, he said to the young male officer, "Pitka, go out to the tank and fill up a couple ten gallon buckets of water. Then bring them back in here and give our new friend a quick shower."

The young female officer snapped, "Sir, that's physical evidence. We can't—"

"That's enough, Liana. We have samples of the blood on the handles of his batons."

Ackerman smiled and said, "Lee-anna. I like it. It suits you, which suits me, which is really all that matters."

The captain said, "Pitka, go get the water. Now, please."

Snapping to attention, the young officer nodded and rushed from the building.

As the door swung shut, Ackerman shot to his feet and attacked the metal bars separating him from the remaining officers. His spin kick struck with enough force to rattle the whole building. Both the captain and his subordinate involuntarily recoiled in fear. Ackerman laughed and said, "That other police captain I mentioned, the one who stole from me, ended up surviving under my care for weeks. I fed him a diet of his own flesh. We made a little game out of it. Perhaps I'll also get to play with you. What do you think, Captain Yazzie? Would you like to know what you taste like? I have to admit that I'm curious. Perhaps we could share a piece."

Officer Pitka, returning with the buckets of water, took one look at the expressions on the faces of his coworkers and said, "What did I miss?"

Yazzie replied, "Dowse him. We need to get a better look at our new friend."

Ackerman could understand where the captain was coming from. He suspected it was quite unnerving for a normal to sit in the presence of a man whose torso was smeared with relatively fresh blood. Of course, Ackerman knew that Yazzie would be no less unnerved when he saw what was underneath the blood.

Most of Ackerman's body was covered in scar tissue of one type or another. Some of the wounds had been inflicted courtesy of his deranged father—who had subjected him to unspeakable horrors and every pain imaginable in an attempt to engineer a perfect killing machine—but many of the scars had been earned during his various exploits. And many more were self-inflicted. Ackerman's father had ultimately found no way to accomplish his goals without a bit of invasive brain surgery, and so, Francis Ackerman Sr. had performed delicate surgery on his son's amygdala, the area of the brain responsible for a person's sense of fear.

Still on his feet, Ackerman stepped forward and closed his eyes as he awaited the water. His hands remained behind his back and much of the gore wouldn't rinse free without some scrubbing, but within a few seconds, the officers had succeeded in washing away a large percentage of the blood, enough to better reveal his face and his scars.

Liana gasped and quickly clamped a hand over her mouth as the roadmap of his pain was revealed. He looked down at himself, something that he rarely did. He didn't like to dwell upon the past. But in this instance, he gazed down at his wounds with analytical eyes, trying to see the scars in the way that Liana saw them. He flexed the thick cords of sinew in his arms and watched the cuts and burns and gunshot wounds ripple in the artificial glow of the fluorescent lighting.

He wondered if the female was appalled or aroused by his naked torso. Perhaps a bit of both. He said, "I certainly feel refreshed. Is Mr. Canyon on his way?"

"Why would he be?" Yazzie asked.

"Don't insult me with a half-hearted attempt at pretending that you're a real cop. You're a glorified security guard. The lot of you are. Keeping watch over Canyon's town and his enterprises. My guess is that you were on the phone with him when the distress signal went out from Liana. And if you weren't on the phone already, then that means that you called your master on the way."

"I'm no man's slave. But you're right. I was on the phone with John, and he is on his way down from the ranch as we speak. I suggest you get a drink of water and get ready to do some talking. You can either talk to me, or talk to John. And when he asks a question and doesn't like the answer, he's likely to tear off all your fingernails."

A grin forming across his handsome face, Ackerman said, "It's been a while since I've had a partner on my dance card who really knows how to tango. And I so enjoy a good torture."

"We'll see how cocky you are when Big John gets here. You'd be a damn sight better off to just tell me what happened before he gets here, son."

"Patience, captain. Patience is the first of two lessons every hunter must learn."

"What's the other?"

"Stay downwind of your prey. A hunter who fails in

either of these arenas will either be going home hungry or will end up becoming someone else's dinner."

"And you're an expert hunter. That right?"

"I'm an expert at many things. And yes, I am quite experienced in that arena. I enjoy the hunt. The anticipation of the kill. But I prefer consummation over foreplay."

The captain pulled over a metal chair, the legs scraping against the linoleum floor the whole way. Sliding down onto the chair, Captain Yazzie said, "We have a forensic kit that can determine whether or not you came in here covered in human or animal blood. What's that test going to show?"

"I love the smell of blood. Researchers in Sweden recently documented that a single molecule of a chemical released when lipids in blood break down after being exposed to air—the same molecule that gives it that metallic smell—causes humans to recoil and other predatory animals to lick their lips in anticipation. I suspect the Swedes would catch me salivating at the smell of blood. It is so sweet and beautiful to me, while it causes instinctive reactions of fear and revulsion in you normals. Perception and relativity, I suppose."

"Come on, give me something. How about your name?"

Ackerman considered that. He couldn't give his real name because the infamous serial murderer Francis Ackerman was officially dead. The Shepherd Organization had even paid for a plastic surgeon to change his face enough that no one could possibly recognize him.

He said, "You may call me…Frankenstein. Or Frank, for short."

6

Ackerman felt his mutilations would fall, on the spectrum of horrific disfigurement, somewhere between the burns of Freddy Krueger and the wartime injuries inflicted upon Rambo. Thankfully, his father had been strategic with the abuse, in order to avoid detection. The scars were all concealable by a long-sleeved shirt, but of course, he wanted them to see the evidence of the crucible that was his life.

The young and rather beautiful Liana couldn't seem to pry her eyes from his torso. His body didn't contain an ounce of fat, but he knew that it wasn't his physique drawing her attention. He could see her analyzing the scars for a method behind the madness. He made a mental note to ask her later about what conclusions she had reached.

Captain Yazzie said, "Frankenstein. Frank, that's cute. I can see from that little roadmap of pain you call an epidermis that torture isn't going to have much effect on you. How about I talk and you let me know if I'm on the right track?"

Ackerman fought to keep his concentration on the Tribal Police captain and the situation at hand, but he could already feel the breath on the back of his neck, the shadow at his back. Over his shoulder, he heard his father say, "I think we should kill every one of these people and be done with it. This is boring me to tears."

Ackerman's father—the serial killer known as Thomas White—walked around to the front of the cell and stood in front of the police captain. Through it all, Ackerman kept his face as stone. Internally, he wanted to scream and break something. For the past few months, he had been hearing the voice of his father in his head, but up until recently, the voice had only spoken phrases that had been lifted from actual memories. But during a recent confrontation with a serial killer who called himself the Gladiator, the voice in his head had begun to speak as if it had a mind of its own.

And then, in the hospital following the Gladiator ordeal, Thomas White had appeared in the flesh. Or at least Ackerman perceived him that way. The hallucination had been so vivid that he had called for the nurse and asked her if she could also see the mad doctor in the three piece suit. She had looked at him as if his tongue had crawled out of his mouth like a large pink leech. The real doctor she summoned had wanted to run more tests on him, but he had better things to do and had convinced the doctor that he would handle the matter with his primary care physician.

Now, with Maggie missing and possibly dead and him back in another cage, he wondered if he should have heeded the doctor's advice.

Thomas White said, "It feels so good to have the band back together again, doesn't it, Junior?"

Behind his father, the police captain said, "Are you still with me, kid? If I get the story right, will you help me fill in the blanks?"

Ackerman said, "I can't stop you from talking just yet, but by that same token, you can't keep me from ignoring you."

The imaginary Thomas White laughed. "That's the spirit, Junior. Try to outthink this. Make a game out of it, just like you always did with everything, in order to deal with the pain. But that was before the gifts I gave you. I helped you to transcend pain and master fear."

Captain Yazzie said, "You were right. Mr. Canyon did call me. But that would be the sensible thing for a man to do when a crazy person has attacked his ranch."

Ackerman said, "I didn't attack anyone. I merely analyzed the current situation and applied pressure where it was required."

"Mr. Canyon claims that you set one of his trucks on fire and rolled it into his reserve fuel depot."

Ackerman nodded. "As I said, the proper amount of force for the situation."

"And what situation is that? Why would you feel the need to do anything to John or his property?"

"I needed to get his attention."

Thomas White leaned against the bars, arms crossed, looking bored. He said, "If you wanted to get his attention, you should have followed my advice and dragged his whole family out of the house and started executing them one by one until he told what he's done with your brother's concubine."

Ackerman gritted his teeth and resisted the urge to defend Maggie's honor. He reminded himself that his father wasn't actually there. Unless the old man had mastered some form of astral projection.

Captain Yazzie said, "You certainly managed to get his attention. I think a better choice would have been to call his office and make an appointment or at the very least knock on his door. That's usually sufficient in getting someone's attention."

Ackerman shrugged. "Let's not split hairs here, captain. Overkill would have been dragging all of them out into the night and chopping off body parts with a chainsaw until Mr. Canyon properly received my message. Your proposed solution, on the other hand, would have been too far down on the other end of the spectrum. I feel my actions were quite proportionate."

"You could have killed a lot of people. He has bunk-houses out there—"

"The variables were considered. As they have been considered ten steps ahead of your feeble mind in this instance. Besides, the point is moot as no one was killed in the truck explosion. It was merely a diversion."

"A diversion for what? Why did you need to get Canyon's attention?"

"You haven't asked me about the blood yet."

"I was working my way up to it."

Thomas White walked around behind Ackerman and placed imaginary hands on real shoulders. Ackerman could have sworn that he could feel actual pressure from his father's touch. White said, "May I suggest a small edit to your plan here."

Ackerman said, to both the captain and his father, "I'm listening. Get on with it."

The police captain leaned forward with his elbows on his knees and asked, "What did you do with Tobias Canyon and the others with him? Are they dead?"

"Consider this, Junior," Thomas White said. "If you really want to convey the dire nature of these straits, then you should kill these three, pose them like marionettes, and secure yourself back in the cell. Now that would get the attention of this Canyon fellow."

Ackerman said, "No one need die here. Your benefactor, John Canyon, took someone from me. So I took someone from him. Perhaps it's a bit simplistic. Schoolyard logic, for sure. But I think it holds up. If he returns my friend, then I'll return his son."

He could imagine the wheels turning behind the dark black glasses covering Yazzie's eyes. The captain said, "Who's your friend?"

Leaning forward, Ackerman slowly asked, "You can see him too?"

"What? See who? Try to stay with me here, kid. You said Canyon took your friend. Who exactly is he supposed to have kidnapped?"

"Oh, that makes much more sense. She is a federal agent who went missing while investigating Mr. Canyon. Her name is Maggie Carlisle. Surely you remember her, captain."

"I'm afraid not. Just like I told the FBI agent and BIA agents when they asked. She never came here."

Thomas White was suddenly standing behind Captain Yazzie. Ackerman's hallucination cocked his balding head and said, "You see that. He's lying right to your face. Are you going to stand for this kind of malicious disrespect, Junior?"

Ackerman said, "That's interesting, Captain Yazzie. We were able to track her cell phone to this exact location. She made a call while she was here, one of her last before disappearing."

"She must have stopped by while we were out on a call. None of my officers saw her either. But we can discuss that later, Frank. I'll help you find your friend. I really will. But right now, I need to know if Tobias and those other boys are okay. Do they need medical attention?"

With a roll of his eyes, Ackerman dropped onto the bunk against the back wall and said, "I really wish all of you normals would stop asking me stupid questions. I need you to understand something, captain. When you look into my eyes, you are looking into eyes that have watched countless die. I have felt all pain. I have known all depravity. I have experienced the heights of sadistic ecstasy, and I have endured the pits of hell and the valley of death. Now, you look me in the eyes and answer me one question. Do you know where Maggie Carlisle is right now?"

With a small shake of his head, the captain replied, "No, I have no idea."

"Then you're of no use to me. I have a suggestion. Let's all sit here quietly until the man who can actually answer my question shows up."

The impetuous Officer Liana said, "And what if Canyon can't answer your questions either? Or what if your friend is dead? What will you do then, Frank?"

Ackerman could tell that her question was genuine. She was asking out of fear of his retaliation, not trying to be facetious. Thomas White—who he could now only hear in his head—said, "That's a good question, Junior. What will you do if Ms. Maggie is no more? Maybe that will be my opportunity to take your flesh suit for a little spin. Or maybe you'll merely resort back to your true nature and do what you were born to do. It could be just like old times. Father and son, together again."

As he looked up into the eyes of the frightened young American Indian woman, Ackerman answered honestly, "If Maggie's dead...then God help us all."

7

One month earlier…

The house hadn't changed much in the eight years since Maggie Carlisle had been home. Not that she had expected anything to have fallen into disrepair. Even in her seventies, Grandma scrubbed out the gutters with soap and water once a week. Maggie caught a large whiff of grandmother's home-made vinegar cleaning solution as she called out, "Grandma? Mom?"

Having called ahead and left a message so that her grandmother could prepare her room, Maggie had expected at least some sort of welcome. She passed through the kitchen, seeing the faded magnets stuck to the fridge warning about soda and cellular phones causing cancer. Judging by the silence, her family wasn't home. The kitchen led right into the dining room, and from there, she took the hall to her old bedroom. The rolling wheels of her luggage created a steady thrum over the creaky wooden flooring, but the boards still shined liked diamonds under Grandma Helen's diligent care.

The bedroom, like the rest of the house, smelled of vinegar, indicating that Grandma Helen had cleaned her room in expectance of her arrival. Maggie moved to the window seat of her room, setting her luggage down. She would set her clothes up here, organized to her specific standards before she placed them into her dresser. Unzipping her suitcase, she pulled out a clean, precisely-folded sheet from the top and spread it over the window seat, carefully moving her favorite stuffed animals from her childhood. Once the sheet was down, Maggie began to unpack her clothing carefully. The perfect squares of fabric were organized by day and adjusted according to the forecast. She then organized her toiletries on top of her dresser before going to the bed and stripping the sheets off to wash them. She knew her grandmother would have already washed the bedclothes, but Maggie wasn't taking any chances. Bed bugs were becoming an epidemic, and the mere thought of the vermin made her skin crawl.

Maggie lifted the mattress to free the sheets before carrying them to the laundry room down the hall. She made to leave, but hesitated. Grabbing the gallon jug of vinegar and a cleaning rag, she returned to her room. Her grandmother wouldn't have cleaned inside the dresser or side tables of her old bedroom since she left. Helen was a private person who respected the privacy of others, and the drawers had been where Maggie kept all of her private journals and drawings. Grandma Helen had always cleaned around and under the dressers, but to her knowledge, her grandma had never opened them.

Leaning over the drawers to scrub them had caused her short blonde hair to fall into her face before she'd smoothed it back into a ponytail. She'd worked her way down from the top drawer of the three positioned in the dresser. The top two held several childhood mementos—old pictures of friends and family, certificates of excellency for school subjects, colored pencils, and other odds and ends of little significance.

The bottom drawer, however, was stuffed so full that Maggie could barely open it, nearly toppling backward when it finally came free. Inside, she found her collection of Beanie Babies. She smiled at the little animals, arranging them on the chair nearby. She couldn't quite recall why she'd liked them so much, just that they had made her happy. At the bottom of the drawer, she found a brightly colored Lisa Frank notebook. Maggie vaguely recalled the sparkly unicorn on the front from her childhood. After retrieving the spiral-bound tablet from its hiding place, Maggie resisted the urge to go wash her hands again. Her tanned skin was already ruddy from the three preceding washings from the past hour. While she waited for her family to arrive home and for the vinegar in the drawers to dry, Maggie knew she should have been unpacking her MacBook Air and reviewing her notes on the Taker case, but the blindingly bright colors of the notebook caught her eye. She sighed in frustration at her urge to waste time away from the case to look through the old pages.

She opened the Lisa Frank cover and was immediately appalled by the imperfect, crooked handwriting of her childhood self. Grimacing, she scanned a few pages and was about to put the notebook away when she felt something stiff between the pages.

The short stack of photos she found tucked inside the crinkled pages brought back a flood of long lost memories. Her family looked so happy. Her little brother with her and her mom on a wooden bench, their grinning faces smeared with butter and sweet corn. She vaguely remembered that day. An American Indian event called a "Powwow" had been taking place at the local university. Her dad, who was a Discovery Channel junkie, had insisted on them all being in attendance. He had taken the picture. Maggie could only remember vague flashes and emotions from that day. She wished that she could remember those happy times better. It would have been one of the last outings while her family was still together. But she had been so young, and it seemed that everything about her childhood, except for the day her brother was taken, was nothing more than an obscure collection of shadows.

A folded, yellowed piece of paper had been tucked away behind the photos. She unfolded it to reveal a child's eye view of the Powwow–bright colors and triangle-shaped teepees interspersed with feathers that looked like cattails. In the center of the drawing was a group of American Indian dancers depicted in colored pencil. The view of the dancing men was from the side with their rectangular arms twisted in strange ways to help illustrate their movements.

But there was one dancer who Maggie had drawn facing her. He was dressed just like the others, except that his eyes were piercing black holes. The hair on her arms and neck stood up and a chill shot down her spine. Maggie felt like she was going to throw up as the fear swept over her. She frowned at the drawing, not understanding why those black eyes had such an effect.

Then Maggie's ears, honed by years of training, caught the sound of car doors opening and closing outside. Folding up the drawing and tucking it back into her old journal with the picture, she went to meet the new arrivals, expecting it to be her grandma and mom, but not blind to the possibility that Marcus had found out where she'd gone. She'd told him she was fine and not to come after her before ditching the burner phone so he couldn't trace it, but her team was good. She imagined it was only a matter of time before they located her.

She felt bad, sneaking around like this, but Marcus wouldn't understand... No, Maggie was lying to herself. She knew Marcus would have understood, probably would have dropped everything to help her, but she didn't want him involved unless he really needed to be. This was her burden, not his.

She reached the living room window that faced the driveway and parted the lace curtains to see an old silver Buick and two women carrying groceries toward the house. Maggie rushed to unlock the doors, smiling at her grandmother's surprise. "Hi Grandma, let me help with these."

"I've got it!" Grandma Helen told her sharply. "Help your mother."

Maggie obeyed, moving to her mom. The woman, who looked so much like an older version of herself, said nothing, merely releasing the bags without showing any recognition of her daughter. "Hi Mom."

Her mother's blonde hair was graying now, pulled back in the same French braid Grandma Helen had plaited into Maggie's hair for years. Peering at her mother's pale face, Maggie could see the blue of her veins just under the surface of her skin. After a moment, she smiled at Maggie in a vague way, her eyes almost looking through her. "Hello, Magpie."

Maggie let out a breath she hadn't known she'd held and smiled at the old nickname. "It's me, Mama."

The older woman looked away and walked toward the house, chuckling and saying, "Magpies are one of the smartest birds in the world. They're one of the only animals that can recognize itself in the mirror."

Maggie held her tears in check. She'd hoped, perhaps naively, that her mother would have gotten better, but it seemed her mom was still sleepwalking her way through life. Maggie knew it was mostly the drugs—everything from antidepressants to antipsychotics—that caused the haze. Her and Grandma Helen had went round and round for years about her mother's meds and dosages, but for Grandma, the most important thing was that her only daughter remained calm and didn't try to hurt herself.

Maggie let her mom go into the house ahead of her, knowing that she wouldn't close the door behind them. Juggling the bags as she twisted the deadbolt, Maggie followed the two older women into the kitchen. Grandma was already organizing the new purchases to perfection in her cabinets. Helen said, "I was expecting you later today, Maggie. How long have you been here?"

"Not long. Thirty minutes or so," Maggie answered, staying out of the older woman's way as she bustled around the kitchen. She still remembered the painful pinches her grandmother would give her ears if she was caught underfoot. Grandma's silver hair was cut short and curled, as Maggie knew, nightly with rollers. The old woman's face was lined by age and a sour disposition. As items were slid into their proper places, Maggie noted that Grandma Helen's organizational pattern hadn't changed a bit. All canned foods in the same cabinet, divided by vegetable or fruit. From them on, they were further broken down by color, cut, and can size.

Maggie felt her shoulders relax. She followed the same

pattern at her own apartment. Having things in proper order made her realize how much she had actually missed being home.

Then Helen said, "So... Maggie, how's everything with your boyfriend? Marcus is his name, right?"

Maggie blinked at her grandmother. How had she known that she had a boyfriend, let alone his name? Maggie had never told her about Marcus. Maggie didn't really talk to anyone about her relationship. Who would she tell? It had been years since she'd had any girlfriends. She was slowly making a few friends–Emily Morgan was one, Lisa Spinelli another. Even then, they already knew about Marcus.

Her mouth opened, then closed. She wasn't sure how to respond. Her grandmother seemed oblivious to Maggie's shock. She merely went about her dinner preparations, rinsing and peeling some potatoes she'd taken from her pantry. Grandma had acted the same way when Maggie was in high school and the old woman had something to hold over her granddaughter's head.

Maggie asked, "Has Marcus called here looking for me?"

"He's worried about you."

"I know."

"I'm worried too."

"Don't be."

"He seemed like a nice young man."

"He is."

Grandma Helen stopped mid-peel and turned to look her granddaughter in the eyes. "Magpie, I need to ask you something... Something important about you and your man friend, Marcus..."

Maggie tensed up fearing that she was about to get a lecture on premarital sex. She replied, "Okay..."

With a slow nod and sad eyes, Helen said, "Are the two of you...eating organic?"

The tension fell from Maggie's shoulders. Shaking her head, she started to say, "Grandma—"

But Helen interrupted, "I know it's hard to maintain when you're on the road as much as you are, but you just have to plan ahead."

"Grandma—"

"The government is trying to kill us with all the chemicals in our food. You have to protect yourself. What are you going to do when you go to have my grandbabies, and your womb is a shriveled up wasteland from all those preservatives and pesticides and Lord knows what else."

The comment stung—since Maggie had in fact learned that she was unable to have children—but her grandmother had no way of knowing that. She said, "We take very good care of ourselves, Grandma."

"Really. Are you drinking soda? I remember when you were using those pink sweetener packets in your coffee, and I caught you. Nothing artificial, girl. How many times I have I said. You haven't moved onto the blues have you? And don't let them fool you with those new yellow ones. Those are the worst of the lot!"

"No, Grandma, we eat all organic, chemical free, all natural products. I drink nothing but water and black coffee."

Grandma Helen narrowed her eyes with the don't-lie-to-me look that she had perfected over the years.

Maggie held up her hands in surrender. "Do you want to examine my next bowel movement?"

"How about I just go check the passenger floorboard of your car?"

She winced, knowing that she had been busted.

After a few seconds, Grandma Helen said, "We can talk more over dinner. Go finish unpacking and clean yourself up. Must have been a long trip." Then, with a teasing smile, she added, "Now get out of my kitchen and let me prepare some real food for you."

Maggie obeyed, leaving her grandma to her preparations and heading back to her bedroom. The drawers should have been dry by now. She could put away her clothes, arrange her personal items, and replacing the newly cleaned bedclothes.

She had just finished when she heard her grandmother yell that dinner was done. It had taken her nearly an hour to get things the way she wanted them.

The three women were quiet at first as they took their assigned places and loaded their plates, but then as Grandma handed Maggie the porcelain bowl of fried potatoes, Helen said, "So tell me more about Marcus."

Maggie took the bowl, scooping some potatoes onto her plate, making sure that none of her food touched, "I thought we were done with this."

Her grandmother scoffed. "You thought. No, I want to know who caught your fancy, Miss Magdalania."

Magdalania… Maggie winced. She hated her given name. It was so old-fashioned, but her grandfather had used her real name all the time during her youth. "What do you want to know?"

"Is he cute?" Grandma Helen asked, chuckling as Maggie's face flushed.

Clearing her throat and changing directions, she said, "His older brother works with us too. They're both highly intelligent. Do you remember those brain teaser puzzles that Tommy and I used to play with Grandpa? Marcus and his brother would probably solve them on the first try." Maggie continued on for a while, telling heavily-edited stories of Marcus and Ackerman's exploits. She realized halfway through her own stories how much she missed Marcus. And maybe even Ackerman, a little. She added, "I feel like I'm the Batman of the group. I'm a mere human being, but everyone else on the team have superpowers. It's a little surreal at times."

On her last sentence, Maggie matched gazes with her mother and thought she saw a vague flash of understanding or interest. But then the haze returned, and Mom mumbled, "Sounds nice."

The idle chit-chat carried on through the rest of the meal, and it wasn't until the three were working together to clear the table that Maggie worked up the nerve to ask, "Mom, I need to ask you something important... about that day. The day that Tommy was taken."

Standing halfway between the table and the sink, her mother stared at the plate in her hands as if it held the meaning of existence. The older women's facial muscles twitched ever so slightly, but Maggie noticed her mother's hands turn white and begin to shake.

Maggie tried again, "I know it's hard, Mama. But I can't just let it go this time. What happened the day we lost Tommy? I need to know everything you remember."

The plate fell from her mother's hands and shattered against the kitchen's tile floor. Mother merely stood there as if in a dream. There was a sort of strange confusion in her eyes as she fled the room. Maggie heard her mother's footsteps dragging toward her bedroom and then the click of a door's lock.

The kitchen fell eerily quiet.

After a moment, Grandma Helen sighed and said, "Maggie, you know better than to talk about Tommy around her."

"But I think I can find the man who took him. And… Tommy could still be alive, Grandma!"

Meeting her gaze, Helen reached out and took Maggie's hand. Her grandmother seldom ever showed signs of physical affection. They were not huggers and hand-holders in Helen's household. The old women's eyes displayed the same kind of gravitas as she said, "I know that you want to find this man. And maybe you can. But Tommy is gone, and we can never get him back."

Grandma's eyes filled with tears, and Maggie tried to remember the last time that she saw her grandmother cry. Grandpa's funeral perhaps?

Helen continued, "That evil man has taken so much from us. He took my grandson, he destroyed your family, broke your mother's heart and then her mind. He has stolen so much happiness from this family. Please, Maggie, don't let him take you from us too."

Unable to hold back her tears any longer, Maggie broke down and joined her grandmother in mourning yet again for all the Taker had stolen from them.

8

John Canyon had killed in both hot and cold blood. He had cut his teeth on the Rez inside the Native Mob, and he had the scars and the tattoos to prove it. When he had decided to escape that life and join the military, the teardrops of ink that ran down his left cheek were converted by a skilled artist over to small eagle feathers. He had kept that tradition going during his two tours in the first Gulf War. By the time he returned to the Rez, as a war hero, he had nearly half his face covered with feathers and other small icons which held significance to each life he had taken.

When he returned to civilian life, the gang had tried to bring him back into the fold. He accepted them with open arms at first and then killed a few of the leaders as examples. The gangs on the Rez were typically not connected to the larger organizations from which they derived their names. They were just kids modeling another oppressed society of which they empathized. But after the war, John Canyon had a vision. A dream of a better kingdom for The People.

And he was pleased with the contribution he had made to the Diné so far. He had united several of the gangs into a true criminal empire, and then he had turned his attention to the belegana's greed.

When Canyon had killed to unite the scattered bangers of the Navajo nation, he had done so with ice in his veins. This was what needed to happen, for the good of his people.

But tonight, as John Canyon brought his brand new GMC pickup truck to a halt with a screech of brakes in front of the local tribal police outpost, his blood boiled and murder was certainly on his mind.

He had built something in this valley, a kingdom built of hard work and blood. He had a family and a good name and a legacy to leave behind for his son. And then this blonde-haired blue-eyed agent from the Department of Justice had come around digging up the past, speaking the names of the dead, and inviting the victim's chindii into his home. And as he had feared, the spirits had called another dark wind down upon him in the form of this stranger, this coyote, who had blown into the valley and disappeared with his son.

It was a good thing that John Canyon didn't fully believe in the old superstitions. He only believed in things that he could see and touch, and right now, he was about to reach out and touch the man who had taken his son.

The Roanhorse Navajo Nation Police Substation was one of those old mobile offices that schools and bureaucracies fell in love with during the mid-80s. It was little more than a fancy double-wide trailer, and just like everything else that had to contend with constantly blowing sand and the sun's barrage, the corrugated metal shell of the station was faded and in desperate need of a coat of paint.

He knew the inside of the building didn't look much better. It was a large open room with one partition for the captain's office and one for the drunk tank. But as John Canyon entered the station, all he could see was his enemy and the only emotion he could feel was rage. Before exiting the truck, John had grabbed his semi-auto Remington shotgun from the gun rack and loaded it full of double-aught buckshot.

Now, as he stepped into the police station, he ignored the three uniformed officers standing in the middle of the room. Instead, he headed straight for the drunk tank and the man sitting on the bunk in the back of the cage.

The bastard on the wrong side of the bars didn't even flinch when Canyon raised the shotgun. The shirtless man simply cocked his head in curiosity. The strange white man didn't even blink when John squeezed the trigger and unleashed a volley of pellets into the wall beside the prisoner.

Yazzie yelled, "What the hell, John?"

But Canyon ignored him. Instead, he redirected the aim of the barrel at the prisoner's chest and said, "Tell me where to find my son, or I swear to any and every god listening that I will kill you where you stand."

The prisoner said, "You seem upset, Mr. Canyon. Perhaps you should take a moment."

"What have you done with Toby, you son of a bitch!"

"First of all, don't ever talk about my mother like that again, or I will force you to consume your own testicles. Now, I'd love for you to sit down so we can have nice little chat, but you don't seem to be in a very receptive mood. Perhaps you'd like to leave the room and come back in, but this time without the childish temper tantrum."

Canyon had never wanted to end a life as much as he did at that moment. The rage threatened to overwhelm his reasoning. It had been a very long time since anyone had disrespected him as much as this man. In his younger days, he would have blown the stranger's head off and sorted out the consequences later, but age had a way of driving home the fact that every action had a consequence, for every choice a man made he had to pay a price. Whether it be overworking a deteriorating body or having one too many pieces of cake, repercussions were assured. And now, he wanted to kill this man with all his being, but the potential cost would be too high to pay.

Ignoring the young officers, who had drawn their weapons and trained them on him, Canyon laid the shotgun across the faux wood top of one of the station house's old desks. Returning to the bars, he said, "Is my son still alive?"

"For now."

"What about the sheep?"

"Pardon me?"

"What did you do with the truck you stole from my ranch? You kidnapped my son and then stole a truck hauling a livestock trailer already loaded down with sheep? Are you tracking all this, you crazy son of a..."

Canyon let the insult trail off without finishing his statement. Ackerman smiled at the small act of acquiescence.

"Crazy is all about perspective, and I understood the question. It just seems like an odd order for your concerns. You haven't even asked about the five men you sent to retrieve your son and your lost sheep. Rest assured, , Mr. Canyon, your property is still intact. My demands are quite simple. Return DOJ Special Agent Maggie Carlisle to me, and I will return your son to you."

"I had nothing to do with that agent going missing. The FBI and BIA have already questioned all of us. I can't tell you anymore than I did them."

The man in the cage shook his head and sighed. "I find that response completely unacceptable. Try again."

"The truth doesn't change by saying it with different words."

"Truth is a subjective term and an elusive concept. but let's make it simple and speak in terms of facts. You have four hours to produce Ms. Carlisle unharmed or your son will bleed out from his injuries."

"I can't give you what I don't have!"

"For the sake of expediency, let's say that's true. If that's the case, and you really don't know where she is, I would suggest that you bring every iota of your power and influence to bear on finding her. But please realize that if my demands are not met within the next four hours, then it will not only be your son who dies. I will sweep across your little kingdom like a Biblical plague. Like the angel of death visiting the Egyptians, I will unleash my wrath upon you and everything thing you love until you let my Maggie go."

"I think you're forgetting that you're the one behind bars. You're not in a position to be making demands."

The prisoner chuckled. "Are you familiar with the writings of Laozi?"

Canyon resisted the urge to tear his way into the cell with his bare hands. Through clenched teeth, he answered, "No."

"Loazi was an ancient Chinese philosopher. He has actually attained the level of deity among religious Taoism and some other traditional Chinese religions. One of my favorite quotes from him is that 'There is no greater danger than underestimating an opponent.'"

"What makes you think that I'm underestimating you?"

"Because you have yet to accept the inevitability of my Xaviery. Now is not the time to stand up and fight, Mr. Canyon. Now, is the time to dust off the white flag and start waving. You now have three hours, fifty-eight minutes, and thirty-seven seconds to produce Ms. Carlisle. Those are my demands. They are not subject to debate. This is not a negotiation. It is a hostile takeover by a superior force. I'm going to take a little nap now. I think you have some work to do."

"And what if I can't pull this missing agent out of my ass?"

Laying back onto the metal cot of the drunk tank and closing his eyes, the scarred stranger said, "Then, Mr. Canyon, I will burn your whole world to the ground."

9

Liana Nakai sat at her desk and willed her hands to stop shaking. This couldn't be happening. She was a police officer on the largest American Indian reservation in the United States, a nation within a nation. Which basically meant that she had all the same duties as a belegana cop, but with more ground to cover and less resources to do it with. She was an officer of the law, and this was still a police station. Liana had one day dreamed of moving east and becoming a detective or even applying to the FBI academy. This was supposed to be a pit stop on her way to better things. Instead, she probably wouldn't leave this backwoods excuse for a police station with her life, let alone her career, intact.

She had always known that police work was dangerous, but she had seldom really considered that this place could be the end of the line. And then a man walked into her station on her shift covered in blood. This man who called himself "Frank." He had altered the course of her life in a way that seemed irreparable. A federal agent was missing, and her captain and the most powerful man in the valley seemed to be complicit or directly involved with the disappearance. By extension, that meant she was an accessory to their crimes as well.

Ejecting the magazine from her Glock 22, the standard issue sidearm for the Navajo Nation Police, she checked to make sure that it was in perfect working order and ready to fire.

Her grandmother had once told her that we each have two coyotes that follow us wherever we go. One coyote was love, and the other was fear. The two were constantly at war, and the one who would rule your life was the coyote you chose to feed.

As she sat at her desk, checking her weapon, trying to remember her training and searching for a way out of this mess, Liana imagined that Love was hiding under the desk and Fear was clawing at her leg demanding to be fed.

Having learned long ago that life was all about choices and consequences, Liana knew that one simple decision could change a person's life forever. She had seen such causality in the life of her father when he had chosen to rob an armored car in Albuquerque and wound up eating a bullet. Simple choices, permanent consequences. And she had already made her bad choice two days earlier when the FBI and BIA had come knocking and asking about the missing agent. Instead of revealing that she had in fact seen the missing woman when she had come to visit the station and had spoken with the captain, Liana did as she was told and remained loyal to Yazzie.

She had thought nothing of the woman's visit at the time. It wasn't until the next morning that Yazzie had called her into his office and said, "Remember when I hired you for this job, and I told you that some times up here in Roanhorse, you just have to follow orders, even if those orders may contradict the letter of the law. I told you that you have to be loyal to this community first and the law second, because sometimes we have to let some things go for the greater good of our people. One of those moments may be coming soon Officer Nakai, and when it does, if anyone asks you, we haven't seen any blonde federal agents in this office. Is that clear?"

That night, Liana had been unable to sleep. When she had accepted Yazzie's offer of employment, she thought that his cryptic words about looking the other way for the greater good involved letting the kids of the town council off the hook for drinking—which was illegal for anyone on the Rez. She had never considered that Yazzie had meant she would need to lie about missing federal agents.

And now she had just witnessed a man—whom she was relatively certain was responsible for more than his fair share of illegal dealings—discharge a shotgun in their station house.

It was clear that John Canyon was a man capable of murder. A federal agent had come around asking questions about John Canyon and then went missing. She didn't need her criminal justice degree to put the pieces together. Maggie Carlisle had come here investigating Canyon, and he had probably killed her and buried her in the desert somewhere.

Protecting the community and serving the greater good sometimes meant that you couldn't just look the other way. Choices had consequences, and if Canyon killed someone, federal agent or not, then he deserved to go down for his crime whether he was a pillar of the community or some punk kid.

She had known all of that on the day when an FBI agent had come to ask the captain some questions about the missing woman. But when her moment came, she had lied, and in that moment, she had become an accessory to

Canyon's crimes, whatever they may be. For the past two days, her choices had weighed heavily upon her. She had imagined that at any moment more agents could be back with more questions.

But she had never expected the devil himself to walk through her door to collect on her debt.

They could all end up in federal prison over this. At the very least, her career in law enforcement would be over. Forget Quantico. She would never make it off the reservation at the rate she was going. If she made it out of this night alive.

The thought of her impending doom was fresh in her mind when she felt breath on the back of her neck. Liana spun around and prepared to deflect a blow with her left arm while holding the pistol close to her abdomen but ready to fire at point blank range.

Officer Ernie Pitka raised his hands in surrender. He had overly large cheekbones and a thick brow, which gave the impression that his eyes were sunken back in his head and squinty. Something about him reminded Liana of an old desert tortoise. Now, Ernie's deep-set eyes were wide with fear.

She quickly lowered and holstered her weapon. "I'm sorry, Ernie. I'm just on edge."

The danger of being shot taken away, Ernie Pitka returned to his normal turtle-like self. She knew that he had a crush on her, but there was just something about him that wasn't for her. And it wasn't the turtle thing. She had actually thought long and hard on the subject. She had certainly dated worse guys, and Ernie was kind of cute, in his own way. But there was just some spark of intelligence missing from his eyes. When she spoke about anything of importance, his eyes became two glazed donuts, and he did a lot of nodding.

Liana wanted someone who would challenge her intellectually and force her to grow as a person. And Ernie, the old tortoise, wasn't the guy for that job.

The many reasons why became evident as Ernie slowly settled down onto her desk and caught his breath in deep slow gasps. Everything Ernie did seemed to be slow and steady. He said, "I thought you had me there."

"Sorry."

"No, it's very understandable with everything going down tonight."

Liana looked to the prisoner—who still laid upon the cot in the back of the cell, eyes closed. "It certainly has been an eventful evening."

"Who do you think this guy really is?" Ernie asked.

"I've been trying to figure that out myself. He says that he's here looking for the missing agent, but if he's a fed then what's with all the angel of death talk."

"If the whole badass killer thing is just an act, then this guy should win an Oscar. Did you see the stranger's face when that shotgun blast went off? Dude didn't even blink. In fact, he looks like this whole thing amuses the hell out of him."

Liana's throat felt as dry as sandpaper. Grabbing a cup of coffee from the desk, she took a swig and then remembered that the cup had been sitting there since yesterday. No matter. It was wet, and she was beyond the point of caring. She said, "What are we doing here, Ernie?"

"We're guarding the prisoner."

"No, I mean... Canyon's going to end up killing this guy... And I think he may have killed the missing agent."

Ernie slowly blinked his eyes at the revelations and said, "You think the prisoner killed the missing agent?"

"What? No."

"That could have been where all the blood came from."

She closed her eyes and shook her head, so that Ernie wouldn't see her eyes rolling. "Why would Frank be demanding that Canyon bring him the missing agent, if Frank is the one who killed her?"

Ernie still looked clueless. "Who's Frank?"

"Try to stay with me here. Frank is the prisoner. I'm Liana. You're Ernie. Any of this ringing a bell."

"I just asked a question. You don't have to be so condescending about it."

Taking a calming breath, she said, "You're right. I'm sorry. What I was trying to tell you is that I think that John Canyon killed that missing agent, and the captain knows something about it."

"Keep your voice down," Ernie said. "The prisoner might hear you. And I would't believe anything he offers. Your buddy Frank is obviously insane."

This time she let him see her eyes rolling. "Is that your professional opinion?"

"Yes, it is. And I think I'll take the word of two men I respect over some drugged-out lunatic. He's probably hopped up on bath salts or something. I mean, look at him." Ernie gestured toward the prisoner, and they both glanced in the direction of the drunk tank.

Liana gasped as she noticed the prisoner leaning forward against the bars closest to them. The man had moved like a shadow, without making a sound. It had been like he had simply vanished from one spot and appeared in another.

The prisoner cocked his head and said, "You do realize, Officer Pitka, that I've heard every word that you've said. To be honest, I resent the implication that my performance has been somehow chemically enhanced. I seldom even drink."

Pitka placed his hands over his Taser and said, "Sir, I need you to step back from the bars."

Frank laughed. "Or what? You mentioned earlier about how I wasn't afraid of Mr. Canyon and his shotgun. Yet, you choose to threaten me with a Taser. That's adorable."

Pulling the Glock instead of the Taser, Pitka said, "When he left for the Ranch, the captain told us not to take any chances with you. If you don't sit your ass back down on that cot, then I'm going to shoot you in the leg. How adorable is that?"

The prisoner didn't speak. He merely smiled and locked gazes with Pitka for a long moment.

Then he abruptly took a step back from the bars and, with wild eyes, said, "I'm really starting to enjoy you two. While we wait for the grownups to play their parts, how would you kids like to play a little game?"

10

John Canyon had agreed to ride with Yazzie. He was regretting that decision now as the police captain drove with no trace of urgency. Canyon said, "I just bought the station new Yukons last year. Tell me these things go faster than this."

"I'm watching the road for signs of where they went and what happened."

"The pickup was found nearly a mile up this road," Canyon said and gestured toward the dirt and sparse gravel road that lay before them. "At this rate, Toby will die of dehydration before we reach them."

Yazzie didn't take his eyes off the road. "You pay me to do a job. I actually think I'm not bad at it, so shut up and let me work."

Canyon thought of the large hunting knife sheathed at his side. For not the first time, he considered what it would be like to slit Yazzie's throat with it. He said, "If you were anyone else—"

"But I'm not anyone else. I'm the guy in charge of peace and security in this valley and making sure that our people have a better way of life. You supply the money and commerce to make that possible. But if you'd prefer that we call in the Bureau of Indian Affairs to assist in this matter, I completely understand."

Canyon cracked his knuckles to keep from cracking open Yazzie's head. "It's just over this hill."

They crested the rise and the dirt road turned into a straight away until dirt gave way to blacktop as the farm road met a more traveled route. Illuminated in the beams of the Yukon's headlights, the wreck of another vehicle he had paid for lay alongside the road, sticking out from a dry creek bed. It was a jacked up old Chevy pickup that four of his men from the Ranch had hopped in to pursue the intruder.

Yazzie said, "You mentioned there were drag marks in the dirt?"

"That's right."

"So you checked the vehicle and walked around the scene of the abduction?"

He sighed. "Yaz, what's your point here?"

"I just need to see your shoes."

With a roll of his eyes, Canyon raised his leg to show the captain his boot. Apparently satisfied, Yazzie stepped from the truck and crept up on the wreckage, shining his Maglite over the ground and the damaged vehicle. Canyon joined him and said, "As I told you, the boys ran off the road, flipped the truck, and that lunatic dragged them from this truck over to the other truck he stole from me."

"Hmm."

"What's that mean? We're wasting time here."

"Do you think our guy Frank carried off all four of those big boys by himself?"

"I suppose so. He certainly looks strong enough."

Shining a light on the blown front and rear tires of the pickup, Yazzie said, "They went off the road because someone popped all their tires with a spike strip like we would use when stopping a suspect. I noticed a spot just up the road where it was probably laid out."

"You're saying that this guy wanted to stir us up like a nest of hornets and then lure a group of my men up here to kidnap them?"

"I would agree with that. But there's something you're still missing. Who laid the spikes out? Frank's tires didn't pop. But when your boys drove through there were spikes on the road. Unless this Frank can run like Carl Lewis or be in two places at once, then he had help."

"Okay, but where did they take my son?"

"We'll lose the trail up ahead where the road is paved."

"That's just great. So this whole trip has been a waste of time."

Yazzie shrugged and adjusted his small wire-framed glasses. "I don't know. I think I learned quite a bit. Now we know that Frank has collaborators. And I can see from the tracks here that the vehicle Frank stole was a loaded semi-trailer. Which makes me wonder what was in the truck?"

"Sheep."

"Just sheep?"

"What difference does it make," Canyon snapped.

"It matters because if it's what i think it is, then someone is going to being royally pissed when it doesn't show up. Maybe enough to send some of their own people looking for the missing shipment."

"That's not going to happen."

"But it could."

"All the more reason for us to find that truck."

Yazzie wiped the sweat from his close cropped hair. "I might as well ask you point blank, John. Do you have any idea what happened to Maggie Carlisle?"

In Diné culture, it was considered rude to look a person

directly in the eyes. Yazzie broke that practice now to demonstrate the seriousness of his question.

Canyon replied, "Not that it should matter to you, but I never saw her. Somewhere between her talking to you and coming up to see me, she must have been bitten by a rattlesnake or fell into a ravine. I have no clue where to find her. And the crazy bastard in that cage is demanding something that I can't give him."

Yazzie shook his head. "I was afraid of that. I don't scare easily, but this guy Frank… I don't know who he really is, but I know what he is. He's an apex predator. He won't take 'I don't know' as an answer."

"Then I guess you had better use your deductive powers to find my son. He can't have gone that far."

"Far enough to make finding a single truck that could be hidden in one of a thousand ramshackle sheds across the valley like finding a specific needle in a cactus field."

Once again, John Canyon felt like slitting Yazzie's throat. "Then what do we do, smart guy?"

"Do you ever pray to the spirits, John?"

"No."

"I would suggest now as a good time to start."

"You better have a plan B. Otherwise, I'm going to turn your station into a slaughterhouse."

Yazzie raised his hands in surrender. "Okay, let's take things one step at a time. And right now, I'm ready for another little chat with our prisoner."

11

The boy hated the men who visited his mother, especially those who did so on a consistent basis. Mother said he should be grateful toward the regulars. They were the clients who put food on their table. But the boy couldn't help but daydream about murdering those men with the sweaty palms and hungry eyes. He drew dark pictures of them in small speckled notebooks at the tiny schoolhouse that served this part of the Rez. He kept the notebooks hidden, which wasn't hard to do. His teacher was usually hungover and merely handed out worksheets. But the boy knew he would be sent to the principal's office if anyone saw the pictures of blood and knives and severed male genitalia. The principal would call his mother and probably force him to see another counselor. And so he kept the notebooks, which also held his personal musings, in a form small enough that he could slip them down the front of his pants if a teacher came sniffing. And if they felt him up to get at the notebooks…well, then they wouldn't be a teacher anymore. Simple solutions to everyday problems.

The boy was almost twelve now. That meant thirteen was just around the corner. And being a teenager, in his mind, meant that he was enough of a man to stand on his own, to take charge of the household and the family business. Being a good business man meant that he couldn't actually go around killing the clients. He had to restrict those desires to the realm of fantasy. But he could still daydream; he could still create his art in the small speckled notebooks.

Having acted as his mother's cashier, receptionist, and booking agent since the time he could add and subtract and mark appointments on a calendar—he wrote out the receipt for Dr. Chee without even looking at the paper.

The receipt was to be given to his mother as proof of the transaction and contained a few pieces of vital information. The first was the length of time each client had with her. The second was the types of sex acts they had paid to engage in. And the third was a small number code that he had developed in order to communicate other personal info about the client, including marriage status, number of children, and whether or not they had gotten rough in the past.

Dr. Chee—the man now standing in their front room sweating through a cattleman western shirt, the puddles of perspiration gathering on the sides of the man's large beer belly—was one of those who liked to occasionally slap his mother around. She had told him that a little bit of that was to be expected, but that he should call his Uncle Red if things ever got out of hand. The boy, however, had no plans to call for help. If the situation presented itself, then he would handle it using grandfather's old hunting knife, which rested nearby him always in the small table beside a couch that also served as his bed.

The boy handed the doctor his change and said, "Let me check that she's ready for you." Then he gestured toward a chair of green plastic that rested between the living room and the hallway leading back to mother's bedroom. Dr. Chee knew the drill. He was a regular customer. And being a regular who liked to beat on his mother, the boy had featured Dr. Chee as the focus of his artwork on many occasions.

The hallway smelled like sweat and burning plastic. Mother must have been smoking some of her cheap crystal meth between clients. When he was younger, he had tried to get mother off the drugs and had failed miserably. The older he became, the less he cared. His mother was merely a cow to be milked until she couldn't be milked any longer. And if smoking some cheap drugs helped the cow to produce more milk, then all the better for the farmer.

He knocked on the door, and after some shuffling, his mother answered in her bathrobe. She was an attractive woman, he supposed. Or at least, she probably was in her youth. His sister, who was less than a year his junior, was gorgeous and petite, and the boy could see the faint traces of the same beauty in his mother. But she was far from thin, with wide hips and a round face filled with half rotten teeth. Coughing as she cracked the door, she said, "I thought my next appointment wasn't until 4:00."

"It's ten after four now. I took my time getting his change and next appointment so you could have a few extra minutes."

"Thanks, baby. Such a good boy," she said as she stroked his cheek, her eyes filled with the ethereal dreaminess of the high.

"I'm sending him back now," the boy said, his expression stone.

Before closing the door, he grabbed a can of air freshener

from a chipboard table in the hall and sprayed the bedroom and the hallway. His mother mumbled, "Such a good boy," as she dropped onto a mattress on the floor.

Dr. Chee was waiting patiently at the end of the hall. The boy said, "I'll give you a couple of minutes before I start your timer, since you had to wait, Dr. Chee."

Standing and adjusting his belt and beer gut, the backwoods doctor said, "Hey, kid, cut the doctor crap. We're all named John, remember." He punctuated the sentence with a wink.

The boy replied, "Well, John, you just remember to watch how rough you get with my mother."

With a little chuckle, Dr. Chee shoved the boy hard enough to throw him back into the brittle wooden paneling of the trailer, cracking the wall and his back along with it. The pain shot up the boy's spine, and tears welled in his eyes.

Standing over him, the doctor said, "I'll be damned if I ever let some ghost-eyed little freak or his junkie whore of a mother tell me what to do. And don't bother checking your little files, kid. I already pulled mine while you were cleaning up mommy. My wife's dead and I don't have any kids, so there's no one to blackmail me with either, you little shit. Next time I come here, you had better keep the commentary to yourself, or I'll really give you something to cry about."

The boy kept his eyes on the floor. He had found that it was often best to adopt the strategies of the opossum and the armadillo. Dr. Chee had already sauntered down the hallway by the time the boy raised his gaze from the floor.

He thought of what the doctor had called him: "A ghost-eyed freak."

The boy had been born a partial ocular albino, which meant that his right eye had no pigment. He still had perfect vision, but the eye had always seemed to unnerve people. One of the older, more traditional Navajo men in their community had actually prayed over him as a baby, fearing that the boy's white eye meant that he lived half in this world and half in the spirit realm.

The other kids teased him about it, and grownups seemed uneasy around him. Many times, he had considered whether or not it would be better to wear an eye patch, even though he could see perfectly. He had read in a science magazine that they now had colored contacts that could cover his deformity, but his family could barely afford to eat. Colored contacts simply weren't in the budget.

One day when he had come home from school crying, his mother had sat him down and said, "Anyone who is worth knowing will take the time to get to know the real you. And a little problem with your eye won't matter a bit." He hadn't spoke the words aloud at the time, but in his head, he had thought: But what If I'm also a freak underneath?

Now, laying on the floor covered in chips of rotting wood and tears, the boy's rage threatened to overwhelm him, and his thoughts focused on grandfather's knife. But rather than going for the weapon, he pulled out a small speckled notebook and began to draw. His pencil flew over the page as he considered what he would like to do to Dr. Chee. The boy covered the white space of the page like a wildfire burning out of control, his rage and pain flowing out in the dark strokes of his pencil.

After a few moments, he paused to examine his work. The picture was of the boy slipping a condom over his grandfather's hunting knife in preparation for violating the doctor in much the same way the doctor did the boy's mother.

His pencil stopped mid-stroke as he heard a piercing scream from down the hallway. His thoughts once again turned to the hunting knife waiting for him in the drawer only a few feet away.

12

Ackerman had been considering what it would be like to stand on shore as a tidal wave approached. He imagined the water pulling back from the sand like a parting curtain, revealing a vast underwater kingdom. Creatures of all kind flopped and flailed about after having been thrust suddenly into a totally alien environment. The wave gained force, gathering up into itself like a mighty titan taking a deep breath. And then it rushed toward him, all the thunder and ferocity of nature amalgamated into one thrust of ultimate power. It was as if the fist of God himself was sweeping toward the coast. It had been beautiful, and he was a bit perturbed when the two children had drawn him out of his mental palace with their blathering.

But this wasn't a pleasure cruise. He was here on business and listening in on these two oblivious fools would most definitely fall under the purview of his mission parameters.

Having decided it was time to take advantage of having the two young officers all to himself, Ackerman had walked to the bars and said, "How would you kids like to play a little game?"

It was an old and familiar phrase he had uttered in many variations to victims over the years. Unfortunately, sometimes his lack of fear had the bi-product of his mouth making promises that he wasn't sure he could make happen in real life. However, his lack of fear also made it so that he didn't care, and more often than not, in his experience, he could come through on nearly any promise.

In this instance, he had muttered the old familiar phrase out of habit and then searched his recollection for a game to play. Typically, he had an entire cerebral storehouse of little games he wanted to play with people. Things that he wanted to learn about the normals. But as of late, his thoughts had not been on such matters, and so he had no game in mind to play.

Which was even more fun. He loved improvisation.

Officer Pitka said, "We're not supposed to speak to you. Please stay back from the bars, sir. Or I will be forced to incapacitate you."

Ackerman had been about to respond to Pitka when the impetuous Liana surprised him once more. She said, "I like that idea. Let's play a game. How about truth or dare? You ask first."

With a shake of his head, Ackerman replied, "Sorry, I don't play that game. Bad things happen when I do. You see, I have this deep compulsion to complete every dare. Which can be a problem if say someone dares you to assassinate the president of Zimbabwe."

"Okay, let's just play truth then."

"Fair enough. I'll ask first. Your captain is lying to me. Maggie has been here. And I saw the look on your face when he said it. You know more than you're saying."

She said, "Is there a question in there?"

"Did you see my friend before she went missing?"

Pitka interrupted, saying, "Liana don't tell him anything. We're not even supposed to talk to him."

Ignoring her counterpart, she asked, "If I tell you the truth, will you answer a question for me?"

"Those are the rules of the game, but if it sets your mind at ease, you have my word."

"And I want your answer first."

Ackerman narrowed his eyes at the young officer. "That would be a deviation from the rules."

"I'm merely adjusting the rules before we start."

"So you want to hear both questions and my answer before you give your own answer? Where's the trust? My nature would be to make you pay dearly for thinking that you are in any position to dictate the terms of a game to me. But I admire your spirit. Ask me your question, I will tell you no lies."

He noticed that she hadn't stopped trembling during the entire exchange, although she mostly kept the quiver from her voice. Officer Liana was clearly terrified, and yet she had still pushed forward to find the ever elusive "truth." He respected that. It also meant that her acts were born of courage, not of defiance. This was important because he needed to be sure that everyone recognized his superiority under the present circumstance.

She said, "Who are you really?"

"That's a terrible question. It would take you a decade to know who I really am. Plus, it's more of an existential quandary than a practical one."

She shook her head. "What is your relationship to the missing agent?"

"Professionally or personally?"

"Both. Pick one. Maybe answer my question with a statement rather than another question."

He smiled. "You're feisty, I like that. But be careful that you don't turn my mood from feisty to fiery. I'm sort of like that mythological hero known as The Incredible Hulk. Like him, you wouldn't enjoy my company when I'm in an enraged state."

"Angry. It's supposed to be angry, not—"

The nice thing about the drunk tank being so small was that Ackerman could easily reach one side or the other with one movement. He did so now as he spun away from the bars and rammed the sole of his tactical boot into the paneling that lined the rear wall of the cage. He aimed the kick into the same area of the thin barrier where Canyon had discharged the shotgun. The entire side wall of the station seemed to shift and crack with the blow.

In the same motion, he spun back and returned to his original position. The lights in the trailer flickered and dust shook down from the ceiling. It had the effect of making Ackerman seem to move in flash. Both of the Tribal Police officers now had their guns at the ready and very serious looks on their faces.

He smiled and said, "That's the kind of thing I'm talking about. Don't for a second forget that I'm on this side of the bars because I've chosen to be. And for the record, I was paraphrasing."

Liana looked at him over the barrel of her Glock and said, "You didn't answer the question."

"Maggie Carlisle is a member of my team. She has also engaged in unmarried carnal relations with my brother on countless occasions. Well, not really 'countless,' I'm sure we could figure the variables and average out those numbers if you were so inclined. However, I will say that I consider her to be my little sister, despite my brother's issues with commitment."

Gun still drawn, she grimaced and said, "You and her are on the same team? Does that mean that you're also a federal agent?"

"That's a second question, and I've yet to receive your first answer."

"Yes, I saw your 'little sister' before she went missing."

"Then why did you tell the FBI and BIA agents that you had not?"

"That's another question. But I don't need the answer to mine now. You must be a federal agent if you know what I told them."

"Technically, I'm not. I'm more of an expert consultant."

"I knew it. You're here on some kind of sting operation."

"Now you're avoiding your obligation. Why did you lie? And if you lie to me..." Ackerman fixed her with his most intense gaze, letting a bit of his old gleeful madness find its way into his eyes.

"I was under orders."

"That defense will not hold up in court. You should know that. Or did you learn nothing from your criminal justice degree?"

"How do you know I have a degree?"

Liana holstered her weapon, but the male officer kept his sidearm aimed and ready to fire.

Ackerman rolled his eyes. "You have a framed diploma sitting on your desk, as if you need to keep reminding yourself that you're worthy. And the truth is that you lied because of that same fear. Not the fear of retaliation from your captain or his superior. But for fear that when they go down, they will take you with them. And deeper than that, a fear that you will never escape the reservation."

She said, "I've heard enough. I'm calling our BIA overseer and getting him and a whole team from the FBI out here to sort out this mess. If you're really an expert consultant for the government, then that should be fine with you."

"It"s not fine with me."

Officer Pitka said, "What exactly are you an expert of?"

"I've put in my ten thousand hours on a great many subjects and disciplines." Ackerman answered Pitka, but didn't take his eyes off Liana. He added, "You asked me earlier who I really am. The truth of the matter is that I'm an infamous serial murderer whom the government recruited to be part of a clandestine task force that hunts other individuals with bloody tastes. Does that information make you feel better or worse in regard to your current situation?"

She looked at him with skepticism written across her squinting eyes and furrowed brow, and then she reached for the phone on her desk.

He said, "I can't allow you to call in your BIA colleagues. They are not privy to knowledge of this operation."

"I don't see how you're going to stop me. I should have come clean before now."

She picked up the receiver, retrieved a card from her desk, and began to dial the number.

Ackerman said, "Now is not the time to be stubborn and naive. I shared the details of my former life with you so that you may better understand that my threats are not idle ones. If John Canyon doesn't return my little sister within the next three hours and twenty-nine minutes, then I'm going to let the demon in me come out to play. And if you don't put down that phone, you'll be the first to glimpse what's coming."

Liana's finger hovered over the last number. A few seconds passed, and finally, she set down the receiver. "Your friend was here. I was filling out some arrest reports and playing receptionist. The walls of Captain Yazzie's office are paper thin. We can hear everything that goes on in there. I don't think Yazzie even realizes it."

"And what did you hear through those paper thin walls?"

"Nothing. She asked him a few questions, standard stuff. Then she took a phone call—which was strange since cell reception here is usually pretty bad. And then she left. There were no tough questions, no disagreements. Just a friendly chat, and then she left. She was still talking on her phone when she walked out the door."

"She didn't ask him any questions about John Canyon?"

"My guess would be that she was leading up to it, but then the call she received must have been more important than talking to Yazzie. I would suggest that you look for the person on the end of that call."

"We have. It was an untraceable burner phone, which was purchased with cash at a store with no cameras."

Lowering her voice to a whisper, as if they were forming some sort of secret alliance, she said, "You talk an awful lot like a cop for being some psycho killer. You can drop the act with me. I want to help make things right."

"You think I'm faking? That I'm some sort of cop merely pretending to be menacing? I find such an assumption to be downright unsettling. I propose we play another game so that I may redeem myself."

"There's no need. I don't—"

"No, no. Don't speak. I'll just ignore you anyway. This is a simple game that I'm sure transcends cultural barriers as being a staple of childhood. I wouldn't know of such things firsthand because I was being tortured and witnessing terrible atrocities during most of my youth. The process did succeed in my father's goal of metamorphosing me into what is basically another species. An abnormal mutation. But from what I've gathered from observing normal human development, this would most assuredly be a universal childhood game. I'm going to hold up a group of fingers on my right hand. You guess the number I'm holding up. If you're correct, then you win. Otherwise, I win."

"You want me to guess how many fingers you're holding up behind your back? Why? What does that prove?"

"Come on, you've been a good sport so far. What's the harm in guessing a number?"

His hands were already behind his back and cuffed, and so he didn't need to move in order to play the game. At least, not yet. Ackerman said, "Go ahead. How many fingers."

"Two."

"Is that your final answer?"

"Yes, two."

And then came the moment that Ackerman had been drawing out with delicious deliberateness. He raised his right hand in front of his face and said, "You lose. It was three."

Liana's eyes went wide, but Ackerman guessed her shock was not at her defeat but rather at the open handcuff which dangled from his right hand. Then, before Liana could recover, Ackerman leaped into action, heading first in the direction of Officer Pitka.

13

The bars of the small cell were exactly what Ackerman would have imagined as having existed in the old west. He wondered if that was where the remote station had acquired the materials to build their drunk tank. It was only another small step to conjure images of such famous outlaws as Jesse James or Billy the Kid staring out through the same bars. And if that was the case, it would also be fair to say that they may have reached through the bars and grabbed hold of some famous lawmen of a bygone era. In the fictional history he had projected for the bars of the cell, he was about to join esteemed company who had once possibly spilled blood on the same iron that Ackerman was about to.

Having already choreographed and mentally practiced the maneuver—which he prepared as he distracted the normals with words—Ackerman rammed his arm through the bars. One ring of the handcuffs was still attached to his right wrist, but the other side of the cuffs hung free. As he had predicted, Officer Pitka had hesitated to fire. Maybe it was a second, maybe much less. But Ackerman knew from experience that the time it would take for Pitka's brain to process the proper reaction and for his finger to slide from the trigger guard to the trigger itself would be more than sufficient.

With a twist of his arm, Ackerman swung the open ring

of the cuffs at Pitka's wrist. The metal loop snapped closed, and Ackerman yanked the shocked kid toward the bars.

Caught off balance, Pitka slammed into the bars headfirst. Somewhere amid his plunge, he released a blast into the ceiling, but he dropped the Glock when his head collided with the iron.

Ackerman had made special note of the pocket of the utility belt where Pitka had placed the key to the cell door. Liana was screaming for him to get down, but any shot she may have had was blocked by her partner. Yanking again, he slammed the young officer's body into the bars to keep him positioned as a shield. Then, with his left hand, Ackerman keyed the cell's lock and opened the door. As the latch disengaged, he tore his right hand free of the cuffs. The pain from the skin he left behind was like a cool breeze against his face.

The handcuffs were now free from his wrist and still attached to Pitka's. Twisting the kid's arm up at an awkward angle, he snapped the cuffs latched against a rung of the cage. Stepping to the other side of the bars, Ackerman pulled the Taser free from Pitka's belt.

Liana was still yelling something and trying to get a clean shot. She was wearing body armor, which would make an effective shot with the Taser unlikely. Instead, he flicked his wrist and tossed the weapon like a boomerang directly at Liana's forehead. It collided with a thwack, and Liana reflexively pulled back from the pain, which gave him the chance to rush forward and disarm his impetuous new friend.

Ackerman heard the screeching tires of a vehicle in front of the station house, most likely Canyon and Captain Yazzie having heard Pitka's wayward pistol discharge.

Lucky for them, further violence wasn't necessary. He felt his point had been made.

Instead of fighting back, Ackerman returned to the cell, leaving the gun behind, and laid down on the cot.

To the figure of Thomas White watching from the corner of the cell, he said, "Happy now."

His imagined father released a low chuckle and replied, "Poetry in motion. Although, you should have killed them both. That would have sent a much better message."

Leaning back and closing his eyes, Ackerman said, "See, right there. That's how I know that you're only in my mind. My real father would never allow me even that much of a compliment."

14

John Canyon had seen a lot of frightening thing. Headless corpses. The charred remains of children. During his second tour in the Persian Gulf, he bore witness to terrible atrocities inflicted upon the Kuwaiti people by the invading Iraqi soldiers in what was essentially organized rape and murder. He had faced enemies with hearts full of the worst kinds of depravity. Even then, he had never faced an enemy that frightened him like the man in the cage.

Canyon sat in front of the bars and watched his enemy watching him. He was reminded of a tiger he had once seen behind glass. This man, Frank, seemed to be a predator of equal magnitude, a powerful force of determination and skill.

His instincts told him to unload the shotgun into Frank and let the chips fall where they may.

With no preamble, he asked, "Is my son already dead?"

"No. He's alive. For now."

"I don't know what happened to your missing agent. You're declaring war on the wrong man."

Frank leaned forward, the old cot protesting beneath his shifting weight. "You still don't understand, Mr. Canyon. This is not a war. This is an extermination. But then again, I suppose the termites being sprayed with poison would feel that they are at war. To the exterminator, it's just another day at the office."

79

"You seem a bit overconfident for a man behind bars."

"Please, look at your officers."

Canyon glanced over to the other side of the station where Yazzie was dressing a small wound on Liana's forehead.

Frank continued, "I could have killed them both. In the old days, I would have had some fun with the girl. She has fire. I bet she would surprise herself with how strong she could be. The other officer I would have probably just killed outright. He bores me. And I don't like his name. Pit-cuh. What's his first name?"

"Ernie."

"That's terrible. I would have killed him for sure."

"This is all just a big game to you, isn't it?"

"When viewed in a certain light, life is always a game. One with no rules, but definite winners and losers."

"It's the middle of the night. And I'm sitting here listening to fortune cookie philosophy from a guy who kidnapped my son. In most instances, I would be of a mind to start cutting on you until you answer my questions, but I get the feeling that you would never talk. I can see from your scars that you're no stranger to pain. So what do I do with a man who I can't force to talk?"

Frank shrugged. "It is a dilemma, and your only real option is to acquiesce to my demands. Return Maggie Carlisle to me, and you'll get your son back."

Canyon shook his head. "Would I? Even if I knew what had happened to your friend, why would I trust that you to hold up your end or that those boys are even still alive? No, I think I do have one other option."

Standing and crossing the room, Canyon retrieved his shotgun from where he had rested it earlier. Yazzie called from the other side of the station, "John, what are you doing?"

"What I should have done from the start," Canyon said, heading toward the prisoner.

He raised the gun to fire at a spot between the iron bars, but before Canyon could take aim, Frank launched himself across the cell and collided with the back wall of the makeshift prison. Frank was a large man, and he appeared to be aiming straight for the part of the wall damaged by the earlier shotgun blast. Dropping his shoulder and balling up, the prisoner broke through the paneling, the two by fours of the wall, and the fiberglass shell of the station.

Canyon stood dumbfounded as the man called Frank disappeared into the night through an exit of his own making. Trying to recover, he fired three volleys of lead into the back wall of the station, hoping to get lucky. But as he peered through the hole in the wall, he saw no bodies outside.

Turning to the three officers, who had drawn their weapons but seemed unsure of what to do now, Canyon screamed, "What the hell are you waiting for? You have a prisoner escaping!"

Coming to his senses, Yazzie barked orders to his two underlings, and the four of them trailed the man called Frank into the night.

15

As Ackerman burst free from the building—after having cannonballed himself at the least structurally sound point of the wall, where the shotgun blast had been centered and where he had aimed his previous kick whilst educating the children—his first thought was: Find the closest darkness. The quote was from a childhood memory in which his father had been instructing him in ways of escaping pursuers. His father had elaborated, "Darkness is our friend in nearly every instance, Junior. Why is that?"

"If you seek the deepest darkness, then you will be able to see them coming by their light."

Now, as he hit the ground with the balls of his feet and rolled away, his first thought had been his father's teaching of embracing darkness. His second thought was that an exquisite pain had bitten into his arm, probably a cut from the metal or building materials of the cheaply made outpost. Either that or Canyon got lucky with one of his shotgun blasts.

Ackerman knew that John Canyon had been a decorated soldier, and his skills were obviously still sharp. Canyon had responded almost instantly to the escape. Perhaps not as fast as Ackerman himself would have performed, but the speed of Canyon's reactions spoke to Ackerman of a soldier who was years from a battlefield but still looking for a war.

The surprise had led to a piece of either buckshot or shrapnel to become lodged in Ackerman's back and side. He mostly ignored the pain as he hit the ground running and passed by the officer's parked vehicles, up a small rise, and down and up two more.

It was at this point that he allowed himself to enjoy the pain. The tendrils of cold fire had spiderwebbed out from the point of the wounds. The faster he ran and the harder he pumped his arms, the more the pain burrowed inside like a rat fleeing fire.

The pain didn't slow him down, however. It rejuvenated him, refreshed him.

He listened for the sound of feet slapping dirt, and using echolocation, he surmised that the officers were clinging to the perimeter of the station's pole light. That was good. It meant that none of them had witnessed the direction into which he had fled. But the officers would soon find his tracks and retrieve flashlights to mount a search.

If they stayed on foot, then he would have no problem outpacing any of them for any amount of time. The issue was that they would take to their four wheel drive vehicles and try to cut him off, a pincer maneuver placing armed officers at his back and armed officers at his front. He couldn't outrun a truck or a bullet. He had tried to do both on multiple occasions to no avail. Although, he had yet to be killed by either, so maybe he was being too harsh on himself.

As Ackerman half-stumbled down a hill of jagged rock, which was barely visible in the sparse light of the moon, Thomas White appeared beside him, matching his pace and stride. Ackerman said, "Yet another example of how you differ from my real biological father. He could never hold a candle to me physically."

"Perhaps, but mentally there is no question of his superiority."

"That's preposterous."

"Really, which one of us spent half their life in a cage and which one of us operated under the radar for years, killing and never being caught. The police even believing him to be long deceased. Thanks for your help on that, by the way."

"The important thing is which one of us is in the cage now. You may have been the most prolific murderer in history," Ackerman said, "but who cares if no one will ever know a thing about it."

White laughed and said, "You can't keep the devil chained forever, Junior. Just ask John the Revelator."

"As if you believe in any of that. And you're not the devil. You're just a sick and broken man who spent so much of his life in crippling fear that the only way he could function was to let that fear and pain flow out onto others."

Changing the subject, White said, "They're going to catch you. This is all open desert and rocks out here. You could try for the mesa and find a cave or head for town and maybe take a family hostage. But unless those four are entirely incompetent, they should be able to run you down out here with a couple of officers on foot and the others in vehicles."

"You always did underestimate me."

"Or perhaps I drove you to be even better than we both could have imagined. But they're still going to catch up to you within a matter of minutes. Hell, they could be waiting for you over this rise."

"I haven't heard any engine noise or seen headlights, so that's pretty unlikely."

"When they find you, there's only one thing you can do… You have to kill them all."

"Oh, dad, that's what you always say."

"I'm serious. You're only way out is through. Canyon will shoot you on sight. I suppose when the moment comes, I could just take control and dispatch them. I certainly can't allow your stubborn refusal to take life result in the same being done to us."

"There is no 'us.' You're just a figment of my imagination. Nothing more than a minor and likely temporary glitch in my programming. You cannot 'take control.' You don't exist."

"I exist within you, just like you exist within you. I don't see why I couldn't take the reigns for a bit."

And then Ackerman heard what he didn't want to hear: the sound of tires rolling over dry ground and rock. A vehicle was approaching, and he had nowhere to go.

16

Liana felt like she was wandering through a bad dream. Her world grew more terrible by the moment, and yet, she just kept moving forward, kept pretending to do her job. She felt like a puppet being pulled in a thousand different directions. And yet, somehow, she kept moving forward, sweeping her flashlight over the dirt and scrub-brush, checking for tracks or hiding places.

One of her puppet masters, John Canyon, did the same twenty yards to her left. She had to fight in order to match his pace as he ascended a rocky outcropping and sprinted his way to the summit of the next rise. Out of breath, Canyon paused for a moment at the top, shining his light into the small valley below.

Liana joined him at the top and matched his actions, thankful for a chance to rest, even for a second. Not that she was out of shape. Yazzie had instituted his own regulations in regard to fitness at their small outpost. Despite being over twice her age, she knew that the captain was surprisingly strong and fast. Still, she wasn't surprised when Yazzie elected to take one of the trucks up ahead to cut off the stranger. She had been surprised, however, when John Canyon threw the keys of his truck to Pitka, grabbed a flashlight, and reloaded his shotgun. Canyon had to be close to the same age as Yazzie, yet he seemed to be imbued with a warrior's fire where Yazzie was acting like his usual dreamily indifferent self, despite the dangerous circumstances they faced.

Closing the distance between them, Canyon said, "I found his tracks and some blood, looks like I may have hit him with one of my shots."

Liana said nothing.

"What did the stranger say to the two of you in there?"

"I already told you."

"Tell me again. Every detail."

"He said that he was a serial killer who now worked as a consultant for the government and that the missing agent was his friend and colleague. He called her his 'little sister.' But I'm sure that was all just a story to scare us."

In a low growl, Canyon said, "I wouldn't put anything past the white man and his government. They've certainly employed serial killers in the past."

"When?"

"How about the cavalry men who bashed in the skulls of our ancestors, using their boots to save on bullets?"

"Those were soldiers acting under orders."

"I'm not talking about them fighting us warrior to warrior. They did this to women, children, babies. Unless you want to argue that our people are less than human, then I would consider all of those men to be serial killers."

Liana heard the whine of engines in the distance. She said, "We had better get moving, Mr. Canyon."

"When we find this guy, Frank... I'm going to kill him. Do you have a problem with that, Officer Nakai?"

Liana wanted to scream that she sure as hell did have a

problem with that, but she held her tongue. Considering her words carefully, she replied, "No offense or disrespect intended, but to be perfectly honest, from what I've seen, I'm not overly concerned about protecting him from you. It's more the other way around."

17

30 years earlier…

The boy had been taught that a little screaming was okay. His mother had explained that some men needed to hear her scream, to see her in pain, in order to be satisfied. She had instructed him to call for help only if she screamed his name and "help" specifically.

His mother didn't really need to explain the desire of some clients to hurt her. The boy's favorite hobby was torturing small animals and imagining doing the same to his mother's clients. He wondered if the shrieks of terror issued by various animals as they met their ends were also cries for help. Were those animals afraid to die? Did they know what it was to die? Or were his torture victims merely reacting to the external stimulus of pain.

He sharpened his grandfather's knife on a wet stone as he sat on the ratty old couch and watched one of about ten VCR tapes that he had viewed at least a thousand times a piece.

Only if she screamed his name… A name he'd always hated and planned to change when he was old enough. Still, he longed for the day when she—

Bugs Bunny had just met Marvin the Martian when he heard a crash and his mother's voice calling his name in a voice he had never heard before. "Xavier! Help!" she shrieked. Her screams reminded the boy of the high-pitched keening of a desert hare when caught in a trap and dying.

Xavier sat ramrod straight, unmoving, unsure whether or not he was merely daydreaming.

Out of the television's crackling speakers Bugs Bunny asked Marvin, "What's up, Doc?" The cartoon rabbit's iconic line was followed by another crash and more choked screams for help. Another scream of "Xavier!"

This time, the boy leaped into action. He ran to the kitchen where a mint green rotary phone hung on one wall. He spun the dial for his uncle's house, just across the valley. But the phone kept ringing, and his mother kept screaming. He considered running to a neighbor's or calling the police, but then he looked down at the knife stretching from his right fist, and the boy knew that this was the moment which he had been patiently awaiting, the day he would turn daydream into reality.

He hurried down the hall to his mother's bedroom and workplace, but he paused at the door. The room on the other side had gone quiet. He worried that he was already too late. He had failed. His hesitation had cost his mother her life. He placed his ear to the door and listened.

The barrier was made from cheap particle board with a hollow core. In the room beyond, he heard what sounded to him like someone gurgling water in the back of their throat. It took a moment for the boy's rich imagination to picture the room beyond and realize that the sound was Dr. Chee choking the life from his mother.

He opened the door and let it swing inward. Dr. Chee was naked atop the mattress, straddling his mother, the doctor's large hands wrapped around his mother's neck.

The pent-up rage of watching years of "Johns" walk though his front door fueled his courage, and he yelled a guttural war cry as he rushed toward the doctor, the knife held out in front of him like the horn of a rhinoceros.

The boy realized his mistake halfway across the bedroom when Dr. Chee whirled around and, taking advantage of his longer adult reach, backhanded the boy with enough force to send him flying across the room and smashing into the small table and mirror that his mother used to repair her makeup after each client. Pain shot down his left arm, and his vision went white.

Barely clinging to consciousness, Xavier heard his mother scream his name again as she fought to free herself, his attack apparently having given her an opening. Tiny shards of glass stung his left hand. He picked some of the larger pieces free from his flesh and ignored the rest. Attempting to push himself to his feet caused snakes of fire to shoot through his shoulder. The world spun, growing and swelling, as his stomach flipped in circles.

Dr. Chee screamed unintelligible obscenities as he began kicking Xavier's mother and then dropped back onto her. The doctor's eyes were wide and wild with rage. In that moment, the boy knew that Dr. Chee had no intentions of stopping. If he didn't act now, his mother would be dead, and he would follow shortly after as the crazed physician covered his crime.

It was now or never. Kill or be killed.

Swallowing down the waves of pain, he retrieved his grandfather's hunting knife from the floor and rushed once more at Dr. Chee.

This time, however, the boy didn't scream. Instead,

having learned his lesson about announcing an assault to an opponent, he attacked from his opponent's blindspot and moved as quickly and quietly as possible.

The doctor was hunched over Xavier's mother, his flabby rear-end tensed up and sticking up in the air as the doctor pushed his weight down onto his victim's throat.

The boy aimed for the biggest target. He threw all of his weight into the stab as he plunged the hunting knife straight between Dr. Chee's two hairy butt cheeks.

Xavier would never forget the sound the doctor made. It was shrill and animalistic, more the squeal of a dying pig than the screams of a man. But the boy detected traces of intelligence, a fear of imminent death, that didn't seem present in his animal victims. The notes of Dr. Chee's death song sent shivers of pleasure up Xavier's spine.

Bucking and writhing, the doctor knocked the boy backwards, but he kept hold of the knife, pulling it free with him. Blood spurted from Dr. Chee's rear and stained the whole room as the doctor flailed about, fighting the throes of death.

Blood loss and shock soon tired out the dying man, and he fell back atop the mattress amid a growing stain of crimson red.

His mother rushed to the boy's side and helped him off the matted green carpet. She tried to lead him from the room and cover his eyes, but he shoved her away and said, "Get off of me. I'm staying!"

Then the boy approached the dying doctor, while remaining a safe distance away. He knew that animals were often most dangerous just before death. One of Xavier's favorite pastimes was capturing rabbits and stray cats and, after playing with them for a bit, slitting their throats. That was his favorite part: watching the look in their eyes as they realized death was coming for them.

But he had never seen that look in the eyes of another person, a person whose fear gave him power, until this moment. He had imagined it. He had fantasized about it. And he wasn't disappointed. The look in Dr. Chee's eyes revealed a whole new level of fear that no animal other than a human could attain.

The boy watched as the doctor sobbed in pain and tried crawling toward the door. The old man grew paler by the second as more of his lifeblood stained the carpet. Rolling onto his back, Dr. Chee struggled for breath and reached out toward the boy. He begged, "Please…Help…Ambulance…"

The boy smiled in response and said, "What's up, Doc?… Oh, sorry, I forgot again. You're all named John!"

Xavier felt like he was a soaring eagle now. He had never been so light and filled with joy. He had never known true happiness until that moment. Overwhelmed by some unnamed ethereal emotion, repeating the name "John" over and over to himself, the boy began to laugh uncontrollably and couldn't stop until Dr. Chee had passed into the darkness.

Closing the doctor's lifeless eyelids, the boy cackled even harder at the thought that a ghost-eyed freak laughing in his face was the last thing that the doctor ever saw.

18

Ackerman watched the lifted jeep rumble toward him over the hard-pack of the desert floor, trampling over scrub brush like a metal elephant. The driver had turned off the headlights, apparently to approach without being seen. Ackerman—accounting for the roar of the big engine, the crushing of desert foliage, and the telltale cloud of dust—surmised the attempt at stealth to be an exercise in futility. Still, he knew that his brother was merely trying to buy them every spare second using the variables he could control.

Special Agent Marcus Williams—Ackerman's baby brother—pulled the Jeep to a stop and said, "Looks like you could use a ride."

"I have the situation under control."

Marcus shrugged. "Says the guy bleeding all over himself."

"A mere flesh wound."

"You sure about that? Looks like a lot of blood. To be clear, I'm not worried about you. But this Jeep is a rental, and so I really need you to try not to let your 'flesh wound' stain the seats."

Now it was Ackerman's turn to shrug. "If it's an issue, I can find my way on foot. Do you perhaps have a water bottle or—"

"Get in the damn jeep, Frank," Marcus said, his head swiveling around to watch for the pursuing vehicles of the

Tribal Police. The reaction caused a smile to spread across Ackerman's face. His brother was perhaps the toughest man he had ever met—besides himself, obviously—but his superiority was always proven in moments like this. No matter how tough Marcus pretended to be, his brother was still afraid to die, while he was afraid of nothing.

Climbing up inside the open cab of the Jeep, Ackerman said, "If you insist on hurrying off."

Throwing the big jeep into gear and cutting a path up the rise, toward the rock wall of the mesa and away from their pursuers, Marcus said, "It looks like your plan didn't work out like you had hoped."

"On the contrary, dear brother, the reconnaissance phase of this operation was a resounding success."

"Reconnaissance phase? I thought Canyon was supposed to take you to wherever he's keeping Maggie. I thought this 'operation' only had one phase."

"What is it you like to say?… Improvise, adapt, and overcome."

"Maggie could be running out of time. If she's still…" Marcus's words trailed off as tears welled in his eyes.

Ackerman said, "I'm more aware than most of the true enemy of all mankind. The name of the unconquerable foe of humanity."

Swiping at his cheeks, Marcus shifted into third gear and asked, "Death?"

Cocking an eyebrow, Ackerman replied, "Death is but a doorway for those who believe. I was referring to a power only transcended by God himself: Time. Time is the real Taker. An adversary every living soul must battle and a force by which we will all be defeated."

Marcus said, "Focus for me, Frank. What did you learn in there?"

"I discovered quite a bit. For example, Mr. Canyon was almost as worried about his sheep as he was his son."

Marcus said nothing, his brow furrowed in concentration. Ackerman loved that his brother didn't ask needless questions of him like the normals always did. His brother merely understood the possible scenarios his information implied and drove off into the night. It all brought a small smile to Ackerman's lips. It was funny how he had lived most of his life without his brother, but now, he couldn't imagine any kind of life without him.

19

As they ate, Maggie stared into Marcus's eyes and noticed an anomaly. "Your eyes are different colors."

"Yeah, most people don't notice. My eyes are kinda gray-green, but the right one is half brown. It's called sectoral heterochromia."

"Is that some kind of disorder? Nothing contagious, I hope?"

He laughed. "It can be related to certain syndromes, but I don't think I have any of them. It can also be a sign that you had a twin you absorbed in the womb. They call it chimerism. In that case, I could actually have multiple sets of DNA in different body parts. I don't think I have that either. I also read once that some believe it to be a sign that you're descended from Swedish royalty, or something like that. I think I'm just a dude with a funny colored eye."

"I told you that you were an odd man."

"I didn't dispute it. What about you? You have any oddities?"

She straightened her silverware and folded her napkin into a perfectly symmetrical square. "No, I'm completely normal."

He grinned. "Nobody's completely normal."

"I am."

"Really. You're not mildly obsessive compulsive?" She started to open her mouth but stopped. After a moment, she said, "What makes you say that?"

"I pay attention. Your apartment is impeccably clean—not a single picture or decoration is out of place. Every grouping is perfectly balanced. When you eat, you cut every bite into the same size. You make sure that the silverware you're not using is in perfect alignment. You folded your napkin into a square. And when you put the sweetener into your tea, you made sure that the markings on the two packets lined up before you opened them. You even put one back because it was longer than the other packet."

She felt naked before him. She started to say something, decided against it, and stared down at the table.

He reached across and laid a hand over hers. "There's nothing wrong with wanting the world to be in order and make sense."

"But my compulsions don't make any sense. They're irrational. I don't have a good reason for doing them. I just feel like that's the way things should be done. Most people don't notice, so I try to hide it. It makes me feel like a freak."

"Does it make sense to you?"

"What do you mean?"

"Do all the things that you do make sense to you? We each see the world through different eyes. We all have our nuances...our little tics. I'll give you an example. I always sit facing any points of ingress. I always know what's behind me. When I walk into a room, the first thing I do is scan it to find the entrances and exits. I consider what could be used as a weapon in this space. I play out in my mind what I would do if someone walked in the door with a gun. Where's the best place to take cover? What's the best route to flank an armed assailant who just entered? And other things. Who in the room could pose a threat? Who's potentially armed? What's here that's out of place? What's missing? All that runs through my head every time I enter a room. Some people call that cop instincts or training. I call it paranoia."

Marcus squeezed her hand, and she met his gaze. "I don't have a good reason to do all that," he said. "Nobody's after me. I don't have any enemies. Even back in New York, I was never in a restaurant that somebody shot up. Maybe one day it'll save my life, but probably not. Odds are that I'll never be in that situation. But I can't help but run through it. It's just my nature."

Her face brightened. "Thank you."

"For what?"

"For being stranger than me."

PART 2

20

John Canyon stared down at the place where the dirt road merged into paved blacktop and the jeep tracks they had been following ended. He clenched and unclenched his fists and looked up to the dark silhouette of the mesa and the foothills. The madman who had invaded his kingdom was obviously not alone. And they had just slipped through his fingers.

Standing beside him, Yazzie said, "Don't you have some kind of GPS trackers on your trucks? Have you tried to—"

"Of course, I have. Are you suggesting that I'm a total moron?"

"Just covering the bases. That's my job."

"You want to do your job now? Then find my son!"

"That's what I'm trying to do, John. I love the boy too. I'm as sick over it all as you are. We know that they can't be holed up anywhere here in Roanhorse, and they're tracks are heading away from Shiprock. But there are thousands of places out here in the hills and canyons where they could have the boys and the truck stashed. It's a—"

Stepping up into Yazzie's face, Canyon said in a low growl, "Don't you dare give me any needle in a haystack bullshit. If that's the case, then get a big damn magnet to find the needle."

"I will, John. I will. We'll bring Toby home. What about your other problem?"

"What are you talking about?"

"Alvarez. The shipment. You both have protocols and schedules to follow I'm sure. He's going to want answers when the truck doesn't show up."

"You don't need to worry about how I run my business. But just to put your mind at ease, I'm going to call Alvarez and ask him to send up some of his guys to assist us."

"Are you sure that's a good idea? He might see it as weakness, and do we really need a bunch of those...people... coming up here."

"It's a preemptive maneuver. Rather than wait for him to call about the shipment being late, I'll call him and ask for help with our problem. Remember, I don't work for him, and he doesn't work for me. We're independent contractors."

"But what about the next guy in the chain who comes to Alvarez asking questions—"

Grabbing Yazzie by the edges of his body armor, Canyon jerked the police captain forward and nearly lifted him from the ground. Through a clenched jaw, Canyon said, "All you need to worry about is getting your ass back to your station and figuring out how to find my son!"

Yazzie shoved his arms up between Canyon's and broke the hold. Then, within the blink of an eye, Yazzie had pulled his Colt Peacemaker pistol and had it pressed to Canyon's gut. His expression stone and his eyes unreadable behind his dark little glasses, Yazzie calmly whispered, "One of us has killed people, John, and the other is a killer. There's a big difference. Let's not forget who's who."

"Don't cross me, Yaz. You're a long way from the enforcer you were when we were kids."

Returning the gun to his holster and taking a step backward, Yazzie said, "I'll get you a location. You just worry about raising a war party. I hitched my wagon to yours a long time ago, John. You had better handle this mess."

Canyon glared at Yazzie as the captain walked back to the two officers waiting in a brand new Ford Explorer police cruiser that Canyon had paid for. After the SUV rumbled away, Canyon pulled out his phone and made two calls. One to Alvarez to let him know about the shipment, and the other to the ranch. He told the man who answered, "Call our guys at the casino and down in Shiprock. Get everyone up to the ranch now, and tell them to bring all the hardware they can carry."

21

Concealed inside the entrance to an abandoned uranium mine, Ackerman stared into the back of a massive cattle trailer, which held the sheep that were John Canyon's "official" livelihood. According to what they could dig up on Canyon, the rancher had gone as far importing a professional from the Basque region of Spain to run his operations. Canyon had descended from three generations of sheep farmers, but his hired head of operations could trace a lineage of shepherding back several hundred years. As far as the US government was concerned, Canyon was a successful businessman, who had invested the money from his farming operations into a now thriving casino.

But Ackerman had looked in the man's eyes. What he saw there was the blackened heart of a stone cold killer. He knew John Canyon was a criminal and a predator. He, however, couldn't say whether or not Canyon was the particular one they sought.

As he approached, the animals retreated to the far corners of their enclosures. Ackerman smiled, knowing they could also sense a predator. To his brother, he said, "These are the fattest sheep I've ever seen."

With the cocking of an eyebrow, Marcus replied, "And how many sheep have you actually seen in person?"

"I always forget that you're a city boy. If you must know,

I hid from the police once inside the livestock building at a state fair. There were several prize-winning sheep I met there, but none of them were as plump and juicy as these fine specimens."

Marcus sighed. "Okay, let's get one of them out, but since you're the expert, you're in charge of the stupid thing. I'm not in the mood to be chasing down runaway sheep."

"Have you slept at all since Maggie went missing?"

"Let's do this before I change my mind."

Pulling out a built in ramp, the brothers opened one of the metal enclosures and attempted to goad a female sheep, also called an ewe, out into the open. It was, of course, stubborn and refused to move. After some prodding, the first creature and two others made a break for it. Ackerman tried to kick the extra animals back up the ramp, but they paid him no attention. It took another ten minutes to wrangle one of the agitated creatures for closer inspection.

Ackerman grabbed the beast in a headlock while Marcus felt beneath the thick layers of wool. Marcus said, "There's nothing here. It's just wool and skin. I can feel all the way down to its back. Wait..."

"What is it?"

"The skin doesn't feel very warm."

"Is it supposed to?"

Marcus didn't answer. He was busy groping all over the sheep's body. Ackerman added, "Did you know that ISIS traffics sheep as sex slaves?"

Ignoring him and reaching beneath the animal's stomach, Marcus said, "You were right." Then he lifted off a fake skin and wool "costume" from the animal. The ewe, which had been shaved down to its skin, actually appeared quite thin.

Marcus flipped the fake covering onto the rock floor of the mine, exposing a lining filled with bags of white powder.

Marcus looked back at the massive cattle trailer, which they now knew to be loaded with cocaine-smuggling sheep. Ackerman could see his brother's wheels turning. He knew exactly what Marcus—whom he believed to suffer from an undiagnosed form Autism Spectrum Disorder—was thinking. Marcus was calculating, analyzing, and surmising.

Ackerman asked, "Is it enough for us to retire?"

"Street value of about twelve to fifteen million dollars. I guess now we have another bargaining chip with Canyon. I'm sure he's pretty attached to his animals."

"But you forget, dear brother, that when I absconded with Tobias Canyon and commandeered this vehicle, they were preparing to leave with the shipment. Which implies a new set of problems in the coming day, when this shipment doesn't arrive where it's supposed to."

"That's Canyon's problem. All the more reason for him to give up Maggie."

"After having spent some time with Mr. Canyon, I'm not convinced that he would surrender Maggie even if she is truly in his custody. He seems more the type to eliminate the threat and worry about the ramifications later. I think we must consider the possibility that—"

"Don't even speak it. Until I see a body, she's out there, waiting for the both of us to come save her. And I don't care if that means we have to wipe Canyon's little operation right off the face of the Earth to do it. We will find her."

Ackerman laid a hand on Marcus's shoulder and said, "I'll hunt with you to the ends of infinity, dear brother. You know that. But where do we go from here?"

Darkness shifting in his eyes, Marcus said, "We prepare for war. Full out, bloody war."

"Does that mean you're finally allowing me the use of firearms?"

"On this case, you can carry as many guns as you want and a whole hell of a lot of bullets." Punctuating his next statement with a finger in Ackerman's face, Marcus added, "But the same rules of engagement apply. No killing."

"What if it's a ricochet, or what if I shoot them in the foot, but they have some anemic disorder and bleed out. Firearms are far too unpredictable to make any sort of reasonable promise that—"

"No killing. Shit happens, I get that. But it's a last resort, even under the circumstances. And we'll both know if someone goes down, and you could have prevented it. Remember, we're the good guys."

As his brother walked away, Thomas White whispered in Ackerman's ear, "You're going to wake up from this dream soon, Junior. Think about it. Could you and I really be considered akin to these so-called 'good' guys? Marcus is a bit rough around the edges, sure. Still, I could see him as the white knight. But what are you? I suppose we'll find out soon enough, when I take the wheel. Maybe I'll kill your brother first. I haven't quite decided yet."

Ackerman spun around, as if to attack a physical enemy, but there was no one there but him and the night.

22

One month earlier…

Maggie parked her rental car—a Ford Focus hatchback that smelled of body odor and take-out food, the former coming with the car and the latter her own addition—in front of a double-wide trailer that seemed held together only by a new coat of paint. The family who lived here had once told her that they would never move. In hope that their missing daughter, Elisabeth, would find her way home to them. The for-sale sign in the front yard, however, told a different story.

She climbed out and headed up the sidewalk toward a screen door that looked like it was about to fall from its hinges. Through the front window, she saw a small living room lit only by the glow of a television set. Maggie raised her hand to knock on the wood surrounding the screen, but a woman with a deeply-lined and leathery countenance appeared on the side before she could. Even through the barrier and with a strong breeze blowing outside, Maggie detected the stink of cigarette smoke and beer. Without opening the door or greeting Maggie, the familiar woman peered through the screen, her lips flattening, and Maggie noticed door move slightly toward her, as if Elisabeth's mother was holding it shut.

Maggie ignored the reaction and said, "Hello, Mrs.

Crenshaw, it's me…Agent Carlisle. Maggie. I was in the neighborhood and just wanted to stop in and check on you and your husband. It's been awhile since I've heard from you. I've tried to call several times, but—"

Mrs. Crenshaw closed her eyes, took a deep breath, and looked into the other room for a moment before replying, "We're no longer going to be sending you Elisabeth's things, Agent Carlisle. Or helping in your investigation in any way. Please leave."

"But ma'am, you would be surprised what difference even the smallest piece of evidence can make to a case," Maggie explained, in much the same as she had all those years ago when she'd first convinced Elisabeth's family to send her the packages that the Taker sent to them every year on the anniversary of the abduction—the scraps of clothing, hair, and buttons—so that she could have it thoroughly analyzed.

Mrs. Crenshaw laughed bitterly as tears streamed down her cheeks. "Every year, we send you everything we have left of our little girl. What have you been doing with it? What difference does it make?"

"Ma'am, as we've discussed—the post mark, the box or envelope, the packing material—every bit of it could contain some kind of trace evidence that—"

"It doesn't matter. None of it has ever made a speck of difference. You're no closer to finding him now than the police were back then."

"That's not true. We're closer than we've ever been. Mrs. Crenshaw, there have been several new developments."

"Have you found my daughter? Or the man who took her? Do you have any answers for me or just more questions?"

"Well, no, I just—"

"You're worse than the Taker! He sent those packages to torture us, keeping our hope alive, keeping the memory of that anguish, that emptiness, alive. We knew exactly when it was coming, and the dread of it infected the rest of the year. At least he knew when to quit, and I'm grateful that it stopped. Our Elisabeth is long dead, Miss Carlisle, and we're moving on. Your brother is gone too. You should do the same. But most of all, and you listen good now, you get off our property and stay the hell away from us."

The inner door slammed shut, and Maggie heard the locks engaging. She turned numbly, heading back to her rental car. Maybe Mrs. Crenshaw was right, what had she been doing to find them all these years? Had she truly put forth her full effort and dedicated everything to locating Elisabeth and the other children and the man who had taken them?

She dropped in behind the wheel and sat a moment without moving, breathing hard. Then, with a wail of anger and frustration, she slammed her fist into the steering wheel over and over.

All her hope had hinged on acquiring Elisabeth's package. The young girl had been the victim taken closest to her brother's date of abduction, and Maggie hadn't received a package for going on two years now. Fearing that the Taker had died, which meant she may never learn the truth, she had prayed to find that she was the only one. But, confirming her worst fears, Mrs. Crenshaw's words about her daughter's package echoed through her racing thoughts: At least he knew when to quit, and I'm grateful that it stopped.

23

The abandoned Red Bluff Trading Post rested twenty miles west from the town of Roanhorse and thirty miles north of the Grand Canyon Hotel and Casino, which had been erected along US 491—a lonely stretch of highway that the locals still referred to by its original name: Route 666. The trading post itself was a weather-beaten structure of faded red that had been out of business for a couple of years. The dilapidated building sat atop a small bluff with one road in and a shear drop off to its back, making it the ideal place to set up their temporary base of operations. The uranium mine where they had stashed the truck was only another fifteen minute drive up a mostly dirt road that led up into the hills.

Ackerman found Dr. Emily Morgan—the other member of their team, who had stayed behind to guard the prisoners—in the back room of the old trading post. The captives sat beyond her on a pinewood floor that was beginning to sag and rot. The place smelled of sweaty young men, rat excrement, and underneath it all, almost imperceptible, the metallic aroma of dried blood. Like a shark detecting a drop of blood in a vast ocean, he zeroed in on the tantalizing odor and felt the carnal desire of a predator to rend and tear flesh and taste blood on his tongue.

"Frank, are you okay? Hello?" Emily Morgan asked, apparently not for the first time.

"Sorry, just indulging a darkly sweet daydream."

She gave him a questioning look, and he changed the subject. "I see the children are nestled snuggly in their beds with visions of my bone-handled bowie knife dancing in their thick heads."

"You should write poetry," she said, and he couldn't decide if she was being sarcastic or merely recognizing that his genius should be shared with the world.

He replied, "Your superiors would never allow anyone to read it. And that's another question. Any progress on the blogging issue?"

Emily stared at him with an unreadable expression across her exotic features, which were a result of her combined Asian and Irish heritage. She reminded Ackerman of a Siamese cat he had once seen in the home of a victim. It was the way he imagined a feline princess would move– confident but not boastful. Powerful. Graceful. But gentle. All at once. Her skin was flawless and smooth like a child's, as if the harmful rays of the sun had never touched her skin.

She fascinated him. Something about her inner strength and calm demeanor. Sometimes he simply had no idea what she was thinking. And as a student of human nature, Emily was one of most intriguing subjects he had ever met. He had thought so ever since the moment he first met her on the day he murdered her husband.

She said, "I didn't advise you to journal so that you could post it on the Internet to make money."

During their last case, Ackerman had met a strange private detective who posted his ramblings on God and the Universe on the Internet and, by selling advertising space, generated a six figure income. He said, "They realize that

I'm not being paid to be here, and it would be anonymous. That's the beauty of the Internet."

"They are fully aware of the concept. And the answer is still no."

He scowled. Sometimes he wondered if the Shepherd Organization's Director was the real villain they should be dispatching. "Please let them know that I'd like to file a formal complaint."

She rolled her eyes but said, "Okay."

A part of him loved cracking her stone demeanor. Having accomplished that mission, he turned his attention to the prisoners. The closest young man was Canyon's son, Tobias. He had bandages over his forehead and arm. Unlike his father, the young Canyon's face was the perfect color of wet clay and was unlined from the years. He looked nothing like his progenitor. Where John was tough and worn like old leather, Tobias was smooth and undamaged.

Emerging from the deep shadows in the back of the room, Thomas White—or at least Ackerman's hallucination of him—said, "You know how you could find your little friend, Junior? Just cut off a significant piece of this one and deliver it to his father. Then you'll get your answers. Perhaps a foot. Or if he has any tattoos, you could skin that portion of his body and deliver it to the old man like an offering of flesh."

Turning back to Emily, Ackerman said, "Have you been able to reach Computer Man?"

"His name is Stan."

"I know his name. I just don't enjoy saying it. Besides, he likes it when I call him Computer Man."

"No, he doesn't."

"Well, I like it."

"And that's all that matters?"

"No, there are many factors beyond my personal tastes that 'matter.' For example, I need the Computer Man to find out everything he can about a Navajo Nation Police officer named Liana Nakai. Also, I'd like to know more about Captain Yazzie. Don't recall hearing a first name."

"Fine, if I'm able to reach Stan, then I'll let him know. I'm not sure what it is, the canyons or hills or something, but even with our boosters, we can't get any signal here. We may have to drive around to the other side of the mesa in order to get an outgoing connection. I wish we would have tracked down a satellite phone or something, but we've never had this problem in the past. The boosters for the cellular signals usually do the trick, even out in the middle of nowhere."

"My sympathies. I'm sure it's difficult for you being out of contact with your child. I know Marcus feels the same about Dylan, and he isn't aware of this, but he grows increasingly cantankerous the longer he's out of contact with the boy. As if he needs to see Dylan's face and hear his voice to ensure that the child is growing to maturity."

Emily's expression was stone, but her eyes were bright and glistened with tears in the light of a battery-powered lantern that hung from the rafters of the back room.

He asked, "Did I say something wrong? I didn't mean to cause you emotional distress."

She said, "Do you miss your mother, Frank?"

The question jarred him to his core. Ackerman was a man who was seldom truly caught off guard, but her mention of his long dead mother took him completely by surprise. He replied, "I never really knew her. I only have a few vague recollections of the time before she fled with my unborn brother."

Coming up behind Emily, Thomas White said, "She abandoned you, Francis. She cared enough about your brother to whisk him away to a better life, but not you. I think she sensed you were a monster from the very beginning."

Ignoring his father's spectral form as much as humanly possible, he concentrated on Emily as she said, "But when you look back on your childhood, do you mourn the loss of not having her there? Don't you wish she had been?"

Thomas White snarled, "Tell her, Junior. Tell your little friend that your mother offered you up to me like a sacrificial lamb, just to save her own miserable skin. Tell Emily that you'll never forgive your mother for choosing herself, and your brother, over you. Tell her your mother was a selfish bitch. Tell her!"

Laying a hand on Emily's shoulder, Ackerman whispered, "My mother was a wonderful woman who did the best she could under impossible circumstances. I respect her for standing up to the...toxic black hole that is my father. Where is your daughter now?"

"With her grandparents."

"Good people, obviously. They did an exceptional job raising you."

"But I'm her mother. And I'm not there."

"She knows you love her. Her development will not be stunted by your absence."

"It's not about that. Every second I miss with her is one I'll never get back. Ashley is growing into a young woman, and I'm missing it. Out here in the desert babysitting thugs."

"I trust you're referring to the Canyon clan and not my brother and I. We could be characterized in many colorful ways, but 'thugs' would be a grand oversimplification. Besides, we need you here. Maggie needs you. I need you."

She looked up into his eyes in a way that caused a warm feeling to course through his whole body. It felt good to be looked upon without contempt or fear or even reluctant acceptance.

He turned away, feeling immediately guilty.

Thomas White said, "Oh, I see. Maybe I won't kill your brother first. Maybe, once I take control, I'll spend some intimate moments with this lovely specimen. But wait a second... Aren't you the real reason that poor Emily has been separated from her child. If you hadn't come into her world, she'd still be living happily ever after in a beautiful Colorado home with Ashley and her state Trooper husband. What was his name, Junior? Ah, yes... Jim Morgan. You remember him, don't you? You gutted him like the pig he was."

Ackerman added, "I simply mean to say that you are one of the few people in the world, besides myself, whose competence I can rely upon."

Wiping her eyes, she said, "Can you keep an eye on these five for a few minutes? Without maiming them any further? I need to use the outhouse."

"I suppose I can restrain myself."

Once Emily had exited the back door, Thomas White continued, "I can see why you like her. I'm a bit too old for such pursuits myself, but when I wear your skin, I have a feeling that I'll be like a whole new man."

Looking the subconscious projection of his father directly

in his imaginary eyes, Ackerman said, "You will never 'wear' my skin, and you will never lay a hand upon Emily!"

Thomas White merely smiled, and Ackerman knew that he had just lost a small battle by rising to the antagonism of a hallucination. The more he acknowledged his father as real, the more real he became. Until one day, perhaps Thomas White would become strong enough to steal the reigns.

Ackerman vowed to never allow that to happen. If it came down to it, he would see to his own end.

Thomas White gestured to the prisoners, raising his eyebrows. Following his father's gaze, Ackerman realized that he had forgotten about Tobias Canyon and his four comrades being with them in the room. The eyes of the young men stared back at him full of fearful questions. Namely, who in the hell was he talking to?

To the young captives, Ackerman said, "In case any of you were wondering, the voices in my head are telling me to kill you all. And then eat you. Or perhaps the other way around. I slowly devoured a person once in the past over the course of a few weeks. I found it to be a very sensual and intimate experience. With a little strategy, I was able to keep him alive for a downright disturbing length of time. But that individual was long past his prime. His meat wasn't nearly as succulent and tender as I'm sure you four youngsters would be."

The looks of fear that passed over the faces of the four prisoners filled Ackerman with another warm feeling, but this time, he didn't feel guilty at all.

24

This was all his fault. He knew it in his head and felt it in his heart. Special Agent Marcus Williams had failed in so many ways he couldn't even begin to count them. Although, he often tried. Marcus would sit for hours on end—usually while the rest of the world slept—replaying past mistakes. Not just out of a sense of guilt, but also a desire to learn from prior missteps. He had screwed up a lot during his life—with Dylan's mother, as a cop, a son, a father, times when he had allowed anger and self-righteousness to cloud his judgment—but he guessed that if all of the times that he had said or done the wrong thing could be totaled up by victim, Maggie would have been the person his poor choices had harmed the most.

And now, he had pushed her away to the point that she...

He couldn't bear to imagine a world without her smile.

Instead, Marcus turned his attention to surviving the moment. In what could very well be his worst decision yet, he had followed the advice of his brother and struck John Canyon's empire with a straight-up frontal assault. He often felt he was overly cautious, and Ackerman seemed to have the variables all figured. But now, Marcus wasn't so sure, and he feared that this latest mistake would get him and the rest of his team killed.

The fact that a full communications blackout had

occurred just after Ackerman's foray onto John Canyon's ranch hadn't escaped Marcus's notice.

By all accounts, Canyon owned this valley and damn near everyone in it. That was a lot of hands holding a lot of guns pointed in their direction. Everything seemed to be working against them, everything falling apart. Under his watch. Because of his mistakes.

He had stashed the rented Jeep SUV inside a small shed beside the dilapidated trading post. The three buildings on the property—an old mobile home, the shed, and the store—had all sat vacant for years, and judging from the wear on the wooden siding of the structures, the place had been on its last legs even before the owner passed away. From the back of the Jeep, he lifted a heavy black gun case, which contained an impressive .50 BMG Caliber Barrett Model 82A1 sniper rifle. While the .30-06 Springfield—a standard caliber for American soldiers in both World Wars and one of the most popular choices for hunters—produced muzzle energies between two thousand and three thousand foot-pounds. The .50 BMG round produced around fifteen thousand foot pounds of force.

Marcus heard the sound of a low exhalation behind him and didn't hesitate. Pulling his Diamond Plated P220 Sig Sauer pistol from its holster, he spun on whoever was sneaking up on him through the darkness.

With disinterest, Ackerman looked down at the gun aimed at his midsection. "Jumpy, aren't we?"

"Damnit, Frank. Don't sneak up on me like that." Slipping the Sig back into its holster, Marcus added, "How's your side? I noticed you were bleeding."

"I'm fine. We need to calculate our next move."

"Before we do that, we need to make this place somewhat defensible. Now that you've thrown down the gauntlet, Canyon will be coming at us with everything he has, if he can find us. I don't want him to catch us with our pants down."

"What do you propose? Do we have access to explosives? I could probably rig up something with gasoline and poor man's C4."

"Actually, I brought genuine military-grade C4, but I'm hoping that we won't have to rain down any hellfire and brimstone."

"I can be very precise when shaping my charges. I've certainly demonstrated this ability during—"

"That's not what I'm saying. I don't doubt your skills, but first, I'd like to try something that's a little less shock and awe and a bit more subterfuge."

"Well, we should figure something out soon. It's only a matter of time before our guests arrive."

Eyes narrowing, Marcus asked, "What did you do?"

"I left them an invitation to the party."

Marcus lowered his head and pinched the bridge of his nose, feeling the onset of a migraine. "And what exactly does that mean, Frank?"

"I found one of the trading post's sale bills and tucked it beneath the drunk tank's mattress. When Captain Yazzie finds it, he'll inform Canyon, and they'll be coming at us with everything they have."

"When did you intend to share that part of your 'plan' with me? And I use the word plan, in the loosest sense of the word. Let's get something straight right here and now. I'm not your little brother when we're out in the field. I'm your commanding officer. If I don't know about a part of the plan, then it's not part of the plan."

Ackerman cocked his head. "You and I both know that, on this case, we have no chain of command. No support. No hierarchical bureaucracy to call upon. We are but two lone warriors doing what we do best in order to save a wayward sister. And as you also know, dear brother, the variables are always shifting. We must adapt, improvise, and overcome."

Gritting his teeth actually helped with his headache, and so Marcus ground down until he felt he might snap something. After a few seconds, he calmly said, "Don't feed me some spur of the moment line. You took the sale bill with you to the station, which means that you had this planned out from the beginning and neglected to tell me about it."

Ackerman replied, "I'm not your pet or your weapon. You can't just wind me up and send me out into the world expecting me to do your bidding. And, for the record, if you didn't have your head up your ass feeling guilty over everything, then I wouldn't need to be executing contingencies."

"That's it. We're done. We're packing up. I'll get Valdas and his friends at the FBI to handle it from here. You're right about one thing. We're off the rails here. It's time to end it."

Ackerman laughed. "You might as well kill Maggie yourself. If she is still alive, we're her only hope. By the time your bureaucracy has mounted its investigation, the evidence of her presence will be long gone. We're committed here. The only option is to stay the course."

"That's difficult," Marcus said, "when you don't know the plan."

With a roll of his eyes, Ackerman explained, "Our

new friends are only aware of my existence, not yours or Emily's."

"They know someone picked you up."

"I could have just as easily had an escape vehicle hidden somewhere. They can't know for sure. We have Canyon's son and his drugs. Simultaneously attacking a man's family and his livelihood is definitely a good way to get his attention, and to keep him off balance and making mistakes. Once they discover the breadcrumb I so graciously left for them, they'll be headed this way. All of them."

Marcus nodded in understanding. "And while they're distracted here with you, the ranch will be virtually unguarded. Leaving an opportunity for me to search the place."

"You and Emily."

"Actually, I'm sending Emily out of here. With communications down, we can't risk it. She needs to update the rest of the team. It's just you and me on this. It's better that way."

"You mean so that's she's insulated legally from what's about to occur."

"That's exactly what I mean. We're going to war. I don't want Emily to be collateral damage."

"Agreed."

"She'll take the Jeep, and I'll use the dirt bike to reach the ranch. It'll be better to stay off the roads anyway. But what about you? You'll be here alone."

Ackerman smiled. "They won't know that. You just worry about finding Maggie, and I'll keep Canyon and his men so twisted up they won't know if they're coming or going. I have to admit... I've been looking forward to this part. You know how it is, a true player is always looking for a good game."

25

The past…

Marcus said, "You did good today. I've come to realize that our job isn't to catch killers. It's to protect innocent people. And that's what you did. You saved a man's life."

She met his gaze. Her cheeks were flushed, but he couldn't tell if it was from embarrassment or the cold. "Thank you."

"Don't thank me. You're a good agent, and if I were any kind of a team leader, you would already know that." Marcus blew out a long breath. "And if I were any kind of a man, you would also know how much I love you. But we—"

Her hands shot out and grabbed him by the sides of his head. Just as quickly, she pulled him in close and kissed him. It was a long and hungry kiss.

His arms folded around her. He could feel her heart pounding, and she was breathing hard. When she pulled away, she said, "Don't say anything else. You'll just ruin it."

26

John Canyon had based the design for his home off a ski lodge he and his wife had visited in Aspen, CO. It was the kind of opulence that was unheard of among the Diné people. But it also sent a very clear message as to who he had become, the empire he had built. As he looked around the two-story great room of his home, which was built like a log cabin, Canyon considered how far he had come from the shack in which he had been raised. The only elements of the decor that didn't mimic the Aspen ski lodge were the mounted trophies of animal heads. Instead, American Indian artifacts lined the walls—everything from glass cases of ancient pottery and weaponry to colorful Diné rugs and artwork. He had even rescued a piece of a rock wall, which displayed the intricate petroglyphs of a hunting party of the Old Ones, that had fallen from an Anasazi dwelling.

Although he didn't completely keep to the old ways himself, he knew that the lodge room comforted some of the more traditional of his men. George Todacheeny, Canyon's head of security, counted himself among those traditionalists. Canyon—having cut his teeth among the gang's of the nation with the no-neck, barrel-chested Todacheeny—knew the man simply as Toad. With a nod of his head, Canyon told his longtime subordinate to quiet the twenty-five men gathered in his great room.

Toad yelled, "Everyone sit down and shut up. Mr. Canyon's about to speak."

As the assembled man found a spot to listen, Canyon made a point to try and look each man in the eyes, which was counter to their culture but necessary to convey the seriousness of what was about to be discussed.

Stepping into the center of the lodge room, which was filled with leather couches and barstools and smelled of cigar smoke, he began, "We're all familiar with the Old Ones who built their homes high in the rocks of the canyons and mesas and hills all throughout this region. Most of us even visited the ruins of the Old Ones as children. Not to desecrate or to deface, but to walk the footsteps of our ancestral peoples. The belegana dirt diggers still can't explain exactly why the Old Ones took to the high places, where life was infinitely more difficult, rather than building their homes on the plains, close to water and other resources."

As he spoke, Canyon walked over to the wall of the lodge room, unlocked one of the glass cases, and retrieved a piece from his collection. This particular stone tomahawk was a meticulously recreated replica, not an original. He would never defile an original in the way he was about to use this one. The reproduction had been constructed from a straight shaft of hickory and a rounded stone axe head with bands of leather holding the two together. His ancestors used the tool, which measured approximately two feet in length, for both labor and self-defense.

Using slow and deliberate movements, Canyon sliced the air with the ancient weapon and continued, "They've found evidence of civil war and cannibalism among those they've named the Anasazi. Many take this as an insult and reject the idea. Personally, I can see it. Look at the Diné people now. We have been scattered and subjugated. This defeat, along with the systematic removal of our culture and heritage perpetrated by the so-called United States, has caused our people to cannibalize each other as well. They locked us in a prison without walls, forcing our people to feed off one another and desecrate our sacred lands. Alcohol, drugs, gangs, the theft of our youth to the false dream of a better life beyond the Rez. All of these things have been slowly devouring the Diné people for generations. But I say no more!"

With a nod to Toad, he gave the order for his subordinate to bring out the two men who had failed him earlier in the night.

As Toad left the room, Canyon declared, "So how do we stop this slow erosion of our people? I say we must learn from the mistakes of the Old Ones. Their people died out and were dispersed. Their ways and their stories lost to time. I've always suspected that it was actually invaders like the Vikings or other white peoples with their inherent greed and diseases who caused the Old Ones to run to the hills. And our people are no different. We have forgotten who we are. We're losing ourselves to time, just like the Old Ones— who the belagana thieves of time have dubbed the Anasazi because even the name of their people has been forgotten."

The door leading to the mansion's west wing opened, and Toad walked through with the two men who had allowed Canyon's son to be taken close on his heels. Both of their faces were swollen and bloody from where he had put them both on their asses earlier, when he had first leaned about

Tobias's kidnapping. After meeting the man responsible, Canyon knew that it really wasn't the fault of his men. He would still, however, need to make an example of them, for the greater good.

Still fighting shadows with the stone tomahawk, Canyon continued, "By learning from their mistakes, we can ensure that the Diné people will never die out like the Old Ones. We have fueled the economy of our town and this valley into something that even the belegana envy, and we have accomplished this by selling their own poisons back to them. Not only their drugs, but soon, even the weapons of war which they created from our sacred land and, in the process, contaminated the life blood of the Diné. The work we are doing will strengthen our people for generations to come and see to it that the Diné, who have the witnessed the rise of America, will also see its inevitable collapse. When that happens, our people will live on, stronger than ever."

As he looked around the room once again, this time holding the tomahawk out toward each man as if he were knighting them, he said, "Have no illusions, the belegana and their government do not want us to flourish. They want us to assimilate and submit to their ways. Now, they've once again invaded these sacred lands and have stolen from us. They have stolen our resources, and they have stolen our sons and brothers. Toby, Shinny, Tuchoney, Jim, and Ahiga. These white invaders have threatened to kill these men. To kill your friends. To kill my son. They have threatened to destroy all that we have built here. Everything we love. They wish to see our children grow up fatherless, weak, and demoralized. Will we allow this?"

He could see the fire in their eyes, the angry shaking of

their heads, the tensing of muscles and clenching of jaws. The only thing that ruined the moment was that some of his warriors still stank of manure from the manual labor they normally performed for him. Besides the smell, they we re a war party of which his ancestors would have been proud. The looks of devotion he saw reflecting back at himself brought to his mind a quote from another white invader: Adolf Hitler—The leader of genius must have the ability to make different opponents appear as if they belonged to one category.

With a nod from Canyon, Toad shoved the two failures forward, into the center of the gathered war party. The two were about the same age, but the Ramirez kid was almost twice the size of his counterpart. Both men stank of sweat, fear, and blood. Jamie Ramirez was a handsome young man who had once been a top notch soldier, but after coming home to serve his own people, Ramirez had fallen prey to the same drugs that were supposed to be poisoning the children of their oppressors, not a member of the People. Even an adopted member like Ramirez. Canyon couldn't remember the other runt of a man's name, but he was fairly certain that he'd heard Ramirez refer to his rat-faced sidekick simply as: Slim.

Laying a hand on Ramirez's shoulder but still addressing the war party, Canyon said, "Make no mistake. This war is no longer cold. We are under attack, and these invaders have declared their intentions by words and action. They mean to see all of us dead or locked up in one of their cages. We have no choice but to fight back. Our people, our families, need us to be warriors now more than ever. But let's not forget the fate of the Old Ones. The dirt diggers say the

Anasazi died from cannibalizing each other and civil war. I say that makes a lot of sense. We only have to look at these two men to see evidence of that."

Ramirez said, "Sir, I—"

"Don't speak. Just listen." Looking to the others, he added, "These two men were busy…sampling our products when my son was stolen."

"We were on watch, sir. That man, he—"

Canyon stopped the young soldier with a look. Then, to Ramirez's surprise, he held out the stone tomahawk and indicated for the kid to take it. Once Ramirez had hold of the weapon, Canyon said, "You see, brothers, these two men were not ready for battle."

In a blur of movement, he snatched the pistol from his belt (what type of gun?) and placed it against Ramirez's head. "Going into battle and protecting our homes from attack requires many things from us. First of all, a clear head. Loyalty. Discipline."

Eyes closed and voice trembling, Ramirez interrupted, "Sir, please, we—"

"Do not interrupt me again, son. Now, see there, damnit, you made me lose my train of thought." With a growl and a shaking head, Canyon continued, "If you choose to be one of my warriors and don't display these qualities, then you are essentially cannibalizing your own people." Digging the barrel of his gun into the young soldier's temple, he snarled, "Open your eyes! Look at these men!"

Ramirez did as he was told. Tears streamed down both his cheeks.

"Do you hate your brothers, Sergeant Ramirez?"

"No, sir!"

"I already told you not to interrupt me, boy! That was a rhetorical question. Now, someone is going to pay for you and your partner's attempt at cannibalizing our families. Is it going to be you or your little friend? Your choice. Either strike him down with that tomahawk, or I will strike you down with a bullet to the brain. It should be easy for you, Ramirez, since you would choose cocaine, heroin, and whiskey over Toby, Shinny, and Ahiga, over your brothers."

Ramirez, holding the tomahawk low at his side, didn't move or speak, and Canyon gave the kid credit for that. At least he was learning something.

Canyon said, "I want you to kill your friend and then eat his flesh. That's what cannibals do, right?"

Ramirez said nothing.

"Have you two learned your lesson? Will you ever betray your brothers again. You can answer this one."

"No sir!" both men exclaimed in unison.

"I don't believe you," Canyon replied. Then he slipped his gun back into its holster and took the tomahawk from Ramirez's hand. "Place your left hand on the table, Sergeant."

The kid looked relieved to have the gun from his temple and, responding admirably, didn't hesitate in placing his hand flat atop the closest end table, which was fitted with a granite top.

Canyon swung the tomahawk in a wide downward arc, trying to gauge the amount of force necessary to break the hand and not cut it off completely. The impact resounded in a wet "thwack" and a stifled scream from Ramirez. Canyon felt blood on his knuckles and forearm. Standing in the center of his warriors, holding a bloody tomahawk,

Canyon thought of the man calling himself Frank, and all the ways he intended to hurt him and everyone he loved.

Turning his attention back to the war party, Canyon said, "We must find these invaders, whoever they are, and we must kill them. If anyone here is not willing to see that through to the end, you may leave now. You are free to go home and enjoy the life that your brothers will be out fighting for tonight. Anyone?"

He gave them all a moment to think and glanced from man to man once again before saying, "Good. Toad will assign the areas that each group will search. Our adversaries are extremely dangerous and have hostages. Do not approach them on your own. We've cut off all communication in the valley, both cellular signals and the landlines. That means the radios will be your only means of communication. Stay in contact with regular updates. Now, for your brothers, for your family, get out their and go to war."

27

Ackerman watched through the window of the old trading post as Emily Morgan loaded her things into the Jeep. He hated situations like this, times when he knew he should act in a certain way, say a certain thing, or display a certain emotion. He often enjoyed going against the expectations of the normals, but there were often times when meeting or subverting the expectations of a person wasn't an issue, because he had no idea what those expectations were. In this instance, he felt that he should see his teammate off, but he hated goodbyes. Based on his observations of normal human emotion, a goodbye under such dangerous circumstances necessitated specific reactions stemming from a fear that one may never see the other person again. But for Ackerman there was no such thing as fear. He didn't worry whether or not he would see Emily again. Either he would or he wouldn't. Worrying over the outcome served no purpose, even if he would've been capable of such a thing.

Keeping one eye on the prisoners and the other on Emily, Ackerman observed as Marcus executed a perfect goodbye hug. He couldn't read his brother's lips at the current angle, but what he read from Emily's face was that Marcus had succeeded in calming her fears. Strangely, Ackerman had always found it much easier to instill fear in someone rather than calm it out of them.

Sensing this was his moment, Ackerman headed outside, passing his brother in the doorway of the trading post. Emily stopped what she was doing as he approached. The wind kicked up, blowing her hair. In the predawn light, he could just make out her pale Asian features and the reddish glow of her dark hair.

She said, "I was wondering if you were going to come see me off."

"It's not as if we'll be apart for long. Marcus and I should have this all wrapped up within a matter of hours."

"Always so confident."

"It's always worked out for me before, and the best indicator of future outcomes is past experience."

"I guess that depends on your definition of something working out."

"Regardless, I wish you Godspeed. Be careful. Obey all traffic signs, signals, and laws. We don't want to risk any further involvement of the Navajo Nation police force."

"I think I can handle it, Frank. Next, you'll be telling me not to take any candy from strangers."

"That certainly is a good rule of thumb by which to adhere."

"Since when do you pay attention to the rules?"

"Well, that's the thing about being extraordinary. The rules don't apply to you. The very meaning of being exceptional is to be the exception to the rule."

A ghost of a smile crossed her lips. With a shake of her head, Emily said, "Could you stop being so...exceptional for a minute? I have something important I need to tell you."

Ackerman didn't like the direction this conversation was heading. He could see the hesitation in her eyes. She said,

"You're the most frustrating man I've ever known, but I'm truly going to miss you."

"As I said, we won't be apart for long."

"That's not what I'm talking about. Once we find Maggie, I'm leaving the Shepherd Organization and going back into private practice. This job isn't compatible with being a parent...especially a single one."

Feeling like he had just been stabbed in the gut, and not in a good way, Ackerman tried to remember the last time that he could think of nothing to say. After a moment, he replied, "You, of course, must do what you feel is best."

She met his gaze, and tears began to form in her eyes. Feeling a strange awkwardness, he stuck out his hand and added, "Working with you has been one of the greatest pleasures of my life. You will be missed."

Looking down at the proffered hand, she shook it with both fists. Then, knowing that she couldn't say the same about him, he simply nodded and walked away, resisting the urge to look back at her one last time.

28

Captain Yazzie stood at the station house's whiteboard, making notes and talking out loud, mostly to himself. Liana tried to pay attention, or at least look like she was, but she couldn't stop thinking about Frank. He was so terrifying and yet so fascinating. There was no point during the entire confrontation during which he was not in total control. He had proven that he could have killed all of them at any moment. But he didn't. In fact, when Liana looked back on the encounter, she saw that Frank had actually been quite strategic in disabling them without causing any real damage.

The longer she considered the situation, the more she wondered if she was on the wrong side of things.

What if Frank really was some kind of federal agent, come to rescue his friend and bring down Canyon's evil empire... But where did he get all those scars? Maybe he was a former special operations commando who had been captured during a top secret mission to North Korea and tortured by the—

"Officer Nakai? Are you with me?"

"Yessir."

"Well...then what do you think?"

The only thought running through Liana's head was "Oh shit," over and over again. But she said—after a long pause during which she tried to seem contemplative and confident rather than confused and uncomfortable—"I…agree with your assessment, Captain."

Yazzie had an annoying habit of flipping and fiddling with his Zippo lighter, which—like the Colt Peacemaker on his hip—was engraved with the symbol for infinity. In this instance, the familiar 8-shaped design was displayed in the form of a black snake eating its own tail overlaid atop a background of white pearl. Nodding his head as he looked at the board, he flipped open the lighter and lit it in one movement and said, "Good, I'm glad we're in agreement."

Liana winced, having no idea what she had just agreed to. Looking to the whiteboard for some indication, she saw Yazzie had written: Tobias Canyon, Missing Truck, Pitka: Drone Sweep. That much of the discussion she remembered. Officer Pitka would take one of the trucks and an expensive surveillance drone that John Canyon had "donated" to the department. Pitka would do a grid search of the valley using the drone, hoping to get a view of the truck or anything to indicate the presence of the suspects or hostages. But the board gave no indication as to what the captain had asked her.

Yazzie said, "Okay, Ernie get going and keep in constant contact on the radio. And don't take any chances."

Nodding to the captain and offering her a weak smile, Ernie Pitka rose and headed out to start his search.

His attention still on the white board, Yazzie announced, "The spot they're holed up has to be less than a half hour radius from town. Frank and whoever is helping him are strangers. We know this area a hundred times better than they do. If you were hiding a truck and four hostages arounds here, Liana, where would you go?"

She had been giving that a lot of thought, yet she had no real answer. She said, "There are hundreds of dilapidated or condemned buildings in the valley alone. There are nearly that many abandoned uranium mine shafts. Even many of the ones that have been filled in still have old outbuildings still standing or caves big enough to drive into. And that's just the manmade caves, not to mention all the natural ones. The Big Mine has a hundred places to hide. There's the old fish hatchery and that warehouse off Route 50. At least three abandoned service stations I can think off the top of my head."

"Okay, let's look at it a different way. We need to narrow our search. Is there anything we're not thinking of that we could use to track them."

"Like what?"

"I don't know, but if anything happens to Toby, John is going to go on the warpath."

"I thought he already was."

Yazzie's eyes remained unreadable behind the glasses he wore at all times, but she saw a small smile break the granite of the captain's typical expression. He replied, "You ain't seen nothing yet, kid."

"Sir, don't you think it's time that we call in help?"

"From who? The main agency? The FBI? Bureau of Indian Affairs? I'm sure John has already talked to Agent Whitley, our BIA babysitter, and informed him of the situation. Besides, we don't need more men or resources. We have plenty of those, but nowhere to send them. We need more thinking."

Liana's eyes went wide with shock at hearing Agent Whitley—their BIA rep—and John Canyon mentioned in the same sentence. She felt her lips trembling and turned away to hide her dismay, but Yazzie was deep in his own thoughts.

Why would Canyon be talking to Whitley? Unless the agent was on Canyon's payroll...

When her superior officer had first ordered her to be complicit in covering up the disappearance of a federal agent, she had almost contacted Agent Whitley and spilled her guts about the whole situation. But if she would have called... She didn't want to think of the things John Canyon did to people who got in the way of his warpath.

Staring at the whiteboard and twirling the lighter between all his fingers, which Liana had found impressive the first thousand times she had seen him do it, Yazzie proclaimed, "Trace evidence!" as if the phrase was the answer to everything. Over his shoulder, he said, "Grab an evidence collection kit. Wait, forget that."

"I can get the one from my cruiser, sir."

"Don't worry about it. None of this will ever see a trial. We don't have time to send evidence off to a lab, and we damn sure don't have our own mass spectrometer. That makes the kit pretty pointless."

Yazzie moved toward the holding cell that had temporarily housed the man calling himself Frank. In order to reach it, he had to squeeze past her, and she was trapped between the cell bars and the front of a desk, unable to get out of his way in time. He lingered in close proximity a few seconds longer than necessary, and she saw his nostrils flare as he passed. Yazzie often did small things that made her feel uneasy. Nothing overly offensive, but she had noticed him coming close and sniffing her hair on many occasions.

Stepping inside the cell, Yazzie pulled the Maglite from his utility belt and shined it back and forth over the floor and the cot resting against the back wall. Surprisingly, Frank's escape through the wall had caused little disturbance to the rest of the cell and most of the dust and debris had landed on the ground outside. Yazzie bent down to the cot, scanning it first with the light. Then he started to lightly run his hand over its surface. A single sheet covered the mattress, which sat atop a steel frame. No blankets. One pillow. The less for the drunks to puke on, the less work in the morning.

Yazzie was about to search beneath the cot when the radio on his shoulder crackled to life. Pitka's voice said, "Sir, I'm having some problems with the battery pack on the drone. Can you give me a hand?"

With a sigh, Captain Yazzie replied into the radio, "Copy that. On my way." Then he looked to Liana, smiled, and said, "I swear sometimes that boy's elevator doesn't reach the top floor. Keep checking here. I'll be right back."

Once Yazzie was gone, Liana felt like she could breathe again. She respected her commanding officer, and he had always treated her fairly. But there was something about being alone with him that made her uneasy. Returning to the search, she examined the areas where Frank had tracked in the blood that had been covering his whole body. Using a piece of Scotch tape wrapped around her hand, she searched the fabric for any particles he had left behind. She didn't find much beyond dust and sand, which could have merely blown in through an open window. There were, however, some small white specks that looked to her like salt.

Then, checking around the mattress, she noticed the edge of what looked to be a yellow piece of paper that someone had stuffed beneath. Pulling it free and checking over her shoulder to make sure that she was still alone, Liana unfolded the thin yellow slip to reveal it as the business portion from a carbon-copy receipt book with the name Red Bluff Trading Post stamped across its top. The handwritten notes on the sale bill were too faded to read, but Frank's message was not in the list of purchases but rather the happy face symbol finger-painted in blood.

29

The brothers walked in step together toward an old shed behind the abandoned Red Bluff Trading Post. Marcus still found it surreal that the man beside him had once been his enemy, and now, there was no one else he would rather have by his side. It was amazing how much things could change within a relatively short span of time. Enemies could become friends, and the people closest to you could just as easily turn away.

Oddly enough, Ackerman was perhaps the only person in the world whom he trusted. Relatively speaking, of course, in the sense that he knew Frank would always have his back. His brother would stand by him to the death. Once, he would have said the same about Andrew, but something between them had changed since the Director had started grooming Andrew for management. Marcus sensed that Andrew was learning all kinds of secrets that he couldn't share with any of them. Every time they talked, he felt the tension, the secrets and lies slowly erecting a barrier between them. And Maggie...he couldn't bear to think of all the ways he had pushed her away.

Ackerman, as if reading his mind, said, "We'll find her, brother."

"I know that. I just have my doubts whether or not she'll be breathing when we do."

Ackerman had nothing to say to that. Instead, he said, "What wonderful toys did you bring with you this time?"

Marcus thought about that. He had packed the four-door Jeep Wrangler with as much hardware as it could carry and had unloaded the cases into the shed before Emily departed in the Jeep. Opening the slide door of the shed like a snake oil salesmen revealing his wares, Marcus said, "We have four MP5s, a .50 cal sniper rifle, a few different types of grenades, C4, and a crap ton of ammo."

"But did you bring the items I requested?"

In reply, Marcus grabbed a rolled up blanket from atop the stack of black weapons cases and spread it out to reveal the series of items that his brother had instructed him to bring. The first was a bone-handled Bowie knife that Ackerman had acquired during the Thomas White investigation. Along with it was a sheath designed for concealment beneath the shirt in the small of one's back. The second was a pair of push daggers that had once belonged to the Gladiator, a killer the team had recently hunted in San Francisco. The third was a bit of an enigma to Marcus, and it had actually stirred some troubling realizations about the items and how his brother had acquired them.

Marcus said, "Frank, what are all these things to you?"

"I'm not sure I understand your question, but they are basically the only possessions I have in this world. I don't count Theodore as a possession. He's more like a lamprey clinging to a great white shark."

A mental image of his brother playing with the small Shih Tzu puppy brought a smile to Marcus's face and a small chuckle to his throat. Emily had felt that it would be good for Ackerman to have another life over which he needed to care. And Marcus had to admit that the animal and Ackerman had formed some sort of strange kinship that seemed to help Frank. The puppy was currently back home in Rose Hill, VA with their technical director, Stan Macallan.

Ackerman—who refused to call Stan by his real name—added, "Are you confident that Computer Man is capable of caring to Theodore's needs?"

"Stan has a doctorate from MIT. I think he can handle a little dog for a few days."

"I still feel we should have left him under Dylan's care," Ackerman said, referring to Marcus's son.

"His grandpa doesn't want a dog in his house. He's allergic. And he's pushing eighty."

"Shih Tzu's are actually very hypoallergenic dogs. They don't shed."

"Stop avoiding the question," Marcus snapped. "Are you keeping these things as trophies from other killers we've beaten?"

Ackerman smiled and shrugged. "They certainly carry with them many fond memories. The bone-handled Bowie knife has pierced the flesh of many, but in particular Mr. Craig—our old friend from the CIA—and our father. The push daggers are, of course, the weapons you used to finish off the Gladiator."

"Yeah, I get those. But what about Judas's watch?" Marcus asked, referring to an accessory retrieved from the body of the Judas Killer that should have been collecting dust in an evidence locker somewhere instead of sitting among his brother's keepsakes.

Ackerman's eyes lit up at the mention of Judas's timepiece.

"Have I not shown you this one? You're gonna love it." Ackerman slid the titanium gray watch over his wrist, and then, with a twist of the watch's crown, he pulled out a long thin wire hidden inside. He added, "All of you thought it was merely a clothing accessory, but I knew better. Our old friend Judas was full of surprises, including a superbly crafted garrote concealed in his watch. I'm not sure of the material, but the wire is quite sharp." When he released the crown, the garrote automatically retracted back into the watch.

"I'm not sure how I feel about you keeping trophies from our cases."

"Other than my books and a few articles of clothing, these trophies, as you call them, are all that I have in this world."

Marcus detected a hint of sadness in his brother's tone and said, "That's not true, Frank. You have me. Dylan. Maggie. You have a family. People are more important than possessions."

Cocking an eyebrow, Ackerman said, "You didn't mention Emily or Father as part of that family."

"Thomas White is not part of our family. He's a sperm donor and that's all. And Emily..."

"Is planning to leave the Shepherd Organization."

"She told you?"

"As she was leaving."

Marcus hadn't wanted to have this conversation with his brother until after they had found Maggie, but he had found that more often than not things didn't work out the way he planned, at least not when it came to his personal life. He said, "Frank, listen, she has to do what's best for her daughter."

Ackerman's face remained stone. "I don't have possessions because they are pointless. Or at least, the emotional attachment you normals have to your possessions is. I've learned over and over that everything you have can be taken away in the blink of an eye. These weapons are useful tools that have been tried and tested in battle, and yes, the remembrances they stir in me bring a smile to my face. But I don't need these things. If they were lost to me, I would simply find other tools to replace them. It's the same with people."

"So all of us humans are as replaceable to you as a new knife?"

"Don't be overly dramatic about it. I'm merely saying that both possessions and people can be taken away from you. There's no sense crying about it. One must simply carry on and make due with the resources at hand."

"You've been crying about her leaving?"

"What? No. Stop being obtuse."

Marcus said, "That's funny coming from you. And you can drop the hard-ass routine with me. I know you care about her."

"I find Agent Morgan to be a very capable and fascinating person. The world is a better place because she's in it. But that doesn't mean that my world will grow dark just because she's not part of my personal circle of acquaintances."

"Well, hypothetically speaking, if you did care about Emily on any kind of deeper level, you would have to understand that things were never going to work out between the two of you. There's too much history there."

"Is that why the two of you have been keeping plans for her departure from me? Do you both share in the assessment that my behavior toward Agent Morgan has somehow implied—"

"Okay, okay. Now who's being dramatic," Marcus said, his hands held up in surrender. "The point is that Emily bit off more than she could chew with this lifestyle, and she's chosen to go back into counseling. Considering how often I get to see Dylan and how terrible I feel about that, I can understand where she's coming from. Once Maggie is safe, she'll be leaving the team. That's happening. You can talk about it or not. You can care or not. That's your prerogative."

Ackerman fixed him with the kind of laser-beam gaze that he hadn't seen directed his way in a long time. Ackerman whispered, "Don't ever patronize or coddle me, little brother. Emily is a beautiful woman with the type of exotic features that I've always found attractive. I would be lying if I claimed to have never experienced a stray thought. But believe me, I am fully aware that the sins of the past can never be truly erased in the minds of men, and that a woman like Emily could never love a monster like me."

"That's not at all what I meant."

In a tone that implied there would be no further discussion on the matter, Ackerman said, "We've wasted enough time on this subject. With Emily taking the Jeep, how do you intend to reach Canyon's ranch? We should have stashed the trailer full of wool and cocaine up in the mine and drove the tractor part of the equation back here as another vehicle. I told you that was a poor use of our resources."

"I can't drive a big rig. How in the world did you learn? Never mind, I don't want to know. I'm sure it would just bring up some horrible story from your past."

"Actually, Father taught me. It's one of the few pleasant memories I have of him from my childhood. I had a natural aptitude for it. It was one of the few times that I felt like he was actually proud of me. I should teach you."

Marcus couldn't help but smile as he looked at his brother's face and saw an edge of excitement at the prospect of teaching him to drive a big truck like their sperm donor had taught him. He said, "If we make it out of this alive, I'd be happy to learn. In the meantime, we're covered. The Director actually came through for us on that."

Ackerman looked skeptical. "In what way?"

"Let's move all of this hardware into the main building, and then you can help me assemble my new toy."

30

After the building of Marcus's "new toy," Ackerman took one look at the strange portable vehicle and said, "It looks like a dirt bike and an four-wheel ATV had a baby and then sent it to military school."

The more he considered the strange motorcycle's various uses and the design, although utilitarian and compact, the more he felt it did provide enough stability and power for a variety of off and on road applications. The pieces had all collapsed and fit easily within the back of the jeep along with the weapon cases and ammo boxes. He and Marcus had assembled the small fat-tired motorcycle in less than five minutes. And with practice, Ackerman was sure he could shave that down to less than two. He could think of many, many uses for such a "toy," and many of those uses had nothing to do with transportation.

Marcus said, "It reminds me of some kind of GI Joe vehicle."

"I'm not familiar with Joe."

"The action figures. They were my favorites when I was a kid. Those and the Star Wars figures."

"Father didn't allow me to have toys. He once told me that toys rot a child's brain."

Marcus made his uncomfortable time-to-change-the-subject face and said, "The bike is called a Moto 2x2 Tarus.

At least, I think that's the name. It's made by a Russian company and currently only available in Eastern Europe."

"Then how did it come into our possession?"

"The Director sent me to a place in DC called Savoy & Sons Pawnbrokers They showed me to their private armory of illegal weapons and told me to take whatever I needed."

Ackerman feigned offense and said, "And why wasn't I invited on this weaponry shopping spree?"

"You would have picked up a ninja sword or something equally ridiculous."

His expression and tone growing serious, Ackerman said, "Don't ever underestimate the usefulness of a katana. But Im fine with the Bowie knife. It's more my style."

"While we're on the subject, what are you going to do with the fishing line?" Marcus asked, referring to the spool of Hi-Seas Grand Slam monofilament fishing line that Ackerman had specifically requested along with his "trophy" weapons. The line was thin but tough, knotted well, and could hold up to four hundred pounds.

Ackerman replied, "Its uses are too numerous to list. After you leave, I'm going to re-wrap our hostages using some of the fluorocarbon line and the burlap sacks I found in the trailer. But since you're keen to discuss weaponry choices, you won't be able to carry much more than an MP5 and your sidearm with you on your assault."

Marcus nodded. "I'll be going in light. Besides, you're the distraction. You need the fireworks more than me. But remember, no killing unless there's no other way."

Feeling the perfect segue into a subject he had been wanting to breach with Marcus for some time, Ackerman said, "Speaking of which, I would like to revisit our policy regarding murder."

"That one is pretty much a commandment, not like a guideline where we can make amendments."

Ackerman noticed his brother's Brooklyn accent become more prominent whenever the conversation became heated. He had also noticed a certain way that the accent could indicate when his brother was lying to him, which often came in handy. He said, "I wasn't suggesting that we rescind the policy. In fact, I was thinking that we should broaden our definition of the life forms protected under the divine directive."

With a roll of his eyes and a crack of his neck, Marcus replied, "This had better not be about eating your dog again."

"You took those comments out of context. I was merely putting forth the idea that I would be considered a monster if I decided to kill and eat my dog. But the same people who would judge such an action harshly have no problem consuming cows and pigs, which by the way are just as intelligent and trainable as canines. Don't you find that a bit hypocritical."

"That's totally different than killing and eating your pet because you find it annoying."

"Your culture has placed an idea in your head that some creature's lives are more valuable than others. If I had the newborn offspring of a domesticated animal like a puppy or a kitten and a baby piglet, between the two, which would you prefer I bludgeon to death with a baseball bat?"

"You're telling me that going through the drive-thru at

McDonald's and ordering a quarter-pounder is the same thing as killing puppies?"

Cocking his head in contemplation, Acking considered the merits of the analogy. "Yes, I am saying that. Explain to me why a dog's life is more valuable than a pig's. Both are classified as vertebrates and mammals with comparable IQs. Why is it not hypocritical to stuff your face with bacon and hamburgers, while curling up your nose in disgust when I hypothetically suggest eating my dog?"

"I don't know, Frank. It just is. Maybe it is hypocritical, but somewhere back in time, our ancestors decided that pigs and cows and chickens were good livestock and dogs were good companions and helpers."

"And you're willing to accept your ancestor's views on the matter without question?"

Marcus rubbed his temples. Likely another headache coming on. Ackerman wondered when the last time was that his brother had slept. Marcus replied, "I don't even know what we're talking about anymore. Are you suggesting we become vegans?"

"I was actually thinking lacto-ovo vegetarians. Something where no animals have to die for us to live, but we also have easily accessible protein sources."

Marcus cocked an eyebrow. "You're serious?"

"I'm always serious. Let me ask you this... Why can't we just run around killing people?"

"Lots of reasons. It's wrong, number one."

"From whose perspective?"

"God's perspective, and pretty much everyone else too. Killing someone is universally considered inappropriate. Murder takes away everything that a person has and will ever have. If you believe in almost any kind of god, then by taking a life, you're interfering with God's plan."

"Didn't the same God create the animals your society tortures in order to consume their flesh?"

With a sigh, Marcus offered, "Fine. If we survive this, we can discuss joining PETA or something."

"Lacto-ovo vegetarian. It means that we would still eat eggs and dairy products but abstain from consuming animal flesh."

"I know what it means. When this is over, we can talk about it further. Right now, I need to get ready to leave and you need to prepare yourself for visitors. It won't be long before they search that jail cell and find the invitation you left for them. You need to be ready."

Ackerman smiled. "I'm always ready."

With another look of skepticism, his brother said, "But ready for what exactly?"

"Whatever comes my way."

"Do you have any plan at all for dealing with Canyon and his men? How are you going to keep them busy long enough for me to find Maggie?"

With a wink, Ackerman replied, "I'm confident that it will come to me in the moment. Besides, since when do you need to worry about me."

"I always worry about you. You're not indestructible or invincible. One day, you're going to learn that the hard way."

Ackerman shrugged. "Perhaps, but remember, dear brother, that I've honed my skills over years. I know exactly how far I can push myself and of that which I'm capable, both physically and mentally."

Marcus looked him directly in the eyes, a rare occurrence for his brother, meant to convey the seriousness of what was about to be said. Rubbing at the tattoo of a cross on his chest—a nervous habit Ackerman had often noticed—Marcus said, "I hope you're right, Frank. But I still worry that one day, all your calculations will be off. I know that you don't fear death, but Maggie's life is on the line this time. I can't do this alone. So, if you're going to screw up and get yourself killed, make sure it's not today."

"You handle your end of things, dear brother, and I'll come through on mine," Ackerman said. "A word of advice in return, if I may. There are a lot of coyotes running around these hills, but there's also at least one true predator, a wolf. Besides myself, of course. Don't forget that."

"John Canyon is the right age to be the Taker. Do you think he's our guy?"

"I have no doubt that he's a killer. I'm just not sure if he's the killer who has absconded with your would-be bride," Ackerman said. "Now, you need to get on the road, and I have a bit of tidying up to do before this place is ready to receive guests."

31

His younger sister had screamed hysterically when she saw the blood covering their mother's bedroom carpet. The boy had simply walked over and smacked her across the face. Then he grabbed her by the shoulders and said, "Get the bleach from under the kitchen sink. Mom and I have to go dispose of a body."

Xavier knew that a long and intricate journey of questions from Navajo Police and Federal agents alike would lay ahead of them if they allowed the death to look like foul play. Luckily, he already had a plan in mind. Not one formulated on the spot in a rushed panic, but machinations he had been contemplating for years. He had a similar plan for disposal of every one of his mother's regulars.

In the case of Dr. Chee—the dead man who had tried to murder the boy's mother and probably wasn't much of a doctor, otherwise he would have been working for real money off the Rez—the boy had instantly instructed his mother to remove the dead man's clothes. Dr. Chee was a short man, the same height as the boy's mother. With a little padding, it had been an easy task to make her up like the deceased doctor. At least, from a distance. Then he and the fake Dr. Chee had driven away together in the doctor's rickety old station wagon, in plain sight of all their nosey neighbors.

Once they were out of town, he instructed his mother to drive down an old field road bordered by brush that would conceal the vehicle. Then the boy had left his mother with the station wagon while he followed a dry creek bed through the darkness back to his home. He retrieved the body, which he and mother had already wrapped in garbage bags and loaded into a wheelbarrow. Tracing the creek bed back to the station wagon and loading the body into the back, they drove several miles into the hill country.

The boy explained his plan along the way. "We drive until we find a good spot. I have a few places in mind. Then we dump the body for the coyotes. Hopefully, any evidence will be destroyed by the time anyone finds him."

His mother sobbed as she drove into the night. She asked, "What about the car? What are we going to tell people?"

"We'll say that he invited me to go on a ride, and then he tried to molest me. But I fought back. I have the wounds to prove that already. I drive the car back into town and call the police. I tell them that I shoved him out the door and took his car. They go looking for him, but I tell them the wrong direction. And there's way too much ground out here to cover."

"What about me? The neighbors will see me coming back into town with you, especially old Ms. Begay. I think she gets off on spying on who comes to visit."

"She can't see the house or drive from where she is. I've checked."

"Don't be so sure."

"It doesn't matter. I'll drop you off outside of town, and you'll follow the creek bed back to the house. I'll drive the car home, and we'll finish cleaning up before we call the pigs."

In a trembling whisper, she said, "You have everything figured out, don't you?" In the breathless anxiousness that permeated her words, the boy knew that his mother now truly feared him for the first time.

Xavier said, "Just so we're clear...I'm in charge now, and things are gonna change."

32

Liana Nakai pulled her Ford Explorer patrol vehicle to a halt in front of the old trading post. The place had been shuttered nearly two years ago. The owner had actually been a bit of a relative, their grandmother's both descending from the Bitter Water clan. She didn't bother to hide her approach. In fact, she left the engine running and her lights cutting the darkness for a moment, mainly as a habit of Diné culture, since it was considered rude to advance on another's hogan unannounced. After stepping out of the Explorer and killing the engine, she half-expected Frank to step out onto the front porch and greet her like an area resident would have. She waited beside the vehicle for another moment, even after the 3.5L EcoBoost motor had grown silent.

Unfortunately, the lack of greeting necessitated that she search the creepy old structure by herself. While gambling that Frank was here and wouldn't kill her on sight.

The dust kicked up and carried with it the scent of juniper, and somewhere beneath that the smell of blood and sweat. Pulling her Glock 22 from its holster with her right hand and grabbing the Maglite from her belt with her left, Liana made a mental note to keep her overactive imagination in check. She wasn't some little girl chasing whiptail lizards into the scrub brush. She was an officer within the Navajo Nation Police. It was time she started acting like it, time she made a stand.

The front stairs protested under her weight as she ascended onto a porch that she remembered once held a variety of wood art that the former proprietor dabbled with. It made her sad for the loss of several locally owned and operated businesses that had gone under since the Walmart opened in Farmington.

"Frank?" she whispered as she pushed her way through the open front door.

Only the wind whistling through the broken windows replied.

Most of the homemade wooden shelving units still lined the left side of the front room. Liana imagined that it was exactly what an old general store from the wild west would have looked like. She called out again with no more of reply, but she did hear the shuffling of movement coming from the back store room. The front room had windows, which provided at least some ambient light from the moon and the headlights of her cruiser that she had left on out front. The back room was different, however. The shadows seemed impenetrable even beneath the barrage of her Maglite.

Frank sat in the center of the space, the shadows seeming to swirl around him as if they both obeyed his commands and feared him. He was no longer shirtless. He had changed into a fresh pair of tactical cargo pants and a tight-fitting black long-sleeved shirt made of some type of dry-fit material. Beneath the shirt, she could see the rock hard curves of his body. After receiving her placement with the Roanhorse Navajo Nation Police Department, Liana had joined a gym down in Shiprock, and she had met plenty of body-builders during her time there. But Frank was different. His muscles weren't as massive as the steroid junkies she had encountered at the gym. Instead, his body looked rock hard and densely packed with thick coils of muscle fiber, an unforgiving combination of sinew and bone. She wondered if his body fat percentage was even half a percentile. For a fleeting second, she considered what that body would feel like pressed against her.

"Keep your hands where I can see them," she whispered, almost not wanting him to hear. He sat atop a milk crate with his arms crossed and his head down. As she traced his form with the flashlight, searching for hidden weapons, she noticed that his left side was soaked in blood, visible only as a dark and wet spot on his shirt. Blood dripped from the wound and pooled on the floor. She wondered if he was dead. Canyon must have done more damage with the shotgun blast than they had previously thought. Or perhaps the metal shell of the station house had cut Frank as he made his escape. Either way, the man bleeding out on a milk crate in front of her now did not look nearly as imposing as the one who had burst free of the drunk tank only a few hours earlier.

Taking a step forward, she added, more forcefully, "Get your hands up now, Frank!"

Then she saw the knife. A massive bone-handled Bowie knife, which was embedded in the floor with the handle sticking up just a few feet in front of the stranger. The blade was bloody.

Her chest felt tight, and her heart hammered so loudly that she felt as if she were caught in the middle of a stampede. The room was still and silent, but her internal thundering was deafening. The stranger hadn't moved. She said, "Frank, if you can hear me, I'm going to place you in these cuffs. Then I'll check your wounds, and we'll get you medical help."

When he spoke, she jumped back like she had been struck by a rattlesnake. The deep but dry rumble of his voice reminded her of the hiss of the same reptile. He said, "Do we really have to go through all of this again? I thought our relationship had grown beyond the need for another display of my physical superiority."

Holding the gun out in front of her like a religious talisman warding off the devil, she repeated, "I need you to slowly raise your hands."

"I need you to pull up another crate and have a seat, Officer Liana. We have much to say but the time for only a few words."

"What have you done with Tobias Canyon and those other men?"

"They're in the front room. You passed them on your way in," he said, raising his eyes to her for the first time.

"I didn't see anyone."

"You didn't look hard enough. That's not important now. I don't have the time, energy, or inclination to give you another lesson at the moment. But I truly admire your spirit." He smiled and shook his head as he looked her up and down. "You are adorable. That little uniform, and you waving that hunk of nylon-based polymer around as if it could do a damn thing to protect you from me. I wish we had more time to play, Ms. Liana, but alas, fate has other plans. Now, I'm going to ask you nicely once more. Put that thing away and pull up a seat."

"And if I don't? What if I choose not to play by your rules?"

He fixed her with his piercing gray eyes. The beam of the flashlight reflecting in them made them seem like two pools of fire. He said, "We all have to play by certain rules, my dear. Even I am bound by space and time and other laws of physics. You can, of course, abstain from playing or make up your own rules in this game called Life. But bear in mind that every action has a reaction, every choice a consequence. And if you don't play by my rules, then I'll be forced to put you in timeout, little lady."

With a growl, Liana slipped her Glock back into its holster and pulled up another wooden milk crate, making sure to keep several feet between her and the outsider. As she sat down, she said, "Let's get one thing straight... I'm not your darling, your dear, or your little lady. I'm Officer Liana Nakai of the Navajo Nation Police, and I don't care who you are, I won't be talked down to like that by anyone."

As he sat up, he smiled and gave a little nod. "As you wish, Liana. I respect a woman with some grit. But not too much."

"What the hell is going on here, Frank? I want the truth. The whole story."

Rolling his eyes, he said, "My patience is growing thin, officer."

"You told Captain Yazzie that any good hunter had to be patient above all else."

"I don't think I said it quite like that, but it's nice to know you were paying attention. And touché, I merely meant to convey my annoyance at always having to repeat myself with you normals. It's like I have to tell what I'm going to tell you, then tell you, and then tell you what I already told you. It can be quite frustrating. Especially when..."

Liana watched as Frank's sentence trailed off and his head drooped forward. He looked pale and empty, a mere shell of the man who had seemed invincible earlier. She said, "Frank, wake up. I need to look at your wounds."

"You lick your own damn wounds," he mumbled, but then his posture straightened and his eyes came open.

Making a move to stand, she said, "You're bleeding out. I'm taking you to a hospital."

"Preposterous. I'm fine."

"You just passed out mid-sentence."

"No, I didn't."

"What do you mean, 'no, I didn't.' I just sat here and watched you nearly fall off your seat."

"Prove it," he proclaimed.

"What?"

"Where I'm from, one is innocent until proven guilty."

"You need a doctor, Frank."

"Let's play a game. Kids on road trips everywhere play I-Spy, or so I'm told. How about we play a variation on that? We'll call it I-Smell."

"You do have an odor."

He smiled again, but this time it was the grin of a shark. "My apologies. I've worked up a sweat kicking all of your asses tonight. You stink of fear and anxiety and dime store perfume. But we were supposed to say 'I Smell' first. Your turn. What else do you smell, Officer Liana?"

With a growl of frustration, she closed her eyes and said, "I smell Juniper, dust, rotting wood, and blood."

"Very good. But there's more, so much more."

"What does this have to do with anything?" she shouted.

"You remember me telling Yazzie about a good hunter's

need for patience. But what did I tell him was the second rule of thumb when stalking prey?"

She tried to recall more of the conversation, but the whole night seemed like it had happened in a blur now, a jumbled mess of fear and confusion. It was something that had seemed very arbitrary to her at the time. As she struggled to remember, Frank's head began to droop again. After a moment, she said, "Wasn't it something about staying downwind?"

He chuckled, but even the small effort seemed to exhaust him. His eyelids fluttered as he said, "That's right. You see, the most important thing is to always..."

Then, the outsider—who earlier had seemed as invincible as a cyborg from the future and now seemed as helpless as a child—trailed off again. But this time, he passed out completely and dropped forward from his milk crate to the floor.

Liana ran a hand through her raven black hair and rubbed the base of her skull as she wondered how in the world she was going to drag the muscular strange out of the trading post and load him up into the Explorer by herself. Moving to his side to check his pulse and see if she could rouse him, she heard him mumble something under his breath. When she bent closer, he said in a clear and precise whisper, "We're about to have guests. When this goes down, get into the front room and stay out of my way. I'll handle the rest." Then, with a wink, Frank's head drooped back to the plank flooring.

33

When Liana Nakai was a little girl, she was present when her grandfather passed away. She supposed now that lung cancer had been the cause, but they hadn't had the money for belegana doctors and the traditional Diné singers and ceremonies had little effect. She remembered men from their clan carrying her grandfather outside when they felt his time was near. This was done to allow his chindi to disperse and so that they wouldn't need to burn down their hogan for fear of ghost sickness. Grandmother had explained that the chindi was everything bad about the person, which was left behind when they passed into the spirit world. It was the dark residue that the deceased had been unable to bring into universal harmony.

Liana had always been close to her grandmother and refused to leave her side, despite the risks from evil spirits. Grandmother had explained that they were not to speak grandfather's name or show any emotion at his passing or anytime afterward. Outward signs of grief were believed to draw the spirit back and interrupt their journey to the next world.

Now, as she stared down at the lifeless form of the man calling himself Frank, Liana felt he looked every bit as dead as her grandfather had. On that day, Grandmother had said that Grandfather would leave a weak chindi anyway so there was little danger, but Liana didn't want to run into the terrifying chindi this outsider would leave behind.

She tried to decipher Frank's cryptic warnings, but a part of her wondered if he was merely delirious from blood loss.

Then she heard movement outside.

Boots struck dirt and wood in a steady series of shuffling thumps. Someone was coming up the back steps of the trading post. But that was impossible. The building had been constructed on a large bluff with only one narrow road winding up to the abandoned structures of the storefront, a storage shed, and a trailer that the couple who had owned the property had lived in for nearly thirty years. The old man had fought in Vietnam, and from what Liana had heard from her grandmother, he had built his business up on the bluff because he came back from the war always wanting his back to the wall and his eyes on all points of ingress. She supposed that was why Frank and his team had chosen this place as well.

She would have heard the sound of an engine approaching, which meant their attackers must have parked a good distance away and snuck up behind the building on foot. This was someone who had been observing them and was now rushing in for an assault while Frank was down. Her mind resorted to her training, and she snatched the Glock 22 from her hip and aimed it at the door coming in from the back steps.

In the fraction of a second before the door burst open, Liana wondered if she would have time to yell "Police!" or if the attacker would be coming in guns blazing.

The back door crumbled like it was made of paper mache, nearly falling off its hinges from the force of the impact. Splinters of wood and dust filled the air, but not nearly enough to obscure Liana's view of the young man who had just burst inside brandishing an AK47.

She recognized him immediately as one of John Canyon's hired hands. Captain Yazzie had thrown the same man into the drunk tank on more than one occasion, whenever the Canyon boys acquired a new batch of homemade moonshine or, as she had always suspected, a new shipment of drugs.

"Don't move," she screamed, preparing to fire if he didn't comply.

The young man, who she remembered as a half blood Mexican and Diné named Ramirez, had yet to acquire a target. She directed the beam of her flashlight directly into his eyes and screamed, "Police! Drop the weapon now!"

Ramirez reacted instantly, the assault rifle at his shoulder swinging its barrel toward her with a precision that gave evidence of rigorous training. She recalled that—like the majority of Canyon's thugs—Ramirez was a military veteran. Canyon had even started a program for gang members to take advantage of the benefits of a short stint of military service. Most of the young men he had mentored in the program had come to work for him on the ranch after their tour was over. The rumor was that was always part of the plan, for them to receive combat training on the government's dime, so that his thugs were a cut above. Not just men who had been drummed out of the service for their conduct or addictions, but young men who excelled at military life, under the tutelage of Master Sergeant John Canyon.

Ramirez said, "Stand down, officer. We're on the same team here."

"I'm not on Canyon's team."

The former soldier slowly pulled the AK47 from his shoulder and raised his hands in surrender. Bloody bandages covered Ramirez's left hand, and his face was bruised and swollen. He said, "I simply meant to say that we are both here to rescue Tobias Canyon from this crazy SOB. Did you find him in here like this? Have you checked his pulse?"

Liana opened her mouth to respond, but a twitch in the back of her mind ordered her to stop as questions started to rise. How long had Ramirez been outside? Had he been listening in on them the whole time? Had he been lying in wait for the right moment to attack? That would have certainly adhered to Frank's observations on the hunter's need for patience. But why would Ramirez be asking her questions to which he already knew the answers? The only explanation was that he was testing her, which implied that they were definitely not on the same side.

Noticing that his right hand still held the rifle's pistol grip, albeit with the barrel aimed at the ceiling, she said, "Put the gun down, and we'll talk."

Ramirez smiled, and she saw the devil in his eyes. "Are you getting sweet on this belegana, Officer Nakai?"

"I told you to put that gun down. I don't want to be forced to restrain you, Mr. Ramirez."

"So…you remember my name. That's interesting. Maybe you're just looking for an excuse to get closer to me."

"It's my job to know every scumbag in my district, and repeating myself is one of my biggest pet peeves."

Ramirez's lip curled up, and his left eye twitched. A part of her wanted him to try something. She felt confident that she would be able to drop the ex-soldier before he could make any kind of move on her.

But then a cold dread crept up the back of her neck, and she knew that she had made a grave miscalculation. First, she felt a disturbance in the air, the wind of movement against her skin. Second, came the cold steel of a gun barrel against the base of her spine. Ramirez's partner—who held the assault rifle to her back—said, "I think you should be the one to put down your hardware. And I really, really hate repeating myself."

Cursing under her breath in Diné bizaad, Liana complied and laid her Glock gently on the plank flooring.

Ramirez said, "Good girl. Now, get down on your knees. Hands on your head. We don't want to hurt you, officer. But we will if you give us any trouble."

Liana quickly complied. She knew that Canyon would have ordered his men to avoid confrontations with police officers, not murder them, and his thugs never strayed too far from their mission parameters.

Moving the rifle back to his shoulder, Ramirez took aim at her, gestured at his partner, and said, "Roll him over. I want to get a look at the guy who's causing all the fuss."

The partner said, "I thought you saw him at the ranch, earlier tonight."

"I didn't see a thing. He came out of nowhere and choked me out. It was over before I could catch a glimpse."

The partner took a cautious step toward Frank, the assault rifle trained on the outsider. Then the skinny little man nudged Frank with the barrel of his gun.

"Would you roll him over already. Dude is probably dead. And I'll be joining him at the rate you're moving."

The other man shot Ramirez a scathing glance and asked, "How's your hand?"

The comment incited a string of Navajo curse words from Ramirez. With the two men's attention on each other, Liana's eyes strayed toward her Glock, which rested on the plank flooring just a few feet away. But it wasn't worth the risk. Maybe she should have kept her gun and stood her ground with these two hired thugs? Or better yet, she should have anticipated that Ramirez wouldn't have come alone and that his backup would have been coming in through the front of the building.

"If you want to look a dead man in the eyes so badly, then you turn him over. I'm perfectly happy to let him bleed out right where he is until Mr. Canyon gets here."

Apparently, the thin man feared Frank's chindi may follow him home. Liana would never call herself a traditionalist, but that thought frightened her as well.

As the two grumbled and scowled at each other, a strange thought struck Liana. Frank's knife that had been stuck into the floor in front of him was now missing. She had laid her gun right beside the spot where the bone-handled Bowie knife had been embedded into the wood. She had seen the fresh gouge, but the knife was gone. She hadn't seen Frank or either of the goon squad grab the knife. But it was definitely gone, which meant that Frank must have…

She looked away from the gouge and the Glock in time to see Ramirez finally step up and roll Frank over himself.

When he did, the former soldier's eyes went wide, and he yelled, "Grenade!"

34

Ackerman had nearly dozed off as he listened to the normals make fools of themselves. The posturing coming from both sides of the equation had entertained him for a moment, considering that none of the people arguing and threatening to hurt one another truly wanted to make good on their threats. All the while, they ignored the true threat.

He had been waiting for one of the the three to attempt to roll him over and check for vital signs. His arms were tucked up under his body where the others couldn't see, and he had plenty of practice performing similar maneuvers in the past. Although, those were always when he was on the opposite side of the law. He supposed the concept was the same, and therefore, Ackerman considered himself an expert in looking lifeless.

As he waited—and calculated the odds that the children may shoot one other before he could diffuse the situation—Ackerman considered Emily Morgan's departure, not only for the moment but potentially forever. There were very few people in his life whose absence he would notice in any meaningful way. Emily was one of them. The thought of her not being part of the team or his life filled him with a strange empty feeling that he couldn't identify. Or perhaps the sensation merely stemmed from the shards of metal embedded in his side, that were possibly pressing against his spinal column.

Finally, the one Liana had called Ramirez rolled Ackerman over and set the tumblers in motion. He had premeditated his response since the moment he smelled the cheap aftershave and sheep feces that stained all of Canyon's men. That scent—being carried on the strong updrafts crawling up the side of the sharp drop-off at the back of the property—was a dead giveaway to the presence of additional playmates. Ackerman had even detected the smell of a well lubricated assault rifle. From that point, it had been simply a matter of holding Liana's hand while he handled the situation.

Now, Ackerman greeted Ramirez with the sight of a grenade in his right hand and the pin for that grenade in his left.

He watched Ramirez's eyes go wide, but Ackerman decided to sell it even further and released the detonation mechanism of the grenade.

Ramirez shouted a warning and dived toward the back door. His partner and Officer Liana rushed into the front room.

Ackerman tossed the grenade, which was already beginning to spill smoke, into the front room of the trading post. Then, he pulled the bone-handled Bowie knife from where he had tucked it into his waistband and rolled toward the fleeing form of Ramirez, whom he had deemed as the greatest of the two weak threats.

Still in motion, Ackerman swung his arm out in a wide arc and connected with the back of Ramirez's leg. The blade, which Ackerman had sharpened to a razor's edge, easily sliced through skin and sinew and dropped the fleeing former soldier onto his face against the rotting plank floor.

Ending the roll by shooting to his feet—which stabbed

sweet pain into his side—Ackerman grabbed Ramirez by the belt and pulled the fleeing attacker away from the exit.

His opponent's training was evident in the quick recovery the man displayed despite his wounds, as he turned on Ackerman and started striking and grappling. Perhaps, under different circumstances, Ackerman would have enjoyed testing his ground game against Ramirez, who he had pegged as a former Marine. But at the moment, he had another opponent to subdue and an innocent bystander to babysit.

Ramirez tried to his best moves to bring Ackerman to the ground, but the effort was quickly silenced by a knife penetrating Ramirez's left arm, the one holding the assault rifle.

Ackerman left the knife embedded in Ramirez's flesh and ripped the rifle from the screaming former soldier's grasp. As Ramirez reached for the handle of the knife, Ackerman ejected the magazine from the AK47 and cleared the round from the chamber. He then used the butt of the rifle to incapacitate Mr. Ramirez with a blow to the head.

The young man's head snapped back with sufficient force that Ackerman was satisfied that Ramirez was now either unconscious or wishing he was. The rest of the building had filled with smoke, but he could still make out two shadows within the chemical haze. Luckily, the remaining attacker was a head taller than Liana. Unfortunately, the young officer was not doing as he had instructed and staying out of his way. Instead, he watched as the smaller shadow rushed at the larger one and began an attempt at wrestle the assault rifle from the thin man's grip.

Ackerman rolled his eyes. It was so much easier working alone. Holding Ramirez's emptied rifle by the stock, he flipped the weapon over, with the butt facing the front room and the pistol grip point at the ceiling. To do it the other way threw off the weight, as he had learned from experience.

Stretching his left arm out in front of him as a guide, he hoisted the rifle above his right shoulder as if he were throwing a spear.

Once in position, he yelled, "Liana! Down!" Then he cocked back his arm and launched the weapon at the head of the thin man.

As he twisted his core to make the throw, he felt white hot tendrils of pain shoot through his midsection. To Ackerman, the pain that would have likely caused a normal person to pass out altogether was akin to a sexual release. Although, he also felt the metal fragments growing closer to his spine and understood that the pleasure of his pain hid the fact that Liana had been correct in her assessment... If his wounds weren't treated soon, he would bleed out and die.

The rifle he had used as a make-shift javelin struck its mark, knocking the thin man back a few steps. To his surprise, the skeletal attacker stayed on his feet and kept hold of his rifle. Thankfully, Officer Liana had followed instructions, dropped low, and moved away from the intruder.

Ackerman stepped into the fray with two large strides, grabbed the thin man by the right wrist, twisted the arm up, and dislocated the shoulder with an audible pop.

Canyon's thug screamed and released his AK47, which Ackerman emptied and discarded as he had the other rifle. The thin man dropped to the floor and clutched his as he rolled back and forth in pain and cursed in the People's language.

Retrieving the smoke grenade from where he had tossed it previously, Ackerman calmly walked to the back door and threw the handy little gadget over the side of the bluff.

As he passed the dazed and shaking Ramirez, he pulled the Bowie knife from the man's forearm, which woke the former soldier with a shriek of agony. Then he pulled over his original milk crate and sat back down, waiting for the smoke to clear. Once the haze had sufficiently dissipated, he said, "If you boys want to live, I'm going to need you both to kindly remove your pants."

The thin man—still crying in the front room—screamed, "You broke my arm!"

"It's only dislocated. Stop whining. Count yourself lucky that it wasn't your neck."

Ramirez—as he removed his belt and applied it to his leg as a tourniquet—said, "What are you going to do with us?"

Glancing from one man to the other, Ackerman shrugged and replied, "If you play stupid games, you'll win stupid prizes."

35

John Canyon had never really prayed any of the traditional Diné blessings, nor had he ever been all that interested in learning the stories of his people. Not until he went to war. One night during his time in the Persian Gulf—after checking his sleeping bag for camel spiders and scorpions and settling in with the zipper cinched up tightly around his face for fear that the same arachnids, and worse, would try to snuggle in with him—he had recalled the prayers of his grandfathers…

In beauty I walk
With beauty before me I walk
With beauty behind me I walk
With beauty above me I walk
With beauty around me I walk
It has become beauty again
Hózhóogo naasháa doo
Shitsijí' hózhóogo naasháa doo
Shikéédéé hózhóogo naasháa doo
Shideigi hózhóogo naasháa doo
T'áá altso shinaagóó hózhóogo naasháa doo
Hózhó náhásdlíí'
Hózhó náhásdlíí'
Hózhó náhásdlíí'
Hózhó náhásdlíí'

It had been those prayers—or at least the small portions he could remember—that helped John Canyon survive his time at war, and those same prayers that encouraged him to make a new way, not just for himself, but for the People.

He recited the lines of prayer in his head now as he thought of his son and what he would to do the man who had stolen him. John and Tobias had never been close, the elder having decided early on during his tenure as a father that he was better to let the boy's mother handle the day to day maintenance, while he focused on leaving his son, and his people, a true legacy. Despite all the sacrifices he had made, Toby seemed to resent him. But he hoped that it was merely a phase all young warriors experienced, a rite of passage into manhood, and not the influence of the belegana culture.

The road ahead of him was still dark. Canyon sat behind the wheel of his pickup truck, a caravan of his men behind him in various vehicles, a war party on the march. The rest of the world slept. That was where he should have been, at home, in bed. Alone.

Canyon's thoughts turned to his wife, Reyna. His bride—whose resentment of him seemed to outweigh the boy's, had been spending most of her time holed up in the casino's Presidential suite. He took responsibility for some of the chasm that had formed between them, but he knew that a bigger reason for her absence was the five grand a week she snorted up her nose, and his recent intervention of reducing her available supply. But all that had accomplished was causing her to spend all day in bed. For the life of him, he couldn't figure out what she would have to be depressed about. She had everything. The queen of an empire, who was treated as royalty should be. It was certainly several steps above the gutter from which he had pulled her. He suspected that her ailments came from a combination of her drug abuse and her strange religious beliefs, and less from his neglect.

She didn't know about Toby's abduction, and he didn't intend to tell her.

The road ahead wound its way through the hills and up to the top of a large bluff where some damn fool had decided to build a general store. The Red Bluff Trading Post, which served the scattered remnants refusing to leave an area mostly tainted by the belegana's uranium mines, had went out of business when those who lived farther down in the valley had started frequenting the Walmart in Farmington.

Ramirez, one of his lieutenants, must have responded to his earlier lesson, since the kid had been the one to first discover where the outsiders had holed up. The former Marine had always been a good soldier for Canyon. This evening's screwup and a struggle with addiction aside, Ramirez was another shining example of a child he had pulled from the gutter. Without his intervention and guidance of the boy, who had been adopted as an indentured servant by his wife's Uncle Red, Ramirez would have been nothing, just another half-breed banger. Instead, he was a man with a future. A man with hope. Canyon supposed that was what he had really brought to his people: hope.

The belegana had sent his people down a dark road, but just as the headlights of his truck cut through the darkness ahead, he intended to shine a light for all of the Diné with no hope or prospects. He gave them gainful employment, nice homes, and an overall better life.

The caravan cut through a series of hills and then came down into a small valley that marked the bottom of Red Bluff. He couldn't see the trading post yet, but he guessed they were less than a mile out.

His internal musings were cut short when his lights shined upon two men walking down the center of the road. Stopping dead, the others behind him following suit, he jumped down from the big F-150 and approached the two men. Both had been stripped to their underwear with their hands tied behind their backs and their pants stuck atop their heads, flowing down their backs like a headdress. The two were leaning on each other for support. Ramirez in particular seemed to be having trouble walking and now, not only was his hand bandaged from where John had smashed it with the stone tomahawk, but his calf and forearm were also bandaged with blood showing through the white of the cloth.

Ramirez wouldn't make eye contact with him, and neither man attempted an excuse or explanation. They knew better.

Canyon looked from the pair of his incompetent underlings to where the old trading post sat atop Red Bluff like a castle on a hill designed to dispel intruders. He knew that the element of surprise had now been lost, which made taking down the man named Frank all the more difficult. His plan had been to roll up in force, drawing the attention of Frank and whoever was helping him, while Ramirez and his partner, who were already hidden and in position, would be able to slip in the back and take their enemy by surprise.

Canyon didn't look at the two men as he said, "You were supposed to wait for us."

Ramirez, eyes still on the hard-packed dirt road in front

of him, replied, "It was my call, sir. We saw an opportunity to end this. Your man is badly injured and the only other person with him was the Nakai girl."

"Liana Nakai?"

"Yessir, we overheard her and the outsider talking. She kept telling him that he needed a hospital and then he passed out, fell right off his seat, and face-planted into the floor. I saw a shot, and I took it."

"How did that work out for you?"

"I don't know how, but he must have known we were there. When we flipped him over—"

Canyon interrupted, "I think I can fill in the blanks from there." Considering the intel about the injuries and the inside of the building that the two men obviously possessed, perhaps their screwup wasn't a total loss.

"Sir, he totally blindsided us, and he's armed to the teeth. We saw grenades, gun cases, ammo boxes. It looked like he was preparing for war."

"Good. That's what's coming for him," Canyon replied. Then, turning back to the caravan of his soldiers, he called Todacheeney over and said, "Toad, take these two idiots back to the ranch and get them patched up. I don't want either of them dying before I have a chance to kill them myself."

36

At the first sign of engines in the distance, Ackerman pulled out the case containing the .50 BMG caliber Barrett sniper rifle and calmly assembled the weapon from its base components. Completing the task in less than thirty seconds, he slammed home a magazine full of ten armor-piercing five-and-a-half-inch-long bullets and pulled back the slide to position a round ready to fire. He loved the way the Barrett smelled. Brand new, never before fired, virgin steel oiled to perfection.

All the while, in his peripheral vision, he watched Liana pace back and forth. Her breathing was erratic. He estimated that her short and shallow gulps of air verged on hyperventilation. She kept repeating things like: "This can't be happening," "My career is over," and "My life is over." Sometimes in a whisper, sometimes bordering on a scream.

All of her babbling was beginning to give Ackerman a headache, an affliction that was commonplace for his brother but rare for him, until recently.

He said, "Can you please take some deep breaths, or count to ten, or breathe into a paper sack, or something? Some of us are trying to work here."

In reply, Officer Liana barked, "I don't understand how you can be so calm! A group of trained killers are coming to—"

"Yes, yes, I understand and validate your feelings on the

matter. The situation is well under control. You need but to remain calm and enjoy the ride."

"Don't patronize me. I'm a Navajo Nation Police officer."

Ackerman smiled up at her. She was so very beautiful. Hair black as midnight, high cheekbones, and skin the color of wet sand. Her cheeks were flushed, and her eyes full of fear. He said, "My apologies, Officer. I sometimes forget how easily excitable you normals can be. But I would appreciate it if you would stop pacing so close to the nitroglycerine."

Liana froze, wide eyes searching around her feet as if she'd heard the rattle of a diamondback.

"Are you screwing with me?" she whispered.

"Absolutely not. In that shed out back, I found a couple crates of aged dynamite. Normally, the fire department for the area would be called and the danger removed by controlled detonation. It's actually a common task of fire departments in rural America. Aged dynamite, regardless of the sorbent used, will sweat nitroglycerine, which then pools up and creates a sweetly volatile cocktail capable of discharge without the need of blasting caps or fuses."

"So when you found the volatile, sweating, highly-dangerous dynamite, your first thought was to pick it up and carry it inside?"

"You can't very well use your hammer if you leave it in the tool shed."

She sighed. "Please tell me you have a plan."

"Did you see that old cast-iron bathtub sitting alongside the trading post? The one built atop a sheet of plywood on wheels, to make it mobile. I found it beside the trailer. I suspect the former proprietor used it for bathing."

Her brow furrowed, and she said, "What else would you use a bathtub for?"

"You'd be surprised, but I don't think I've ever seen one able to be pulled around the yard."

Liana still seemed confused by his reaction and replied, "They put the wheels on so they could pull the tub out into the sun and have a warm bath."

"Interesting. Mystery solved, I suppose. For some reason, I missed that explanation in favor of other more…fantastical musings. Regardless, I considered turning the tub into a sort of missile to roll down the hill. The long slope and mild curvature of the road would make it possible to reach the bottom of the bluff, where Canyon will be encamping his forces. And the cast iron would deflect any bullets fired at it from striking the dynamite. But I ultimately decided that the bumps, the ease of the the tub hitting a rock and flipping halfway down, and a myriad of other factors would make it infeasible. In the end, there were just too many rogue variables. Wild cards, as they say. Like you."

Liana cocked an eyebrow. "Me?"

"You're certainly unpredictable. And quite a bit of a distraction, if I'm being honest. Don't forget that you were never supposed to be here. My plan all along was to handle this alone. You, Officer Nakai, are a rogue variable. A random anomaly who stumbled into my path. You're like the bug, and I'm the car windshield. You were going along in your simple little life, and then I hit you. No, that's a weak analogy. I'm more like a train than a car. But trains must also hit bugs all the time, so I'm like a freight train, and you're—"

She interrupted, "You realize that they might start

shooting in here, and if any bullets strike this dynamite or—"

He interrupted back, "Yes, I'm fully aware of the properties of my explosives. I don't intend for them to be shooting in here. They should be getting my message any time and reaching out."

"Reaching out with what? The cell towers must be down. Signal is never good, but I had zero service all the way from the station to here."

"I believe that's Mr. Canyon shutting off the flow of communication in and out of his kingdom."

"No way. He doesn't have that kind of power."

Ackerman shrugged. "It wouldn't even be that difficult, but the source of the blackout isn't of paramount concern. We are cut off from the outside world. We typically bring along several different forms of short-range communication: cellular, radio frequency, plastic cups connected by strings. We've encountered killers in the past who have employed jamming equipment. I stashed a handheld radio set to the proper frequency in the pants pocket, or I suppose I should say headdress pocket, of Mr. Ramirez. We also have other forms of staying in touch as a team. Unfortunately, we did not come prepared with a satellite phone. But no one thinks of everything. Not even me. Most importantly, our incoming attackers wouldn't risk shooting the heir apparent to the Canyon empire."

Mention of Tobias Canyon caused Liana to look toward the former main checkout counter of the old trading post. Ackerman had showed her how he had wrapped the hostages in fishing line and burlap and placed them behind the counter like sacks of potatoes.

Ackerman placed his eye to the scope of the rifle and sighted in on his target, which was quickly approaching. Then he reiterated, "Nothing to worry about, officer. Just sit back and enjoy the ride." He punctuated his sentence with a blast from the .50 caliber sniper rifle.

Liana ran over to the window to see what he had fired on and exclaimed, "What in the hell are you shooting at?"

He handed her a pair of binoculars. "As you can see, I didn't kill anyone. Unless you count Mr. Canyon's F-150. With as much as people spend on their vehicles these days, I suppose that you could consider it a member of the family. I mean, honestly, there are many who see no problem in spending forty thousand dollars on a vehicle, but they scoff at spending that same amount on their child's education."

She said, "You could have killed someone with that cannon."

Through the scope, he watched the truck spurt oil and smoke. Canyon fought to keep the truck under control and the top-heavy vehicle from flipping. With expert driving technique, Canyon was able to get the vehicle to the side of the path. Ackerman said, "I merely shot out their engine block. I wanted to send a message that we are well armed and we don't want them coming any closer. And now that the message has been sent, they'll have no other choice but to reach out with the radio I provided. Simple."

Liana asked, "So you planned all of this? You wanted Canyon and his men to come and find you here?"

"That's right. Exactly why I left that little calling card back at your station. You were supposed to be a good girl and tell your superior who would then tell Mr. Canyon. You didn't do that because you're a wild card. But it seems that everything has worked out just fine. Your boss probably suspected what you were doing and tracked you here using the GPS positioning of your patrol vehicle."

She whispered, "My life is over. This may be exactly how you planned things, but what about me? The two men you released are gonna tell Canyon and Captain Yazzie that I'm working with you. You just gave me a death sentence."

He laughed. "Hardly. You were simply traded to the winning team."

"I think you're a bit overconfident."

"Why do you normals keep telling me that?"

"It's going to get the both of us killed."

"I've heard that before many times as well."

"How can you be so damn calm?"

He chuckled. "Do you know the best indicator of future behavior and future outcomes?...Past behavior and past outcomes. And as you can see, despite all those who have tried to kill me, despite all those who have scarred me, tortured me, shot me, stabbed me, burned me… In spite of them all. I'm still standing."

37

The past…

After a few moments, she said, "Do you love me or not?"

The bluntness of the question shocked Marcus and made him hesitate. He wasn't sure how to respond to something like that.

Apparently taking his silence as a negative, Maggie said, "I guess that's my answer."

"It's not as simple as all that."

"Yes, it is. Either you do or you don't."

"It doesn't matter either way. You just don't understand that. What did you think would happen? That we'd get married, have kids, and bring them along on cases? There was a time when all that I wanted was to be normal. Settle down with you and start a family. But I can't do that, because I'm not normal. I'm just as broken as the men we hunt."

"I can't quit the Shepherd Organization, if that's what you want," she said.

"I don't know what I want. But I know now that I can't run from what I am."

A long, cold silence accompanied them down Route 12 past houses and businesses and bare trees. They were all vague shapes at the dark edges of the headlights' beam. The snowfall had tapered off as they drove, and the snowplows were out in force. They had already seen three of them along the way. But Marcus had heard that the worst of the storm was still on its way.

PART 3

38

John Canyon stood beside his ruined truck and seethed up at the dilapidated trading post. He estimated it to be around five hundred yards away, up a sloping lane of fading gravel. He could see the outline of the buildings by the light of the moon and the glow of the caravan's headlights. They were beyond the effective range of most of their guns, certainly the automatic assault rifles and submachine guns that most of the men were carrying. They definitely out of range, however, for whatever kind of military-grade sniper rifle the man named Frank, the man without fear, was using. John Canyon stood there staring, grimacing. His years in the military and his being forced to work with idiots for so many years had instilled in John a definite sense of calm. But this new man, this newcomer, had invaded his home and stolen his calm. People often matched the anxiety levels of those with whom they came in contact. Canyon wasn't sure if it was something subconscious or some learned habit of evolution, but he had found it to be true.

This man Frank was different, however. He was unlike any man John had ever encountered. While Frank seemed to be completely fearless, he caused a strange energy to enter the room which instead of matching his anxiety, his calm caused your anxiety to rise. His fearlessness seemed to manufacture fear in others.

Pulling out the small radio Toad had discovered in

Ramirez's pants pocket, Canyon pushed the button on the small device and said, "You made your point, Frank. We're staying back, for now. Over."

"Salutations, John. Wonderful to see you again so soon. I assume by your presence here that you've located my missing colleague and are ready to deliver her to me. If so, stand by for instructions. If not, follow step number one, before attempting to move onto step number two. I'm really trying to keep things simple for you here, John. Over," came the reply from the small speaker mounted in the device.

Gritting his teeth, Canyon replied, "I'm gonna make you pay. You took my son and now you killed my F-150."

"I'm sure your drug money will have no problem paying for a new pickup truck."

Canyon gripped the small radio so tightly he was afraid he might break it. He wasn't sure how Frank knew so much about him and his operations, but Canyon did know that Frank knew way too much to be allowed to live. Through clenched teeth, he replied, "I don't see my other truck either, the semi you stole from me earlier along with all of my little friends loaded up in the back. Over."

"Don't worry, John. Your sheep and your drugs are perfectly safe. Did you know the Incas believed that coca plant was a gift from the gods or that pure cocaine was first extracted from the leaves of the coca plant in 1859 and was marketed as a coca wine in France in 1863?"

"Is my son in there with you or is he with the truck?"

"They're both safe. I would worry more about myself if I were you. You're the one with crosshairs over your forehead, with an itchy trigger finger caressing the steel of a .50 BMG rifle. Have you ever seen what a .50 BMG will do to a man, John? Oh yes, of course you have, you would have witnessed it several times during your military service. Sometimes I have a tendency to preach to the choir. My apologies. My point is that you should be focusing your tracking skills on more fruitful pursuits. Perhaps hunting down Maggie Carlisle and returning her to me, saving your own life, that kind of thing. Just a suggestion. Over."

"You're not getting out of this place alive."

Frank said, "I could kill you where you stand right here and now and you are completely aware of that fact, and yet you still choose to challenge me?"

"If you wanted to kill me, you would have done it already. I didn't take your friend. You have the wrong man. You're barking up the wrong tree. This is your last chance. You surrender now, you give up your hostages and my truck, and we'll see what happens from there. Maybe you walk out of here with all of your body parts. You and your little partner. Over."

"Well, isn't this interesting. Here we are back in the same position in which we started. You sitting there declaring that you're in charge while I sit here knowing that I'm in charge. Why do you normals keep insisting that I demonstrate my skills to you at every turn? It would be a lot easier for everyone if you merely looked to past experience and put two and two together. I mean, wouldn't that just save us all a bit of time? And make no mistake time is running out, John. For you and your son. Out."

"I'll kill you, you belegana bastard. I'll kill you and everyone you love. I don't have your girl. I don't know where she is. And even if I did, I wouldn't tell you, because this has gone too far now. There's no way you'll leave this place alive. I'm half tempted to just blow you off the face of the Earth and be done with it. I'm starting to have my doubts that my son is even in there with you."

"Oh, is that your issue? If you'd like a little proof of life, I can understand where you're coming from. Unfortunately, you're going to have to give me a few moments."

"What does that mean? You're not leaving this place."

"No, no, I just need a moment to unwrap him. Talk soon. Good times. Over and out."

39

In order to gain intel about Canyon, Marcus had first visited The Grand Canyon Hotel and Casino and, after slipping a bartender a hundred dollar bill, he had learned a lot of rumors about Canyon and his operation. For one, Mrs. Canyon had been staying almost entirely in their suite at the casino instead of living at the ranch with her husband. Marcus could care less about the man's marital problems, but that same intel also told him that he wouldn't have to worry about waking anyone inside the house.

Canyon's ranch consisted of thousands of acres of grazing lands leading up to production buildings, grain silos, and structures that Marcus guessed to house livestock. Maggie could have been locked up in any one of them. With his brother distracting Canyon and his men, Marcus hoped that the ranch would be virtually unguarded. Possibly only a few sentries, and with Mrs. Canyon living at the casino, John Canyon might not have even seen the need to leave any men behind to guard his home.

Moving in the shadows for concealment, he methodically checked the farm's production buildings first, before making his way in a circular progression toward the main house. The sprawling pueblo-style structure that was Canyon's home was a mansion by most standards. Two stories of tans and whites topped with a reddish orange ceramic tile roof and much of its face covered with oversized windows.

Marcus looked from the house to the buildings housing the sheep. He had already searched those to no avail, but one of them had to contain the equipment used to affix drugs to fake skin and wool for transport. Before they showed up, Canyon had quite an operation going. Although they had no hard evidence beyond the drugs they had unlawfully seized, Marcus surmised that Canyon's men received the drugs from just across the border or the Cartels transported it across the border to Canyon. Either way, the ranchers would then strap it to the backs of the livestock. From there, after only crossing one border, the drugs would be insulated and protected for their trips to any prospective US city.

Marcus admired the ex-soldier's ingenuity and his desire to rise above the circumstances into which he was born. And he very much sympathized with the plight of John Canyon and his people—whom the American government had driven out of their homes and basically forced into concentration camps. A people only a couple of generations removed from those living today. That same government had then proceeded to systematically remove that people's culture in an attempt to assimilate them into what they considered civilized society. The thought of it all made Marcus sick. It was an issue that had never really received the attention it deserved.

But he wasn't there to discuss social injustice. He only had one goal. He considered heading straight for the house, but he knew that he should remain cautious and scope things out for a few minutes before jumping in head first. As he watched, he tried to keep his thoughts from Maggie, and so he considered his brother and all the atrocities and injustices that Ackerman had faced down and risen above.

Marcus had been held captive in darkness for months by Thomas White, tortured both physically and psychologically, and had endured many things far worse. Despite all that, he knew that he had never suffered anything close to what his brother had faced. Marcus had tasted pain and fear and death many times, but he had never experienced it in a way that could take away all he knew of fear.

Through his own crucible, he had discovered that enduring something terrible and life-changing had a way of adjusting a person's sensitivity levels. A garden snake wasn't something that scared you after nearly being eaten by an anaconda. Although anacondas may still vividly scare you—in fact, those anacondas might haunt your thoughts and your dreams and your every waking moment—anything short off that level of fear and pain and death suddenly became manageable.

Marcus had once believed that he needed to see all the threats coming. If he could see them, he could fight them. He had been obsessed by the idea. He would sit in restaurants and watch the exits and entrances; the comings and goings, checking each person, watching their eyes, their mannerisms, their ticks. Analyzing, predicting behavior. For fear that a wolf would creep in from the shadows to attack the sheep. But then experience taught him that people who stood in the light were often more dangerous than those who crept from the shadows, and any kind of true protection or security was an illusion. If the wolves wanted you, then they would get you.

Monitoring the main house for several minutes, becoming a fly on the wall, a shadow among shadows, Marcus focused on every detail, searching for signs of movement that might reveal a camera or guard. From what he could see, the ranch had very little in terms of high-tech security measures. But that was the thing about cutting edge security; the best systems were invisible. With as much money as Canyon was pulling down, as many people as he employed, Marcus suspected that John Canyon's home, sitting in this remote area of the Navajo Nation, boasted a security system that would rival any of the mansions out in Greenwich village.

The question he had to ask himself wasn't whether or not the house had cameras and alarms, but whether or not there was anyone watching.

Under normal circumstances, Marcus's instincts would have been to wait and watch a bit longer. Learn the routines a little better. But under the present circumstance, he felt he was showing restraint by not driving his little collapsible motorcycle straight through the front window of John Canyon's house. He had to know if Maggie was inside that building, but getting himself killed wouldn't do Maggie any good. So he waited a few seconds longer. And then a few seconds longer. He knew very well that just because he didn't see any guards didn't mean that there weren't any present or that they didn't see him. In fact, the most deadly opponents were ones that seemed to blend right in.

When his anger and anticipation built to the point that he could contain it no longer, Marcus stepped from cover and headed for the pueblo mansion. Staying low in a tactical shooter's stance, he kept the MP5, to which he had attached a sound suppressor, tight to his shoulder as he scanned for potential targets.

He moved directly toward the house. His brother often said that the shortest distance between two points is always a straight line. It was the kind of statement that Ackerman often made, impossible to argue with because it was true but also typically a vague generalization. In Ackerman's case, it was usually a justification for having cut someone or bloodied someone's nose.

The closer Marcus came to the house, the faster he moved. The momentum built something up in him. He tapped into that well of righteous rage. He was tired of watching and waiting. He was ready to act. He was ready to find out if Maggie was in this building, if John Canyon had truly been the one who had stolen her, and if she was alive or dead. Those thoughts spurred his determination. When he reached the front door of Canyon's desert mansion, he kicked full force at a spot beside the knob, breaking the door from the frame and causing it to swing inwards. He didn't hear an alarm sounding, at least not yet. And he didn't really care anymore. He was past the point of caring. He was past the point of being afraid.

He swept through the first floor of the massive house like a dark wind. He was feeling his aggression rise and a part of him was hoping that a sentry would dare to show their face.

The first floor held a massive foyer, a two-story great room, a dining room, a breakfast room, a fully-stocked bar, a kitchen, multiple bathrooms, and a study. They were all decorated with what appeared to be genuine American Indian artifacts and the memorabilia of Canyon's people.

As he moved from room to room, Marcus kept checking for a set of stairs that would lead to the basement. He wanted to check the lowest levels of the structure first. Although it wasn't completely unheard of for a killer to have his murder room on an upper floor, there was just something about a basement. Something about already being underground and close to your grave, to your final resting place. There was also a sense of insulation and isolation.

It wasn't until the end of his sweep that he located the entrance to the subterranean depths of Canyon's estate. He flipped on the light, stepped down a few steps, closed the door behind him, and steeled his nerves for whatever he might find.

His adrenaline raged, but he fought to keep his body and his emotions under control. He willed his legs to move slowly and calmly. He listened. He reached out with his ears, searching for any kind of disturbance or movement, any indication of something strange or out of place. Most importantly, he listened for a sound to give away an adversary waiting in ambush.

He heard nothing.

The momentary caution now receding, he descended several more steps until his still-focused hearing registered a small but heart-stopping sound, one he had heard before, one that was hard to forget.

It was the sound of stepping down on an active land mine.

40

Marcus gently pulled his arm out from beneath Maggie Carlisle's naked form. She stirred, rolled her shoulders, and said with a moan, "It's time for you got a real bed."

"This is a real bed."

"It's a futon. Death Row inmates have nicer beds than this."

"What can I say? I know how to treat a girl right."

He pulled himself up from the futon, the thin metal frame creaking beneath his shifting weight, "Where you going?" Maggie asked, yawning.

"Nowhere. Go back to sleep. I just need some Tylenol."

Maggie rolled over, exposing the long tanned curve of her back and her golden blonde hair.

41

With every tick of the clock, Ackerman felt his lifeblood pumping away. He felt like a mighty war ship with an oil leak. No matter how hard he could push, no matter how tough we was, how smart he was, or how strong he was, without blood, his gears and pistons would stop turning. In the end, he recognized his body as a miraculous machine, one that needed lubrication and vital fluids same as any mechanical marvel.

But before he could deal with that problem, he needed to handle John Canyon and his caravan of soldiers. A defense against the enemy at the gates needed to mounted before he could allow himself the time to bleed.

With that in mind, Ackerman bent down to the same level as Tobias Canyon, whom he had just restrained to an old wooden chair using high-tension fishing line. Ackerman said, "Now, you're going to be a good boy and tell Daddy that everything is just fine and that you are unharmed."

Tobias Canyon stared back at him defiantly.

With his right arm, Ackerman held out the small walkie-talkie. With a nod, he indicated for the Canyon boy to speak.

Tobias, maintaining his scowl, leaned toward the small black communicator and said, "Father, I'm sorry. I'm alive. I overheard where they have the truck and—"

Ackerman pulled the radio away from Tobias's mouth,

and then he struck the boy hard across the jaw, causing the young man to spit a mouthful of blood in his direction.

The blood splattered across his black shirt. He didn't mind. He expected there to be plenty more blood coming soon. The boy proceeded to curse at him in an unknown tongue, the tone and inflection sounding to Ackerman like a form of witchcraft. After waiting a moment for Tobias to finish, Ackerman asked, "Are you done? Go ahead, get it all out of your system. And when you're ready, I'll actually push the transmit button on this communicator and you can tell your father exactly what I told you."

Ackerman punctuated his statement by pushing the tip of his bone-handled Bowie knife against the soft spot beneath Tobias Canyon's chin. He added, "Now, this time, please play by the rules of the game. I have to say it makes me go a little crazy when people don't play by the rules. My rules, anyway."

42

Marcus had mistaken the small click as he stepped down the stairs as the activation of a land mine. That idea dissolved when the sound was followed by the man hiding beneath the uncarpeted set of stairs saying, "Don't move. Take your hand off the gun and put your arms towards the sky."

Marcus cursed under his breath. He didn't have time for this. He focused on the sound he had heard. He recognized now that it had been the click of a hammer being cocked. But it didn't match up with a sawed-off shotgun or semi-automatic pistol. No, as he thought back on the sound, the reason he had mistaken it for the activation of some kind of explosive had been due to the oiled and rhythmic turning of a cylinder as the hammer was pulled back. That click belonged to an old-fashioned wheel gun. Marcus knew that his MP5 had an advantage over the six-shooter in almost every arena. The trigger pull of his weapon, even with the wheel gun's hammer back, would be much lighter in pounds of pressure. The man under the stairs also had the disadvantage of having to shoot through the slats. All Marcus had to do was to move down the stairs quickly enough and the man's aim would be completely thrown off. The MP5 however, with its automatic firing capabilities, could stitch holes in the entire set of stairs.

Marcus said, "Okay. I'm surrendering. Don't do anything crazy. I'm going to raise—"

Then he dove forward into open air and jerked his right arm up, grabbing the MP5 and pulling the trigger all the way back as he directed the barrage toward his adversary. Splinters of the bare wood exploded into the air to mix with the smoke of burning gunpowder and spent shell casings. Marcus tried to land as gracefully as possible but ended up smashing his shoulder into the concrete hard enough to shoot a bolt of electric pain down his spine. But he didn't have time for pain now. He immediately rolled toward a point of cover while ejecting the magazine and reaching for a fresh load from a pouch on his tactical vest.

But he was stopped short when a shaky voice said, "Mister, I don't want to hurt you, but I will. Navajo Nation Police. Do not move."

Marcus found himself staring down the barrel of a police-issue twelve gauge shotgun operated by a man he recognized as Ernie Pitka, one of the deputies they had learned worked at the local substation of the Navajo Nation Police.

Still fuming with adrenaline and rage, he started thinking of ways he could overtake the kid, but they all had a risk of either himself getting killed or him grievously injuring Officer Pitka. He knew that if Maggie were there now, she would quote his own words back at him and tell him not to lose sight of what it was that they did. They saved people. They didn't hurt people. They didn't kill people. Although it was sometimes necessary to fight back, they always did so with the goal of protecting life, not taking it.

Still, Marcus couldn't merely surrender. He couldn't allow himself to be captured. It wasn't just his own life on the line. Maggie. Ackerman. Who knew how many other lives the Taker would steal if they didn't put an end to his trail of tears, broken families, and unquenchable pain.

But he also had a code to live by, and that code didn't involve hurting an innocent police officer who seemed to be trying to do his job as best he could under a corrupt regime.

He thought of how easy it would be to grab the barrel of the shotgun and direct it toward the ceiling while simultaneously pulling a knife from his tactical utility vest.

Officer Pitka repeated, "Hands up, now!"

Marcus did as he was told and said, "Okay, let's take it easy. We're on the same side here. I know about you, Pitka. I know you're a good cop."

"Slowly get up on your knees."

"Okay, okay. I'm moving slowly."

Stepping from behind Marcus to join his subordinate, Captain Yazzie undid his shirt as he fought for breath. Pulling back the layers of uniform revealed a trio of nine millimeter slugs that had embedded themselves in Yazzie's body armor. In a rasp, the captain said, "Well, goodness gracious, we're all having fun now. This is just like paintball, only it hurts a hell of a lot more." Yazzie ended his statement by pistol-whipping Marcus across the temple with his silver and gold Colt .45 Peacemaker. The last thing Marcus saw before blacking out was a flash of metal and the look of rage in the captain's eyes.

43

Three weeks earlier…

Maggie glanced down at the address Baxter Kincaid had provided for the third time. She trusted the private detective's skills, and yet, this couldn't be the right place. Her father, a deadbeat drunk who had abandoned his family, could never afford a house like this. The yard was professionally manicured, not quite as extravagant as to possess shrubbery formed into the shapes of animals or dotted by fountains of marble, but the bushes were perfectly symmetrical and the flowers blooming and beautiful in perfect aesthetic balance. It was one of those houses where shiny plastic families lived. The two-story brick home wasn't quite a mansion, but it was definitely upper class. While her father was most definitely lower class.

Something about the house made Maggie's skin crawl, despite the fact that everything was in perfect order, just as she would have designed it. The little voices that tugged at the back of her mind when things were out of place were quiet now. But still, she felt like this was a place far out of balance. This couldn't be her father's true address. Her childhood home had never been like this. Her home had been absolute chaos.

Maggie's parents' marriage barely lasted a year after her brother's abduction. Her mother fell into a dark abyss of despair, retreating inward, while her dad tried to drink himself to death. Whenever one of them climbed from their perspective pits of self destruction, they took their rage out on one another, which left her alone and afraid with nothing to think about except how she had failed to protect her little brother. And how she was to blame for the chaos that had poisoned her family.

The day her father left was forever etched into her memory. She had heard him scream many times, but she'd never witnessed him raise a hand against her mother. Having learned to tune out their arguments, she hadn't even registered the ferocity of the hate they were spitting at one another until she heard the "thwap" sound of an open-handed slap and her mother shriek.

Maggie had quickly looked up from the kitchen table to see her mother stumble backward, tripping over a chair and falling. She remembered her dad quickly apologizing and pleading with his mother to calm down, but she was beyond reasoning and immediately called the police.

None of that, however, had been all that traumatic for her. She had become numb after the abduction, somewhat immune to the pain of her parents' vacant stares and the way they had began to ignore her completely. What had haunted her dreams since that day, however, was the look on her father's face as he glanced from her mother to her and then walked out with nothing but the clothes on his back. The look was one of cold calculation. She had seen him size up whether or not there was anyone left in this place whom he loved and decide within a second that there was no one here worth bringing.

A warrant had been issued for his arrest, and they barely

heard anything from or about him for the next couple of years. Everything they did hear was negative. Then they heard nothing at all. A part of her had hoped that he was dead.

One moment of anger. One split second decision. And her father was gone from her life forever. Or at least, he was, until now.

Forcing herself to move, she climbed from the rental and floated dreamily toward the sidewalk. Children shrieked in delight amid the sound of pool splashes and the smells of a backyard barbecue. Maggie trembled as she pressed the little off-white button beside the door and listened for signs of movement inside.

A young girl—maybe eleven or twelve years old—opened the door, and Maggie had more trouble keeping her reaction from showing than if she had come face to face with a mass murderer. The little girl was dressed and coifed in modern styles, but besides that, she was a dead ringer for one of Maggie's school photos. Bronze skin, blonde hair, blue eyes…just like her father.

The pre-teen had her nose buried in her cell phone and barely looked up as she asked, "May I help you?"

Maggie wondered briefly if this was all a dream. If Marcus had been present, he probably would have geeked out that this situation was similar to a scene from Empire Strikes Back. Or at least, the old Marcus would have. She missed him, almost as much as she missed her brother.

Thankfully, the words came automatically as she cleared her throat and asked, "Hello, are your parents home?"

The girl's thumbs danced over the screen, seemingly oblivious to the question, but she screamed, "Dad!"

Maggie was grateful for the fact that the young girl had answered the door and provided a few seconds for her to react and process. Now, her expression could be one of cold indifference instead of confusion when her father arrived to greet her.

He looked better than Maggie had ever seen him look. It was obvious he had been sober for some time, and he appeared to be in better physical shape than he had in the pictures from his high school year book, except for a head of hair that was stark white instead of sandy blonde.

"Sorry about my daughter. She's—"

Maggie had already removed her sunglasses. She wanted him to have a clear view of her when he approached, hoping that he would recognize his other abandoned and forgotten daughter. The way his eyes went wide at the sight of her indicated that she had gotten her wish.

Removing a special germ-resistant leather wallet that Marcus had purchased as a gift from the pocket of her suit jacket, she flipped open to her credentials, and trying to maintain the same tone she would have used with any interviewee, she said, "Special Agent Maggie Carlisle. I have a few questions to ask you."

Her father's hands shook, and his eyes looked as if they might pop from his skull and roll away. He stepped toward her, crowding her away from the front door as he pulled it closed behind him. With that simple movement, he spoke volumes. He had closed the door between his new life and his eldest, forgotten child.

Rage fueling her, she proclaimed, "You have a beautiful home here, Mr. Carlisle."

"Mags, I've thought a lot about what I would say—"

"Don't call me that. I'm here because I need information. So let's be clear, you're nothing more to me than any other random asshole that might cross my path."

He nodded and met her gaze. "I deserve that."

"You deserve a lot worse than that. What do you do for a living, Mr. Carlisle?"

"I run a trucking company. Listen, Maggie, now is not the best time. Maybe we could—"

"Now will do just fine. There have been some new developments in Tommy's case. You remember him? Your son, Tommy?"

"Let's get coffee later. There are a lot of things you don't know. You have a lot of reasons to be angry at me, so you might as well be angry for the right ones."

Maggie dug the nails of her left hand into her palm to focus her anger and remain in control. "You're going to answer a few questions, and then I'll be out of your life, just like you want it."

"I never wanted that, Mags. Listen, your grandmother threatened me. She—"

Raising both hands, she interrupted, "I don't care. I only need to ask you a few questions about the day your son, Tommy, was taken."

"Mags, dammit, that's why I want to explain. Tommy was your brother, but he wasn't my son."

Employing a technique for dealing with rage that Ackerman had taught her, she imagined herself hurting her father in her mind in order to fight the urge to hurt him in real life. She asked, "Are you remarried?"

"Yes."

"What's her name?"

"Teresa."

"Does she know about the wife and kids you abandoned?"

"Dammit, Maggie, there's a lot you don't know."

"How many kids?"

He lowered his eyes and ran a hand through his white hair. "Two boys and a girl."

Maggie closed her eyes and imagined herself pistol-whipping her progenitor. Her father had remarried. She'd been prepared for that, but for some reason, the possibility that he might have more children had never occurred to her. If he didn't want the kids he already had, why go make more?

Sticking out her lower jaw and breathing hard, she said, "So tell me what I don't know?"

"I can't right now, but meet me later, and I'll—"

"Either you talk to me now, or I haul you into your local police station for questioning. Think that would get your new family's attention?"

"I'm sorry, Mags. I really am. Is that want you want to hear? I've been through a lot too, and I've tried to move on and learn from my mistakes."

"So that's what we were to you? Mistakes?"

"No, I just meant that I'm trying to be a better husband and father now. But I'm not the only one at fault in all this. Your mother... Well, did you ever notice that Tommy seemed really...dark-complected?"

"The whole family has naturally dark skin! What the hell are you saying?"

With a sigh, her father replied, "I had a DNA test ran. Tommy was your brother, Maggie, but he wasn't my son. Your mother had been sleeping around. That's when I started drinking. I was trying to work up the nerve to run a test on you too, but it would have broken my heart if it had turned out that you—"

"Don't say another word."

"Your mother blamed me when he was taken, and your grandma threatened to tell the police that I—"

"Shut up!" she screamed.

Her father recoiled and looked toward the windows of his perfect house, not wanting his perfect new family to ask too many questions. Somehow, Maggie had accepted being abandoned, but she wasn't prepared to discover that she, along with the rest of her father's first family, had been replaced.

Closing her eyes and breathing deep, Maggie counted to ten and said, "This was a mistake. Looks like you have a nice life here. Sorry to interrupt."

She turned to leave and had made it halfway to her rental when he called out, "Wait! Why don't you come inside?"

Maggie dug her fingernails into her palms until she felt her flesh tearing, but she didn't turn back. Instead, she willed herself forward to the driver's side of the rental. Sliding behind the wheel, she sped away with an unintentional squealing of tires. Then, driving until she could no longer see through the tears, Maggie Carlisle pulled to the side of the road and wept.

Not wanting Toby to see her tears, she stepped toward the back room, but hearing muffled gasps carried her forward for a peak around the corner.

Illuminated by the light of the moon and a pre-dawn sun coming in through shattered windows, Frank pulled off his black long-sleeved shirt, which was soaked with his own blood and sticking to the side of his abdomen. He looked gaunt and pale.

As he pulled the shirt free, she saw blood oozing from several puncture wounds on his left side. He seemed not to register her presence. He examined the injuries and muttered something under his breath. Then he turned to her, and in his usual calm baritone, he said, "This isn't the first time I've caught you staring at my scars."

Without thinking, she blurted, "I wasn't actually looking at the scars."

"Ahh, so you were admiring my physique?"

"No, no, I was just…," she stammered, "We have to do something about those wounds."

"Yes, I'm aware of that. The body has many wonderful mechanisms in place to expel foreign objects. Unfortunately for me, that means that the several small pieces of metal shrapnel that have pierced my body are also preventing the paths of entry from clotting themselves shut. I thought of cauterizing, but I'm not sure that would even help with as much metal seems to be lodged in my side, and perhaps one even growing annoyingly close to my spine."

"You talk about that so calmly. Like it's tomorrow's forecast or a recipe for tuna salad."

"How am I supposed to talk about it?"

"I don't know. Maybe like a person who's talking about their own death."

He chuckled, and it caused him to cough as he said, "You need to be more optimistic. This isn't going to kill me. It's merely an inconvenience. Perhaps I was a bit overconfident. Or, more accurately, I misjudged Mr. Canyon's abilities. He's quicker than I imagined."

She said, "We're going to have to surrender."

He chuckled and coughed again and said, "Stop making me laugh." Then, after catching his breath, he added, "Despite the Russian fleet signaling for Surrender in the Battle of Sashimi, the Japanese navy didn't get the message and continued firing because they didn't have the word Surrender in their codebooks."

She replied, "What the hell does that have to do with anything? I know, I get it. You're a big tough guy and you don't know the meaning of the word surrender, but you better understand that you're about to learn the meaning of the word die."

He seemed to consider this for the first time and a strange look passed over his face, as if the idea that he might die had never occurred to him. He said, "You're right. I'm going to need you to perform surgery and remove the shrapnel. Then assist me in closing the wounds."

"Oh hell no!" Liana replied. "I'm a cop. I can deal with the sight of blood. But that's a whole different thing than digging around inside somebody and performing surgery. Even under ideal conditions, and these are far from the best conditions. We don't have lights or tools or anything we would need to do any of the things you just said!"

The more she talked, the more she noticed he wasn't listening.

Frank swayed back and forth like a drunk, and a haze had fallen over his normally bright and captivating eyes. His voice grew raspy and decreased in volume as he said, "We can do this, Officer Liana. See how well it worked out that you were here to help me? I probably could have tried to get young Tobias to perform the surgery, but I'm not sure that would have worked out so well."

"There's no way I can perform any kind of surgery."

"Well, what I have in mind is not quite what I would call surgery. I only need you to retrieve a couple of components for me. Just a few simple items and a few simple instructions."

Her eyes narrowed, but she said, "Okay…"

"The first item on the list is one of those milk crates. Because I'm about to fall over."

Seeing him about to stumble forward, she quickly rushed over and helped him sit down.

He continued, "Okay, onto the second item. Behind the building there's a heap of some worthless old scrap metal."

Not sure where he was going with this, Liana said, "Okay…"

"I saw a broken microwave oven out there earlier. I need you to get it and bring it in here for me."

"And how exactly is a broken, rusted out old microwave going to help save your life?"

Frank growled deep in his throat, and then with a wheezing cough, he said, "Can we just skip a step this time?"

"What do you mean skip a step?"

"Can you please just trust me and bring me the damn

microwave? Or would you rather me waste my last breaths giving you a science lesson?"

Unsure if Frank was delirious from pain and blood loss or once again about to do something that would confuse and astound her. She decided that it wasn't worth arguing with him and rushed to the junk heap to search for a microwave.

45

For some reason, Ackerman had been thinking a lot recently about his trip below the border. Specifically, his Rainbow Goddess, whom he had met along the road to Cancun. As he sat atop an old wooden crate, waiting for Liana to return, he wondered to himself why he would be thinking of those days now. Perhaps it was the connection between John Canyon, the king of the Navajo nation and New Mexico, and his business associates in the Mexican cartels.

Over his shoulder, Thomas White whispered, "You're thinking of those days because you're dying and your life is flashing before your eyes. Your brain is trying to replay all of its memories and latch on to something happy to send you off with, but in your case, those memories are few and far between."

Ackerman said, "That's not true. I consider myself a very happy person, with many fond remembrances."

"Oh, come now, Junior. We both know that there's a difference between true joy and the excitement you get from a kill."

"I'm not dying. There's no need for my life to be flashing."

Thomas White laughed. "There you go, Junior. Try to shrug off death himself. We'll see how that works out for you. Perhaps, when you grow weak enough, the grim reaper will allow me to come in and take control."

"I don't know why you keep saying that. That's never going to happen."

"Oh, my boy, it's already happening. You're always standing right on the edge. All you need is a little push."

"I'm not listening to you anymore."

"Yes, that's right. Don't you have some kind of rule about not talking to the delusions. Something about A Beautiful Mind and intellectually rejecting your own psychosis…"

"Thanks for reminding me. You may cease your ignorant ramblings now. I will no longer be acknowledging you."

"You should take the time to listen to me, Junior. I know you better than you know yourself."

Ackerman said nothing.

Thomas White continued, "For example, you're thinking of your perfect woman—your little Rainbow Goddess—because of your proximity to Officer Liana."

Ackerman considered that observation, despite not acknowledging it outwardly.

His father laughed. "You always forget that I'm in your head. I know what you're thinking. Don't overanalyze it. She's a very attractive young lady, and you're a…young-ish man."

"What do you mean young-ish?"

"I was trying to be generous. Which brings me to another point. Perhaps Liana would be a good candidate for continuing the Ackerman bloodline. You're certainly not getting any younger."

The thought caused Ackerman's rage to burn brightly. He heard the old demons screaming. The mere thought of passing on his genetic material, and perhaps his curse, made him want to hurt someone. Not because of his father's insult, but because of the terrible pain it dredged up from the darkest depths of his soul.

He said, "That will never happen."

In reply, Thomas White grinned and said, "Don't you mean never happen again?"

He was about to turn on his father and spout some hate, but thankfully, Liana brought him back to reality as she asked, "Frank? Are you okay? Were you talking to someone?"

Ackerman barely heard her. The tears rained down his cheeks, and he wondered if this truly was the end. Was today the day he would pass from this world?

She said, "Frank, I got the microwave. What do I do now? You're going to be okay. I'm going to help you."

He smiled even as he could feel himself fading from consciousness. "I'm so glad you're here Liana. Have I ever told you the story of my Rainbow Goddess?"

"You've never really told me much of anything. We just met a few hours ago."

"Oh, that's right. I guess I just feel like I've known you longer."

"Um… thanks, I guess. What am I supposed to do with the microwave?"

"First, I need you to get another item for me."

"Oh come on! Are you even awake?"

"Although my physical body is slowly exsanguinating, all is well with my mind and soul. We're going to need a car battery."

"Where in the hell am I going to get that?"

"Out of a motor vehicle."

"But I moved my Explorer into that old shed. Canyon and his snipers would see me!"

"He already knows that you're here, and that you have changed the color of your coat."

"I was more concerned about them shooting me."

"Ahh, yes. That's a definite possibility. They'll be looking for a clean shot at me, but I honestly can't say what they'll do with you."

"You are out of your damn mind if you think I'm going to walk straight into someone's crosshairs. I don't even know if you're with it enough to be giving orders. Tell me what in the hell you need all this stuff for, and then I'll think about getting your battery."

Ackerman could feel his consciousness fading. The darkness growing ever closer. His body was shutting down to maintain energy, and he had no intentions of wasting that precious energy once again explaining himself to a normal. So, instead of replying, he merely leaned his head over and pretended that the healing sleep he expected to come at any moment was already upon him.

46

The biggest thing that changed after that day with Dr. Chee was that the boy truly considered himself to be a man. In fact, he considered himself to be superior to most men twice his age. The second change had been that the boy had demanded that his mother unlock the tin box in the top of her closet that contained grandfather's old pistol.

From that day on, for the next two years of his life, the rusty old gun became his best friend. As he sat in the front room, between clients, he would clean the gun and practice with it. He wore it on his hip whenever he was home, in plain view of every single one of his mother's clients. The word had already spread that he was a hard kid. At school, the others used to stay away from him because they thought he was strange, and he thought they were stupid. Now, they stayed away out of fear, and he liked that. People stayed out of his way and his business, which was fine by him.

The pistol was a single action revolver known as a Peacemaker that his grandfather had purchased at a flea market in Flagstaff, AZ. The boy, Xavier, had researched his new weapon thoroughly, learning that the particular model was known as the gun that had won the west. He translated that as the gun that had drove his ancestors from their homes and then locked them in free-range prisons they called reservations.

But none of that was the gun's fault. One shouldn't judge the tool for how it's wielded.

And Xavier couldn't wait to use his new toy on one of his mother's clients. For two years now, his small speckled notebooks had been filled with drawings of him gunning down his enemies like a gunslinger in the old west. The ones he hated the most were the belegana men who drove in just for a visit. He reserved a special measure of hatred for them.

Xavier imagined that there was money to be made in prostitution, but he found that the lion's shares went to bribing the police and mother's various addictions. Still, it hadn't taken him long to skim enough off the top to purchase a quickdraw instructional video. He had watched the old cowboy explain the various techniques in detail until he had memorized the contents of the VHS tape. Then he sat for hours in the living room or in the brush out behind the trailer, honing his skills with the pistol down to an art.

He dreamed that one day his skills and the protection of the pistol would mean that he would not wake up in the night screaming or fearing that one of his mother's clients would creep into his room at night, looking for a different kind of action. The only problem was that guns were illegal on the Rez, and ammo was scarce. Luckily, he had made friends with an old man in Prescott who reloaded his own. Still, he hated the fact that he was better at pulling the gun from its holster and twirling it around than he was at actually shooting it.

Standing in the brush behind their shack, practicing, he snatched the gun from its holster and took aim. In his mind, he imagined the face of a particular belegana who had been revisiting the trailer for a few months every couple of weeks. The client always pulled up in a big new Cadillac. Xavier imagined blowing Mr. Cadillac's head off as he raised the six shooter.

His sister's voice made him jump as she said, "I figured I'd find you out back playing with yourself."

The boy bristled, embarrassed at having been caught mid-fantasy. His little sister, Reyna, chuckled, but he silenced her with a death glare.

Reyna's expression turned sour, and she said, "Momma's too sick to work today."

"Just make sure she has her fix. She'll be fine."

"She was coughing up blood. We need to take her to the clinic in Shiprock."

Xavier shook his head. "What are a bunch of damn doctors going to tell us that we don't already know?"

"For starters, what's wrong with Momma."

"She's dying, Reyna. She has the same sickness that grandfather had. It's only a matter of time, and there's nothing anyone can do for her."

Tears welled in her eyes. "You don't know that."

"I do, and so do you. You've heard grandfather's stories of working in the mines for the belegana government with no masks, no protection, no decontamination. He would come home with uranium dust on his clothes and hold Momma. His radioactive overalls went into the same water as the rest of the clothes."

"Shut up! I don't want to hear any more. Momma can't work today. Cancel her appointments."

"If she takes the day off, she'll just lay on her back and

get high. She might as well make some money while she's laying there."

"She's going to the doctor today if I have to call the police to give us an escort," Reyna said.

Xavier growled deep in his throat, but after a moment, he slid the pistol back into the holster on his hip and said, "Fine. We'll take her to the clinic in Shiprock. But it's pointless."

Reyna smiled. She was the most beautiful when she smiled. "Thank you," she said.

He merely nodded as he undid his belt and laid the pistol across an old bench. Xavier knew that the trip would be a waste of time, but if it satisfied Reyna and got Momma back to work, then it was worth going through the motions. He knew, however, that mother would soon be another victim of the belegana's wars. Just like Grandfather. And one day, he and Reyna would probably share the same fate. He had heard that their ground water and soil was still contaminated and that the water they drank and bathed in—which they had to haul over in fifty gallon tanks, since like much of the Rez, they didn't have access to water and power grids—was just as toxic.

It made him so angry. He dreamed of one day opening a restaurant out on Highway 666 catering to the belegana travelers. He fantasized about digging up the floor of one of the mines where Grandfather had worked or any of the hundreds of open and uncleaned uranium mines throughout the area. Then, in his daydream, he would feed the uranium dust to the unsuspecting belegana and their children.

Xavier's smile grew wide as he contemplated his revenge and the ways he could use the belegana's own poisons against them.

47

Liana stood at the back of the weather-beaten general store trying to give herself a pep talk. You're a law enforcement officer, she told herself, you can do this. But when she tried to move, her legs wouldn't cooperate. She stood frozen in fear. Assault rifles and pistols wouldn't be able to reach her at this distance, but a .30-06 with a scope was a different story.

She'd been racking her brain for an alternative, something more clever than merely walking out into the open and crossing the divide between the main building and the shed. Some kind of trick that would outsmart the snipers, their high-powered rifles, and their bullets that traveled faster than the speed of sound. Unfortunately, her best plan was to run as fast as she could.

Liana's grandmother, being a traditional Diné, didn't care much for belegana television. She did, however, occasionally get interested in certain programs. One in particular was the show *MythBusters*. On one particular episode of *MythBusters*, Grandmother had been fascinated by a test they did suggesting that you got just as wet running through the rain as you did calmly walking. Liana couldn't wrap her mind around how that could be true, but perhaps there was something to it.

Was it possible she would draw less attention just walking over to the shed calmly and returning with the

battery? Or maybe she should go for something in between.
A light jog, perhaps.

You're stalling, she told herself.

Again, she tried to move, but still her legs wouldn't
cooperate. She needed a better plan, but there wasn't time.
Frank was bleeding out in there.

Finally, after a moment more of inner turmoil, some deep
reserve of hidden courage pushed Liana forward, out into
the open, into the danger zone. She felt crosshairs crawling
over her body and tried to imagine what was happening
right now down in Canyon's encampment. None of the
underlings would fire without their commander's go-ahead.
The kill or no-kill order. Which meant that her life was in
the hands of John Canyon.

Halfway there, she thought.

With the way the road curved up the bluff and the
positioning of the buildings, Canyon and his gunmen would
have a clear view of her from their roadblock. It was only
fifty feet from the trading post to the shed, but to her, it felt
like a marathon.

Three-quarters of the way, she thought.

She allowed herself to hope.

If Canyon was going to give an order to shoot, he would
have surely done it by now.

Five steps. Three. Two.

Then, she was there, throwing open the side door of
the rickety shed and leaning against the side of her Ford
Explorer patrol vehicle as she tried to catch her breath and
keep her body from shaking apart. She held out her hands,
and she shook like a Parkinson's victim. Liana hadn't been
a tribal police officer for all that long, but she had still been

in some tough situations. She had pulled her gun a couple of times during sketchy traffic stops. She had arrested plenty of people for illegal alcohol and possessions of guns, drunken disorderlies, domestic disputes, the usual gamut. But there had been no murders in their area. At least, nothing that she had dealt with. Or knew about.

Liana reckoned that meant that those fifty feet and those few seconds it took her to cross the divide was the closest she'd come to death in her entire life. Obviously, Canyon had chosen to spare her, or the snipers would have taken her down. But her racing mind considered another possibility. Perhaps it had all happened so fast, despite it feeling so slow to her, that the mercenaries had no time to react and didn't have enough time to get the shoot or no-shoot order from their superior. They had likely already been given instructions to take any possible shot at Frank, but she was a different story. And that would imply that the real danger would be in moving back from the shed to the trading post.

As she popped the hood of the Explorer and retrieved the car battery, she tried not to think about the harrowing run she would have to make back to the relative safety of the trading post. She tried not to think of how she would also be lugging a stupid car battery as she went and still she had no idea what any of this was for or if she was merely risking her life for the delusions of a half-dead madman.

48

Ackerman tried to conserve his energy without succumbing to slumber, but the longer he sat atop the small crate and pretended to sleep, the closer he came to actually doing so. Deciding that he needed a distraction and a little movement to keep what little blood he had left flowing, he walked into the front room and carefully surveyed his opponents through the scope of the Barrett rifle. His left leg was growing numb and useless, and he had to drag it the whole way. He supposed that was probably a bad sign.

From behind him, Tobias Canyon said, "You don't look so good, my friend. Things will go much better for you if you surrender while you still have a chance."

Ackerman stood up to full height and turned back to the boy. It wouldn't be long, only a year or two, before Tobias would be sent off to be trained by the US government, so he could come back to fight against the US government. Just like his father and all their other little foot soldiers.

Ackerman sighed and said, "I forgot to gag you again, didn't I?"

"If you don't get medical help, you're going to die soon. And that's a fact."

This time, he didn't limp at all as he took two large strides to put himself within reach of Tobias. He refused to allow his injuries to show. Moving with his normal speed and grace caused terrible pain to radiate throughout his entire body. For a normal, he supposed, this would have caused a blackout or at the very least, an overwhelming sense of nausea. For him, it was akin to getting a nice massage. It made him a little uncomfortable, and he knew it to be a sign that his body was shutting down, but it also deeply troubled him to miss any opportunity to experience or inflict pain.

Rather than going for the Bowie knife, Ackerman pulled one of the push daggers from the quickdraw holster mounted in the small of his back. With a blinding movement that he had practiced thousands of times when shadowboxing, he punched out directly at Tobias Canyon's eye as if he were going to stab the dagger straight into the center of the young man's eyeball. But he stopped at the last second, trying to get the blade as close as he possibly could to the white orb without piercing it.

The pure fear that he saw reflected back at him was exactly what he was trying to accomplish.

Slipping the dagger back into its quickdraw sheath and leaning down nose to nose with Tobias, he said, "I wouldn't be getting my hopes up about me passing away any time soon. I used to think that it was mere luck that I had avoided death under so many extraordinary circumstances, but now, I wonder if it's less of me cheating death and more that death is just plain scared of me. So, if I were you, I wouldn't count on the grim reaper to be swooping in with his sickle to save the day."

"My father is going to cut your nuts off and feed them to you."

Ackerman laughed hard with a wheeze and cough. "You know that's not really something you say to someone in polite conversation. Especially to someone holding so many sharp objects."

The young man merely scowled back at him.

From the direction of the back door, Ackerman heard Liana say, "I thought you were passed out."

"Yes, well, I got bored with being mortally wounded, and so I decided to intellectually reject the idea. Did you get the battery?"

"Yes," she said, "and it was the most frightening experience of my entire life."

He cocked his head in confusion. "Why was there some kind of creature hiding in the engine compartment?"

"No, you freaked me out with all that sniper talk!"

He dismissed the idea with a wave of his hand. "I'm sorry. I was eighty-five percent sure that Mr. Canyon wasn't going to shoot."

"Thanks, that makes me feel much better."

"I'm glad," Ackerman said as he placed a strip of duct tape over Tobias Canyon's mouth and two more over the boy's ears for good measure.

"What do we do now?" she asked.

Rather than wasting time explaining, Ackerman turned and headed for the back room and the derelict microwave. Unfortunately, he took a step forward and then stumbled into one of the shelving units.

Liana rushed to his side and propped him up. She asked, "How's rejecting the idea of being hurt working out for you?"

In reply, he whispered, "The spirit is willing but the flesh is weak. Help me to the back. Lots of work and little time. Let's get started."

49

The past…

"I can't believe that we didn't just kill him," she said.

"He surrendered," Marcus replied.

"What difference does that make? He doesn't deserve to be breathing."

"We need him."

"He won't help us. It's not in his nature."

Marcus turned away from the window and leaned back against the old yellowing plaster of the bedroom wall. "My father is out there right now on a killing spree that has this whole state living in terror. And Ackerman is the only one who knows him. We have no good leads. Nothing. We need every bit of help we can get."

"We can't trust him."

"Who said anything about trusting him? Besides, the only person that hates my father more than me is my big brother."

"That's another thing. I don't like how easily you've started referring to him as your brother. He's not your family." Maggie placed a hand on his chest. "We're your family. He's a monster."

"If he's a monster, then what does that make me?"

"You're nothing like him."

Marcus sat down on the bed and closed his eyes. The room stank of Maggie's cleaning fluids. "You don't know me," he said, "Not really."

50

Marcus was ripped from a nightmare as Captain Yazzie threw a cup of cold water into his face. He spit out the water that landed in his open mouth and smiled at his captor. He found it funny that reality was actually favorable to what he had just woke up from. He had been dreaming that he was back in his high school gymnasium. He sat Indian style on the basketball court's free-throw line. It was dark along the periphery of the gym, but he could see the non-distinct shadowy forms of several people. All standing and watching him. He could feel their eyes judging him, crawling over him. On the opposite free-throw line, there was a medical gurney with a body under a white sheet. Blooms of red slowly grew across the sheet. He heard a noise to his left and looked away from the body. When he turned back, the single gurney had multiplied into four. He shot to his feet as it multiplied again and again, until he was faced with a basketball court full of rolling medical carts and bodies.

In the dream, he had known that Maggie's body was beneath one of those sheets. But now, as he woke up and looked into the face of a man who might know where she was, he felt pleasantly surprised. As if he had just gone from knowing she was dead to having hope that he could still save her.

"I don't suppose declaring myself as a federal agent would do any good," Marcus said.

The tribal police captain's face was unreadable, hidden behind his

Marcus was bound to what looked like a chair from an old kitchen table set. His hands were tied behind his back with the restraints also tied to the chair. His feet were tethered in the same manner. Blinking himself fully awake, he looked from Captain Yazzie to his subordinate officer whom Marcus knew as Ernie Pitka, a local with only a few minor infractions on his record as a youth. Glancing between the two of them, Marcus said, "Good morning, fellas. Can one of you fetch me a cup coffee? Maybe some Tylenol?"

Yazzie said, "You and your partner must have a mutual death wish. And neither of you knows when to shut his mouth. I'm gonna ask you one time, before this gets unpleasant, where is the truck?" Then, producing a switchblade knife from his boot, Yazzie sliced Marcus's tactical pants starting at the foot and running all the way up to mid-thigh. Then he pulled the material apart, exposing Marcus's naked flesh.

"These were my favorite pants, jerkwad."

Yazzie struck him hard across the jaw, and Marcus noticed that with every further escalation, Yazzie's young lackey was growing more and more apprehensive.

He said, "I don't even know what truck you're talking about."

"The one that your partner stole."

"I don't have a partner. I'm a lone wolf."

Yazzie was unperturbed. "We don't know where your friend Agent Carlisle is. We don't know what happened to her. For all any of us know, she could've wrecked her car or gotten lost somewhere up in the hills. It's not all that uncommon. You really want to come in here and go to war with the wrong people?"

Marcus replied, "I think we're barking up exactly the right tree." He then turned his gaze to the younger officer before adding, "What about you, Officer Pitka? Are you ready to die for your boss here?"

The stunned officer looked between the captive and his captain, but said nothing.

Marcus continued, "We're going to find Maggie one way or another. If we have to tear the whole Navajo nation apart to do it. And I'm getting tired of playing this game. I'm tired of talking. I'm a jackhammer, and I intend to get right to the heart of things as quickly as possible. You like to give ultimatums, Captain? Here's one for you: Tell me where to find Maggie Carlisle, or you're not going live to see tomorrow."

"It's not very polite to threaten a fellow law enforcement professional."

"You're not a cop. You're a cockroach."

Yazzie smiled, the first time he had shown any human gesture or expression in the time they'd been sitting there. He asked, "Do you like bugs, Agent Williams? I've got a friend I'd like to introduce you to." Yazzie reached down and retrieved a brown paper bag that sat on the floor beside him, out of which he produced a Mason jar. Inside of that was the biggest scorpion Marcus had ever seen.

Without showing any reaction to the contents of the jar, Marcus said, "That's not an insect or a bug. It's an arachnid, jackass."

After striking him again, Yazzie continued, "My little

friend is an Arizona bark scorpion. But don't let the name fool you, we have plenty of them here in New Mexico. So I had an ample choice when I went out to find the biggest, meanest, and nastiest one I could find. Scorpions show up under a black light, and so it was a simple matter of taking a little stroll with a black lens over my flashlight."

Marcus said, "That's fascinating. Why don't you write me a letter about it."

As he shook the jar a little to get the scorpion riled up, Yazzie asked again, "Where is the truck that your partner stole from the ranch?"

"You guys seem to have gotten pretty wound up over a truckload of sheep. You haven't even asked about the Canyon boy."

"We already have your partner surrounded at the trading post, and we know that he has the hostages there. The only thing keeping us from taking him out is that we need to know where the truck is."

"Do you honestly think that telling me you're going to kill someone if I give you the information would make me want to tell you more?"

Yazzie shrugged. "You know what, I don't even care. It's John's problem anyhow. But either way, you and your partner are both dead men."

Then Yazzie shook the jar, unscrewed the top, and jammed it against the side of Marcus's exposed thigh, giving the most venomous scorpion in all of North America full access to his naked flesh.

51

Liana still wasn't sure what he intended to do with a microwave and car battery, but she nonetheless helped Frank into the back room where he went to work. She watched as he moved with speed and efficiency. He unscrewed and removed the housing and then started pulling out the internal components and wiring until he retrieved a small metal box with wires coming out of it.

She asked, "What are you doing?"

"I just removed the transformer. Now, I'm going to break it open to get at the primary coil."

"But why?"

Still fiddling with the microwave components, he turned to Liana and replied, "All will be revealed in due time. Please fetch me several of the fifty caliber rounds from the front room."

Having learned it wasn't worth asking questions or arguing with Frank, she reacted quickly and returned with the massive bullets a moment later. Handing her a pair of pliers from the small tool kit he was working out of, Frank instructed her to remove the projectiles so that they could access the gunpowder. Then, while she worked on the bullets, he used a cordless cutting tool to break open the transformer box.

As he worked, he said, "Did you know that the first

documented blood transfusion to a human was performed using sheep's blood?"

"Umm, no, I didn't."

"Jean-Baptiste Denys was a French physician who performed the deed on a fifteen-year-old boy in 1667. By pure luck, the boy survived. Emboldened by what he perceived to be an early success, Denys went on to perform another transfusion on a mentally-ill man in Paris. He thought he could cure the fellow's madness by replacing his blood with the pure blood of a calf."

"But human blood often isn't even compatible with other human blood. Blood from an animal would kill a person."

"Quite so. However, it ultimately wasn't the transfusion that ended the patient in question. Instead, the man was poisoned by competing surgeons in an attempt to discredit Denys. Ultimately, the court acquitted Denys of any wrong-doing in the man's death, but nonetheless banned the practice of transfusion. Not because they understood the incompatibility or dangers, but because they feared that the mixing of blood would forge monsters. Half-human, half-animal hybrids, if you will."

"So you're going to use the parts from the microwave to perform a blood transfusion on yourself?"

Still working on removing and combining components, he replied, "No, that would be silly. I've just created a very powerful electromagnet. You'll hold it over my wound, and it will pull the pieces of metal shrapnel back out through my flesh and up to itself."

"Won't that be extremely painful?"

"Oh yes. I'm quite looking forward to it."

"Do we have any kind of sedative or painkiller?"

He grinned. "Pain, my dear, is one thing that I have no interest in killing. To be honest, I only feel alive when I'm experiencing it or inflicting it. Which brings me to something I wanted to mention…. It's a bit awkward."

She cocked an eyebrow, but said nothing.

"As we move forward with the procedure, and as the pain starts to course throughout my body, it will illicit several small physiological reactions that I can only describe as pleasure. During this time, something may happen."

She narrowed her eyes. "Okay…"

"I'm trying to say that as you hurt me, I may become aroused."

Her eyes went wide. "So that's what it takes to get you—"

"Oh no, I function perfectly fine in that department with or without the pain. You see, it's not the only thing that gets me aroused, but it's certainly one of the things."

Unsure of how to respond to such a declaration, she said, "Thanks for the heads up, I guess."

"And we should probably hurry. I fully expect some type of attack from your friend, Mr. Canyon, to be coming very soon. Now, if there are no more questions, your patient is ready, Dr. Nakai." Then he reached out, took her hand, looked deep into her eyes, and said, "I'm so pleased that you could join me on this little adventure, Liana."

"Umm, okay. I'll do my best."

"That's all anyone can ever ask of you."

"But I don't know… I don't know if I can do any of this. I mean, this is—"

"What, crazy? Life is chaos, my dear. You may be sitting here thinking that your world is spiraling out of control and there's nothing you can do about it. But the truth is that you never had any control. That was all an illusion. The only thing that you can ever control, Liana, is what goes on between your ears. You have to be able to find peace and joy in any moment, anywhere, anytime. You can do this. I know that God has placed you here on this night for a reason, just as he has placed me here in such a place as this and such a time as now. You can do this, my dear. I have faith in you. I knew from the moment that I walked into that police station and looked in your eyes that there was something very special about you. I saw that you had a pure heart. And I know that you'll do your best now to save my life, but even if I die, I want you to know that it's been a pleasure knowing you for the short time that we've had together this evening."

"I just hope this contraption works. We've used up a lot of time on it."

"Time is certainly our enemy, but this isn't my first rodeo. It will work." He started to lay down, but then looked back up at her and added, "Oh, I almost forgot, after the magnet has pulled all of the shrapnel from my wounds, we'll need to staunch the flow of blood. So I'm going to need you to pour the gunpowder you stockpiled into the holes and then light me on fire."

52

Two weeks earlier…

The brightly colored beadwork was familiar to Maggie, but her memories had been of duller colors and being surrounded by giants. Now, she was among the giants, and the colors were vivid. Feathers and shells adorned sleeves and skirts. The scent of leather filled the air. It was a beautiful, sunny day, and many of the spectators watched the dancers from picnic tables and blankets beneath shade trees. She moved to the back to observe the festivities more closely. As she scanned the crowd, she considered that the Taker could have been any one of these men, still traveling the circuit all these years later.

Over her shoulder, a husky male voice asked, "May I help you, ma'am?"

Maggie turned back to face the officer. He wore a tan uniform with a gold badge and a gold patch displaying Navajo Police over the year 1868. She estimated him to be around thirty years old with dark hair cut short. He was tall and well-built, possessing a round face already bearing the signs of laugh lines. She removed her sunglasses to look at him directly and gave a half-smile.

"No, thank you. I'm just watching."

She was about to turn back toward the crowd, but then

she added, "It's been years since I've been to a pow-wow. Not since I was a child. I'm just...trying to remember."

His smile was large and genuine. "I hope they were good memories."

Maggie changed the subject. "I didn't realize they had such tight security at these events."

"Most pow-wows are policed by the performers. We have our own rules that almost everyone follows. There's been a rise in gang-related activity recently, but nothing to worry about. We're just here to make sure everyone stays safe."

"Gang-related activity? How long has that been going on?"

Latching onto the detail, her mind started to race through the possibilities. Could a gang have been there when her family had been? Had they zeroed in on her family for some reason?

The officer cocked an eyebrow and tilted back his head in suspicion before replying, "Gangs have been following powwows, selling drugs and making trouble, for as long as I can remember. A big part of our job is trying to help kids find another alternative to joining the gangs, which are often unaffiliated or only loosely affiliated with the larger criminal organizations they mimic. We have our versions of Latin Kings, Bloods, Crips, the usual gamut."

She nodded but was only half-listening now. The gang element made sense with the children going missing, since gangs often involved themselves in human trafficking. She'd checked the dates and locations. There had been a pow-wow within fifty miles of each child that had been taken, but since none of the children had attended, except for her brother, the cops hadn't looked too deeply.

"Do any of the gangs have any specific signs or characteristics? Navajo-specific ways of doing things or traditions? Tattoos? Painting faces? Colored contacts?"

The remainder of the officer's smile fell, and he asked, "Are you a reporter?"

She blinked a few times, surprised by the question. "No, actually, I'm an agent with the Department of Justice. I'm investigating a cold case that could have involved the pow-wow circuit. Would have been over twenty-five years ago."

After examining her credentials, he said, "That's way before my time, ma'am. I could probably put you in touch with some of the old timers, if you'd like."

"No, that's okay. I was just stopping in to see if the environment might spark some new ideas. What made you think I was a reporter?"

Looking uncomfortable again, he shrugged and said, "There have been a lot of reporters around recently asking questions about our beliefs and the like ever since the FBI database made the connections and figured out that a serial killer might be at work around the border towns. Flagstaff and the like. Some people are saying it's a skin-walker, which has made the story more sensational for the people who make up the news."

Maggie asked, "A skin-walker?"

"It's just a myth, and superstitious people being caught up in the hysteria. But in our culture, a skin-walker is a witch with the ability to possess or transform themselves into animals."

"Like a werewolf?"

"More like a werecoyote, but that's the idea. Talking about witchcraft and skin-walkers make my people very uncomfortable. Still, every once in a while, we do get a case where someone claims to have been cursed by a skin-walker or poisoned by corpse powder or the like. It's all nonsense, but no one ever said people were rational."

Maggie nodded in understanding and asked, "What about a man named John Canyon? You ever hear of him?"

The officer's kind face turned to stone. Ignoring the question, he said, "Well, I had better be making the rounds, ma'am. You have a nice day and enjoy the festivities."

53

Sometimes Marcus considered his eidetic memory to be a wonderful blessing. Other times, he considered it to be a terrible curse. This was one of the latter. From a Discovery Channel special he had watched while bored one Sunday afternoon, he remembered quite a bit about scorpions. He knew that the Arizona bark scorpion was the largest variety of the arachnid in North America. It was also the most venomous. But even a mature specimen wouldn't be able to kill him, unless he had some sort of allergic reaction or oversensitivity to the venom. Still, he didn't much relish the idea of enduring a scorpion's sting, or any of the sickness that accompanied it. Perhaps if he kept his leg loose and didn't tense the muscle, the alien-looking creature wouldn't see him as a threat.

Yazzie said, "I think he's taking a liking to you."

"I'm glad because I think he's adorable. Do I get to keep him? I mean after we're done with the whole torture thing. I'd like to name him Harvey, if that's okay with you."

This drew a chuckle from the tribal police captain, then with incredible speed, Yazzie snatched the Colt Peacemaker from his side and clinked the barrel hard against the Mason jar, agitating the massive scorpion. Harvey reared back his tail and twitched, readying a venomous strike, while Marcus prepared himself to accept the attack.

After a few seconds, when the strike didn't come, Officer

Pitka stepped forward and, in a shaking voice, said, "Sir, we can't do this. He's a federal agent. And we're supposed to be cops."

Yazzie barely reacted. He didn't show any signs of anger or yell at his subordinate. Instead, he calmly said, "Ernie, why don't you go outside and get on the radio. Inform Mr. Canyon that we have Agent Williams here in custody and that we're questioning him now in regard to the location of the truck."

Pitka started to say more, but Yazzie stopped him by spinning the Colt Peacemaker on his finger like a gunslinger from the Old West. As he slid the gun back into its holster, Yazzie said, "Now, Officer Pitka."

The scared young man caught Marcus's eye as if to say that he was sorry, but then he rushed from the room, closing the door behind him.

The young and naïve Officer Pitka had no way of knowing it, but Marcus didn't want him in the room. He knew that his chances with one opponent would always be higher than facing down two, even if one was a hesitant participant.

With Pitka gone, Marcus focused his attention back on the scorpion. The agitated arachnid was still reared back and ready to strike, and so Marcus kept his leg relaxed and maintained a calm heart rate. There was a time when being in proximity to such a creature would have truly frightened him. But ever since his days in his father's dungeon beneath Leavenworth, Kansas, Marcus couldn't bring himself to be afraid of much of anything. It wasn't even close to the extremes that his brother had experienced, but he'd definitely undergone a stark desensitization.

Light filtered in from the hallway as the young officer exited, giving Marcus a better look at their surroundings. They were in some sort of basement storage room. The walls were cinderblock and two-by-fours. Shelves, occupied by totes labeled in masking tape and marker, lined the inner walls. He noticed one that read, "Christmas," and another "Easter."

Yazzie said, "Did you know that scorpions are fiercely territorial and cannibalistic? It's quite common for them to devour their mates and offspring."

Marcus replied, "If only your mother would've learned from their example and did the world a favor."

Yazzie leaned close and whispered, "When I was a boy, I lit my mother on fire and watched her burn. I've always felt a kinship with animals like this one. Scientists believe that their cannibalistic ways developed because they are faced with many instances when resources are scarce and the only route to survival is to consume their own species. But this has also allowed the scorpion to hold the distinction of being the world's oldest surviving land animal. They've remained virtually unchanged for the last one hundred million years. Specimens preserved in amber thirty million years ago look exactly like this guy here. There's something amazing and perfect about that. Something we could learn from."

Marcus said, "If you feel such a kinship with this creepy critter, why isn't he crawling around on your leg?"

"You and your partner certainly are hard men. There's no denying that. But everyone has a breaking point, Agent Williams. Everyone has a weakness."

"You may be right, Captain, but you ain't got what it

takes to get me there. I've been tortured by the best, and you ain't got shit on my father. So you might as well give this up."

Yazzie shrugged. "Perhaps, but I think I'll stick with it a bit longer just to be sure." Once again retrieving the switchblade knife from his boot, Yazzie sliced a line of blood across Marcus's exposed thigh, just above the spot where the glass jar held the massive scorpion. Marcus winced involuntarily, but didn't give Yazzie any more satisfaction than that.

The police captain continued, "Scorpions are burrowing creatures. I've witnessed many times what rodents can do when chewing through and burrowing into human flesh, but I've always wondered if a scorpion, with a little prodding, would do the same and dig its way down inside of a person. Why don't we conduct a little experiment and find out?"

54

True to his word, Frank seemed to enjoy the procedure as he made several mewling noises that reminded Liana of a cat being scratched in just the right spot. But eventually he passed out and was so unresponsive that Liana checked his pulse multiple times while she sucked out the shrapnel using the homemade electromagnet like a vacuum and then packed his wound with the gunpowder.

She tried to warn him of what was about to happen, but he wouldn't acknowledge her nudging. After checking his pulse again, she decided to move forward. As she lit the gunpowder, it sparked into a bright mushroom cloud and filled the air with the smell of sizzling meat. Frank only issued a small groan of pleasure, as if the pain coincided perfectly with something he was dreaming.

She tried again to wake him, hoping he would eat or drink something, but he was still unresponsive. She knew that he needed time to heal, but he also needed food and liquids to help with that process. Luckily, the agents had come prepared with an ample food supply and gallon jugs of water, all the resources necessary for a long and bloody siege.

The scent of burned flesh still hanging in the air, Liana rolled Frank over and tilted his head forward. Then she forced some water down his throat, using a collapsible cup she had found among their supplies. She was no doctor, but she had had some EMT training and recognized that

Frank had to be beyond dehydrated. She needed to get his blood sugar up, but most importantly, she needed to keep the water flowing so that his body could rebuild its blood supply.

He accepted the offered liquid, but he never seemed to rouse from his slumber. Deciding to let Frank rest, Liana moved to the front room, where she proceeded to pace a hole in the floor and chew her fingernails down to nubs. She kept reminding herself that she was a trained officer of the law and to remain calm, but another part of her kept yelling that this was far beyond anything she had learned at the academy. Her life was officially off the rails. She was no longer a police officer. She wasn't sure what she was. All she really did know was that, for whatever reason, she felt safer in this room next to an unconscious Frank than she did out there. Than she had earlier in the night out there with John Canyon. Her pacing and chewing was cut short as the tiny speaker on Frank's handheld radio squawked to life and the tinny-sounding voice of John Canyon said, "Don't shoot. I'm walking up the lane, and I'm waving the white flag. I want to make sure that my boy's okay, and then I want to make a deal."

Liana rushed to the window and snatched up the binoculars. Through them, she saw a solitary figure slowly walking up the gravel path toward the old trading post. Rushing back to Frank, she tried to shake him awake again. Her teeth chattered as she repeated over and over, "Wake up, wake up, wake up."

But just as before, Frank responded with only a few small mewling sounds. Taking a deep breath, Liana steeled herself, knowing that she was now on her own.

55

25 years earlier...

Eventually, Momma's illness afflicted her to the point where she could not even work on her back. Luckily, the boy was a smooth operator and was able to come up with other means to pay the rent and keep food on the table. Not to mention the fact that Reyna was becoming a beautiful teenager, and she wanted to look the part. It was a needless expense, but one that he himself enjoyed. He liked to see her beautiful. He liked to see her happy. One of the best ways he had found to make some extra cash was by visiting the ruins of the Old Ones. Or the Anasazi, as the belegana archeologists called them.

He had recently found a remote site among the New Mexican hills that appeared to be a completely undiscovered location. He had been out climbing one day by himself, something he loved to do. He would go up into the canyons and walk in the footsteps of his ancestors. Sometimes, he would sacrifice a small animal to some dark god of the Anasazi now lost to time. But of course, he never received any kind of answer. Until, one day, he stumbled upon the motherlode.

Xavier had several irons in the fire as far as making money and several seeds that he had planted that would soon be growing to fruition. But all of his ideas had their issues.

They all had barriers that would need to be overcome and variables for which he couldn't account. That was why it was so important to diversify.

The problem with a big discovery like the one he had made, high in a canyon north of Shiprock, was that he would need help with hauling out the artifacts. When he had first discovered the remote site, he had been climbing freestyle and had noticed a small path cut into the rock and some ancient handholds. This led him up to what appeared to be a remote religious temple of the lost people.

There were very few individuals in the world who Xavier trusted. One of those was his sister, but she would only be of so much help in carrying the artifacts down the cliff face. He had gone ahead and set up several rope ladders at points where expert climbing would be involved, and Reyna had always been a hard worker. But he would need someone else to assist as well. Someone with a strong back and a dim wit.

The first person who came to mind was a boy from his class named Eugene Bernally. Although Eugene was technically two years older than him, they were in the same grade because Eugene had been held back twice. Xavier had been grooming Eugene to work for him for some time because he knew that Eugene was the kind of guy who would take the cut he was given and never question whether or not it was the correct amount. Not to mention that Eugene was also a very capable climber, despite being overweight. With the promise of adventure and payment, it was easy to get Eugene onboard. Reyna, however, was a different matter, but he always got his way with her in the end.

After all, Momma would soon be gone, and then, all they would have was each other.

Not only was Reyna upset that she had to go on their little scavenger hunt, but she hated being stuck in the middle seat of the old short-bed Cheyenne pickup truck as it rumbled over the hard-packed desert road. She had to sit with the gear shifter between her legs, which caused Xavier to reach over between them to shift, usually allowing a bit of touching as well. And to her right sat Eugene, who had a way of being extra creepy around pretty girls.

Xavier pulled the old truck to the side of the road, parking behind some scrub brush and juniper trees, and said, "We go on foot from here."

They stepped out and adorned their backpacks. Each satchel was loaded with rations to eat once they reached the top. Then they would fill the empty bags with artifacts for the climb down. Spurred forward by either greed or fear, the trio hiked into the hills and ascended the red rock canyons. Xavier had often wondered why the Old Ones built their dwellings in such inaccessible places. They had often constructed villages high in the cliffs under natural stone canopies that were far from necessary resources like water and food.

Xavier led the way and showed the others where the best handholds were. He kept Reyna in the middle, so that he could help his sister and make sure she reached the top safely. Eugene brought up the rear and eyed Reyna hungrily for most of the climb.

It was a grueling climb even with the aid of the ropes he had installed, and this was the easy part. Going down with backpacks weighted with fragile potsherds and artifacts would be the hard part. He had considered lowering the bags of artifacts down the cliff face by rope, but he didn't have enough to reach the bottom. Perhaps with the money they made from this trip, he could finance better equipment for the next.

Finally they reached the top. The ruins were concealed beneath a massive rock canopy that made them impossible to see from above, and the way that the opening was slanted made it completely invisible from below as well. Normally, when the Diné people found a site like this, they would document it but leave everything exactly as it was. The belegana archeologists, whom they called dirt diggers, liked to remove the artifacts and haul them off to museums. Most of the larger sites had already been raided by the diggers and scavengers who wanted to make a quick buck by stealing his people's history. And this place was rich with history. Xavier could feel it all around them. He could feel the ghosts. He knew from the first moment that he saw the ruins, that this was somewhere very special.

56

Harvey, the grandfather of all Arizona bark scorpions, didn't seem to like all the blood. In fact, it seemed to scare the crap out of him. Thanks to late night Discovery channel, Marcus knew that scorpions only stung as a last resort. It could sometimes take weeks for the arachnid to replenish its venom, and so pincers were its weapon of choice. But, as the trail of blood grew closer and closer to the arachnid, as it tried to flee up the side of the Mason jar, it was clear to Marcus that Harvey had reached his limit, and so he braced himself accordingly.

Still, nothing could have prepared Marcus for the speed and power of the attack. With a blur of movement so fast it caused Marcus to jump, the scorpion's tail lashed out like the whip of a lion tamer, struck Marcus's flesh, and came back covered in the already flowing blood.

At first, Marcus felt ice shoot out from the impact site, but the ice turned to fire as the venom spread. Next came pain. Then numbness.

Yazzie laughed. "There you go, little fella. But don't overexert yourself yet. We're just getting started. And don't worry, you'll only need pincers for this part." He then produced a Zippo lighter from his pocket, held it up to the Mason jar, and struck the flame. Harvey spun to face the new threat, and Marcus could already feel the tiny legs digging into the knife wound on his thigh.

Allowing the fire to lick the glass while moving it closer and closer to the increasingly agitated scorpion, Yazzie continued, "Scorpions have an amazing will to survive, and they're almost impossible to keep out of your home because of their ability to slide into nearly any space and burrow their way into any sanctuary. They'll eat their own children to survive. I don't think it will take much coercing for our little friend here to find his way inside your skin. As the air in the jar grows hotter and hotter, the alternative is going to seem more and more appealing… Or you can tell me where you hid the truck?"

Marcus felt woozy from the venom coursing through his system. That gave him an idea. When he was a boy, Marcus and been forced to learn how to control his own gag reflex. He pretty much had to learn how to control all of his senses. At a young age, smells and textures were overwhelming for him. And sounds carried with them all of those connected sensory inputs. The result was that hearing someone blow their nose caused Marcus and his mind to travel up the sound and into the smell and texture of the mucus. It was the same with foods that he didn't like or ones that reminded him of bodily secretions. Eventually, this forced him to be able to control his own gag reflex to the point that he could choose to throw up or not throw up on command. He hadn't been eating much lately, but he knew that there was something in his stomach. And so, this was one of those times when he chose the latter.

Yazzie had been about to speak when Marcus vomited all over him. The police captain jumped back, appalled, looking down at his soiled uniform with disgust written on every line of his face. Which placed him in the exact position that Marcus wanted. The captain's quick-draw abilities were a problem. They made Yazzie a formidable opponent, and so Marcus surmised he would need to knock the captain off his game a bit before attacking.

Now, with Yazzie sufficiently distracted and in the proper position, Marcus placed his feet flat on the ground, shifted forward, and pivoted with his left foot to spin his entire body weight along with the wooden chair like a baseball bat directed at Yazzie's skull. The old wood of the chair collided with a wet "thwap." But Marcus knew that his opponent was far from incapacitated yet. So, as he had planned, he backpedaled himself and the chair into Yazzie, pushing the police captain back against the one wall comprised of nothing but bare cinderblock. Marcus maneuvered his body so that the back of the chair was pressed into Yazzie's throat.

Still disoriented from the blow to his head, Yazzie tried to push himself free, but it was too late. The back of the chair pressed into his extremities, and the pressure on his throat was slowly cutting off the blood flow to his brain.

After a moment of fighting and wheezing, Yazzie was unconscious, and Marcus allowed the police captain to fall limply to the floor as he put all four legs of the chair back on the ground.

The scorpion venom combined with the physical stress of what he had just done made Marcus's world spin and forced him to the brink of passing out himself. He heard the skittering of tiny legs and looked down to see a broken Mason jar and Harvey crawling off into a dark corner of the room.

Marcus said, "Good idea, Harvey. You go get help."

As he waited for the world to stop spinning again, he allowed himself to vomit once more. The violent heaving kept him from passing out. He waited a few seconds and listened to hear if Pitka was coming to assist. But he heard nothing. The young officer must've been outside, radioing John Canyon as he had been instructed.

Numb and nauseous with a migraine throbbing against the back of his eyelids, Marcus tested his restraints, trying to find a weakness. He thought of the switchblade in Yazzie's boot, but getting to it would be near impossible and time-consuming. He cracked his neck to the side and growled deep in his throat. There was only one way he was going to free himself from the chair in the time he had. And it was going to be very painful.

Taking several deep breaths in preparation while forcing some blood flow into the proper muscles, Marcus leaned forward again. But this time, with violent and reckless abandon, he threw all of his weight into a roll, which sent him spinning end over end with all his weight crashing down onto the legs and backing of the chair. The wood impacted with the concrete and separated at its joints with a symphony of snaps and pops. Marcus felt the collision throughout his whole body, deep inside, all the way to his spine and down to his heels. The pain, with a little help from scorpion venom, again pushed him to the edge of a blackout.

But he refused to succumb to the darkness. He forced his aching body to pull itself the rest away of the way free from the broken chair and the now ineffective restraints. As he finally got to his feet, he swayed back and forth, having to steady himself against one of the shelving units mounted to the inner wall.

Once the momentary swirling sickness had abated, he looked to the unconscious police captain with a smile and said, "I think it's my turn to ask you some questions, Cap."

57

Liana stared down at the small communicator, completely unsure of what she was going to say or do. And then she looked to Frank, who lay unconscious on the floor of the back room. She watched and waited for his chiseled abdomen to move up and down and indicate that he was still breathing. He was alive but unresponsive. Peering around the corner of the broken front window, she snatched up the binoculars and watched Canyon for a moment as he hiked up the trail toward her. His arms were raised, and the black handheld radio jutted from his right fist.

Talking to herself aloud, she said, "You're on your own now, girl."

The sound of her own voice chilled Liana down to her spine. As if it wasn't her voice but that of her grandmother, words spoken at her mother's funeral. Grandmother had stared down at a sobbing child and said, "You're on your own now, girl. But that doesn't mean that you're alone. The spirits are always watching over you."

Liana hoped for a little help from the spirits now because she couldn't for the life of her find the words to halt Canyon's march. She had always been a bit impetuous, and sometimes others confused that quality with her being a take-charge kind of person. When in reality, she considered herself more the kind of person to stay to the back of the class, keep her head down, and work hard but under the radar. Now, she needed to channel something that wasn't a natural inclination. Of course, she had no idea how to do that.

She tried to imagine what Frank would do. But that was a lesson in futility. She might as well have been trying to predict the behaviors of a five-headed alien with flippers as trying to figure out the strange man who had walked into her life only a few hours ago.

Holding the radio up to her mouth, Liana said the first thing that came to mind. "This is Officer Liana Nakai of the Navajo Tribal Police. Mr. Canyon, I'm going to need you to return to your vehicle… And then I would ask you and your men to please cease and desist and vacate these premises. The situation here is under control, and you needn't worry about your son or any of the hostages. They are safe and in my custody."

Through the binoculars, Liana watched John Canyon stare in confusion at the radio in his hand. Then, shaking his head, he keyed the mic and replied, "Little lady, you've done bit off way more than you can chew. Where's your new friend? Over."

"He's right here. He's also in my custody. Over"

"I highly doubt that. This has gone way beyond the purview of the law, and you weren't really cops to begin with. More like a bunch of glorified security guards. You have no idea what you've gotten yourself into, or the forces that you're playing with."

"I know this much. My new friend says that if you try to approach this building without an invitation, he's going to put a fifty-caliber bullet through your cranium. The best thing that you and your men can do now is to pack up and head home. This is a law enforcement matter, and law enforcement will handle it."

Canyon laughed. "You really have no clue, do you? They didn't just steal my son. They stole one of our cocaine shipments, worth many millions of dollars. It's worth more than the lives of everyone in this whole damn town. So I want you to understand, Officer Nakai of the Navajo Nation Police, that you are already dead. Your new friend in there, his partner, and anyone else involved are already dead."

Though her heart dropped at the confirmation of what she already knew, she maintained her composure and said, "That's not a very smart thing to say when you have a high-powered rifle aimed at your head."

"I'm just making observations, Officer Nakai. You can let your friend Frank know that we have his partner in custody and that Captain Yazzie is interrogating him at the ranch right now. Things will go a lot better for all of you if you surrender now and tell us where to find the truck. Maybe you can even get through this night alive."

"Like I told you before Mr. Canyon, I'm not all that concerned about protecting Frank from you." To emphasize her point, Liana snatched up the rifle and took aim at the already-ruined truck. Squeezing back on the trigger, she placed another round through the engine block. The recoil from the large rifle, even though she was qualified for high-powered and assault rifles, nearly knocked her onto the floor. It was unlike anything she'd ever shot before, a staggering level of power and the concussion. Although she couldn't hear or feel it from Canyon's or his men's position, she guessed that the massive bullet striking the truck would have felt like a fighter jet flying over.

Into the radio, she said, "I think my new friend is through talking. He says for you to bring him Agent Carlisle and maybe you'll get through this night alive. Over and out."

Laying the rifle back on the table and rubbing at her shoulder, which felt like it was dislocated, Liana looked through the binoculars and was satisfied to see Canyon returning to his men. She allowed herself a deep breath and a few seconds to calm her trembling heart and hands. When she looked back to Frank, she was startled to see him looking back at her with a smile on his face. She asked, "Did you hear all of that?"

His reply was barely audible, and so she moved closer and leaned down until their faces were less than a foot apart.

In a whisper, Frank said, "If Canyon wants you looking at him out the front…"

His voice trailed off, but she finished his sentence outloud. "Then he probably has men coming in the back."

58

After checking Yazzie for weapons and then hog-tying the police captain, Marcus made his way back through the house in order to deal with Officer Pitka. He found the young man inside his patrol cruiser using the radio as he had been instructed. Coming at him from the side and behind, taking advantage of the blind spots and staying out of view of the mirrors, Marcus crept right up to the open window of the Ford Explorer and held Yazzie's pistol up to the young man's head.

Cocking back the hammer of the Colt Peacemaker was definitely a satisfying experience, the well-oiled gun turning exactly as it should, all pieces working together in tandem. Like a bandit of the Old West, Marcus said, "Reach for the sky, partner."

The young officer froze, eyes going wide, bowels possibly evacuating.

Marcus continued, "I don't want you to think about your captain or what's going to happen

The young officer spoke in a flood of information so fast that it was hard Marcus to keep up. "Dude, please don't kill me. Listen, I'm really just a normal police officer. I write tickets. I fill out reports. I patrol. I've only been on the force for a couple of years. We usually aren't involved in anything like this. I mean we knew that something's going on below the surface. We knew that Mr. Canyon isn't exactly the most stand-up citizen, but nothing like this. I mean, heck, I would just be writing tickets tonight and driving around checking on things. Or actually I'd be at home in bed because I wasn't even supposed to be on tonight, but you know, the whole thing with the bloody guy walking into the station, I got called in to help. And man, I didn't even know anything about an agent coming in asking questions and then another agent asking questions about them. I was out on patrol when she came in. I didn't see anyone. But Liana told me that she was there when the agent met with Captain Yazzie."

In his head, Marcus thought: Damn kid, I didn't even have to start counting.

Aloud, he said, "What agent? You mean Maggie? Agent Carlisle?"

"Yeah, Liana was in the office filling out some reports when Agent Carlisle came in to visit Captain Yazzie. They talked. Nothing big. The walls are thin there in the station so Liana would have heard if there was some kind of heated discussion. But she said it was normal, except that your friend was asking about John Canyon and powwows. Liana said that Agent Carlisle asked her questions, thanked Yazzie, and left. She didn't hear anything more until another agent came in from the FBI asking if your friend had been here. From what Liana told me, Yazzie had already instructed her to say that they had never heard of any Agent Carlisle."

Marcus said, "Anything else? Anything you've heard, seen, or know about that you think might help me find my friend? You want to be a real cop? This is your chance. Whatever corruption was going on in this valley, it dies tonight. Your buddy Mr. Canyon is a tumor, and my partner and I, think of us like chemo-therapy. Which means there's going to be collateral damage, like anyone who stands with Canyon or in our way."

The young officer trembled all over as he said, "I don't know anything else. I do my job and keep my head down. It's a crap posting, but it gets my foot in the door, and I'm hoping to transfer down to the main office in Shiprock as soon as I can."

Marcus said, "You're only gonna live long enough to do any of that if you do exactly as I tell you. Are you ready to be a real cop?"

"Absolutely. Name it."

"Do you know where the main cell tower around here is located? The one that provides service for the valley?"

59

Ackerman felt exhausted by the effort required to keep his eyelids from falling. When Liana looked down at him and asked, "If they're coming, what are we going to do?" Ackerman wanted to reply, "I'm going to take a nice long nap." Unfortunately, he didn't have time for rest and relaxation. There was still much work to do on this day.

He replied, "I need you to do exactly as I say. Sit me up, put my Bowie knife in my left hand, and your Glock 19 in my right hand. Place both hands on my lap."

As she did as he requested, grabbing the Bowie knife and retrieving her Glock from its holster, she said, "How would any of Canyon's men sneak up on us now? We have the whole road covered."

"I imagine he sent them around to climb the rock face."

"Maybe I could still get back there before they—"

"There's no time. They're already here."

Once she'd finished getting him into position, she asked, "What about me? What do I do?"

Ackerman felt like ten gallons of feces in a five gallon receptacle. The fact that he was still going was a sheer exercise of will. He wasn't afraid to die. He wasn't afraid to lose. And he wasn't afraid to feel great pain as he did either of those things. He was dizzy and weak, and the world felt like the inside of a clothes dryer on spin cycle. But even he knew that he could only keep this up for so long. He only had so much strength, only so many words that he would be able to speak. His body would soon betray him and shut down in order to focus on the necessary repairs.

With all that in mind, he said, "Use your resources. And remember, losing just means that you didn't cheat hard enough."

Her brow furrowed, and she started to speak but was interrupted when two men, each armed with a 9mm Beretta, stormed in through the back door.

Immediately springing into action, Liana snatched up an MP5 submachine gun from the table, aimed at the intruders as they entered the front room, and said, "Stand down or I will shoot."

The two young men, who appeared to be in excellent physical condition, barked orders at them to drop their weapons as they scanned the front room for the hostages.

Ackerman was now having trouble keeping his mind focused on reality. His thoughts kept wandering. He could feel himself drifting off. His body finally shutting down; his battery finally reaching zero. He had found himself in this situation before many times, but never quite under these circumstances. He was in an odd position where he wanted to simply go to sleep. And he wasn't really afraid of the consequences of what would happen if he did that. Things would either work out or they wouldn't. But it also wasn't in his DNA to give up.

In his ear, Ackerman heard the voice of Thomas White whisper, "You could just let me take over for a moment and handle the situation. I could ring that last bit of energy out of you. Just say the word. Give in and let me have the reins."

Out loud, Ackerman exclaimed, "That will never

happen!" His gaze was directed somewhere at the floor, but in his periphery, he could see everyone in the room turn their attention toward him.

He added, "I will not let you slaughter these men. It's out of the question."

The thought of Thomas White burrowing his way inside of his consciousness provided the anger necessary for Ackerman to keep going. But he still could barely feel his arms and legs and knew that he would not be able to move them. He put all of his strength and spirit into moving his head and forcing his face to make the necessary expressions. If he did this right, all he would need to do was sell it with his eyes.

His gaze moving up to the two intruders and then over to Liana who was also staring at him dumbfounded, he said, "I'm sorry, did I say that out loud? Don't mind me, I was just having an argument with one of the voices in my head."

One of the men, the smaller and younger looking of the two, whom Ackerman pegged as a gangbanger with no military experience, said, "Put your weapons down and your hands up."

Ackerman asked, "What are they saying about me?"

The banger kept his eyes on the Bowie knife and the Glock. "What? Who?"

"Your friends. I've had run-ins with a few of your crew now. Including your illustrious leader, Mr. Canyon. I'm sure that there's been some sort of talk about me during the events of this evening. I'm curious."

With his Beretta tilted slightly to the side and used to emphasize his words, the banger replied, "They say you're a punk. Now put your hands up."

Ackerman met the young man's gaze. The kid was trying to seem tough, but Ackerman had detected the trembling of his voice. He saw all of the kinesthetic markers for lying. And fear.

Fixing the banger with his most piercing gaze, Ackerman chuckled and then said, "We both know that's not true. Let me guess. They've been saying things like: 'He's a dark wind.' Or perhaps that I have one foot in this world and one in the spirit realm. They say that I can dodge bullets. Perhaps there have even been whispers that I could be some kind of witch. What do you call them around here? Skinwalkers?"

He could see the unease fall over all of the room's American Indian occupants. Among the Diné, witchcraft and the existence of skinwalkers was something that was never to be even spoken of.

The banger said, "You ain't faster than a bullet, white boy. From the way I see it, we have you dead to rights. So why don't you drop your weapons and we can end this without anyone getting killed."

Ackerman shrugged. "You may be right. But you see that's something people often become confused about. It's sort of like running from a grizzly bear in the wilderness."

As Ackerman surveyed the expressions of the others in the room, he knew that he had them right where he wanted them by all the looks of confusion. He continued, "You know what I'm talking about. If you're out with a friend in the wilderness and you come upon a grizzly bear. You don't actually have to be faster than the bear…"

The kid replied, "Yeah yeah, you just have to be faster than your friend. What's your point?"

"It's the same principle," Ackerman replied. "You see,

I don't have to be faster than a bullet. I just have to be faster than you. Dodging bullets—especially with small caliber semiautomatic weapons, like what you are wielding this morning, which I assume was due to the climb and the weight that would've accompanied one of the AK-47s or AR-15s—only requires that I be able to calculate and counteract your movements. You see, I've stared down a lot gun barrels over the years, and I've learned how to gauge exactly where a bullet is going to go from the way that you are holding the gun and the angle of the barrel. So I don't have to outrun the bullet. I just have to make sure that I'm faster than you and that I get out of the way before you can pull the trigger. Some have felt that it creates the illusion that I'm dodging bullets, when in actuality I'm merely demonstrating my superior reflexes over the shooter. You've seen what happened to your friends. I won't be as forgiving with you. Let's just say that if you force me into a confrontation right now, you won't be leaving here with all of your parts."

The banger bared his teeth and said, "You ain't no ghost. Not yet. But you're gonna be if you don't drop your weapons and raise your hands."

Ackerman fixed the young man with his most intense gaze and then said, "Do you really want to find out how fast you are? Are you faster than the dark wind? There are only so many ways that this can go down. You have orders to take us alive, because there are a million places out here we could've hidden your boss's shipment. But since you have my partner in custody, those rules of engagement may have been adjusted. Either way, your benefactor is an intelligent man. He's not going to risk killing us quite yet.

At least not if he can avoid it. And if you are able to bring us in alive, you are assured his gratitude and respect. So you may be asking yourself what kind of circumstance or action would allow that to happen. Well, obviously, I'm not going to surrender. And obviously neither are you. So I propose a different course of action. I suggest that the two of you put down your weapons. And so do we. Then you fight my associate Officer Liana Nakai in hand-to-hand combat for the privilege of presenting us to the self-appointed protector of your realm."

Liana looked at him as if he had grown a second head. Ignoring her, he continued, "I'm sure that two strapping young men like yourselves would have no problem in besting Ms. Liana in a fair fight . If you are successful in doing so, then I will surrender without raising a finger. You will have taken us in without a scratch, and you will have earned a place at the table of your grand Mr. Canyon."

The young banger said, "Fine, you drop your guns first."

Ackerman smiled and replied, "I'll do you one better. I'll drop my weapons and have Liana tie me up."

60

The past…

Maggie forced a smile onto her face, but she was shaking so badly and felt so overwhelmed with rage that the gesture was impossible to hold. Marcus sat dumbfounded for a moment, apparently unsure of what to say or how to react. She had caught him red-handed. His betrayal crept inside her heart and made her feel cold all over.

"Aren't you going to introduce me to your friend, Marcus?" He glanced between them and finally said, "Maggie, this is Special Agent Vasques with the FBI. She's working on this case with us. And Vasques, this is Special Agent Carlisle. She works out of my unit at the DOJ."

Maggie looked at Vasques, sizing up the competition. The dark-haired agent was quite beautiful with a tanned complexion the color of light caramel, high cheekbones, and large brown eyes. She resisted the urge to punch the woman in the face. It wasn't Vasques's fault that Marcus had stabbed her in the back.

"Pleasure to meet you," Maggie said in a clipped tone, and they shook hands.

Vasques's thoughts were written across her face. The FBI agent could tell that something was going on here, and she said, "You know, I'm sure you want to get Agent Carlisle caught up to speed, and I want to check in with Belacourt. So I think I'm going to head on out."

"Okay, I'll give you a ride back to your office."

As Vasques grabbed her purse and slid from the booth, she said, "Don't worry about it. I'll just catch a cab."

Marcus opened his mouth to protest, but Maggie gave him a fierce look. His words died in his throat. They sat silently for a few moments, just staring at each other. Maggie broke the silence first. "Now I see why you didn't want me to come along."

"Oh please, Maggie. I don't know what you're suggesting, but you're way out of line."

"You know damn well what was going on here."

"I do know one thing. I have an agent under my command that's disobeyed my direct orders. Just like she did in Harrisburg. What do you think I should do about that?"

She couldn't contain herself any longer. She spun from her chair and slapped his coffee cup off the table and into his lap. Then she stormed out of the restaurant. She felt like falling to her knees and crying, screaming, breaking things. How could she have been so stupid and blind?

She heard Marcus calling after her, but she didn't want to see him at that moment. She wasn't sure if she ever wanted to see him again. His hand wrapped around her bicep, but she ripped free of his grasp. "Don't touch me!"

"Dammit, Maggie! What the hell has gotten into you? You're acting crazy."

"So now I'm crazy, huh? I suppose that's why you don't want me with you on investigations. Because I'm so nuts."

"Don't put words in my mouth. I said you're acting crazy. There's a difference."

"Don't worry about it. Doesn't matter, anyway." She rammed her fist against the elevator call button. "Maybe, if you hurry, you can still catch your girlfriend."

He breathed out with a low growl and cracked his neck to the side. She recognized the gesture. He did it, whether consciously or unconsciously, every time he was getting ready for a fight. "Maggie, let's just calm down and talk about this."

"I don't have anything to say."

"Then shut up and listen! There's nothing going on. And even if there was, it's really none of your business."

Her eyes went wide. She couldn't believe what she was hearing. First, he betrayed her, and then he acted like they'd never had anything going between them to start with. Not knowing what else to say, she just slapped him across the face. The elevator dinged behind her, and its doors slid open. Maggie stepped inside and pounded the button to close the doors again and shut out the rest of the world.

61

Marcus admired Yazzie's silver and gold Colt Peacemaker as he rounded the corner into the small storage that the police captain had converted into an interrogation chamber. Yazzie was now tied in the center of the room to another chair out of the same kitchen table set that he had been earlier, except that Marcus had made sure that the nylon rope was wrapped in such a way to make it nearly impossible for his captive to get free. The faux police captain's weapon was an exquisitely-detailed replica Peacemaker. Silver plated with gold accents. The handle was pearl with the infinity symbol made from a snake devouring its tail in the standard eight shaped infinity sign. Marcus noticed the exact same symbol had been tattooed on to Captain Yazzie's wrist.

Walking over to the corner of the room where the old table and chair set had been stacked to collect dust, Marcus grabbed another of the chairs, carried over in front of Yazzie, wiped the dust away, and sat down. The pistol still in his hand, he said, "I love the Colt. Did you do the modifications yourself?"

Yazzie didn't respond.

Without looking up, Marcus continued, "An old time Colt Single Action Army revolver. 4 and 5/8 inch barrel. I've seen guns with the sights filed down, but nothing as perfect as this. And you removed almost all of the knurling on the hammer. This is a fast draw competition gun."

Yazzie still didn't respond. Marcus looked up at the police captain and chuckled. He said, "Oh yeah, I forgot about the gag." Then he reached out and pulled a black Nike sock from Yazzie's mouth. Giving it a shake and slipping off his combat boot, Marcus slid the sock back onto his bare foot and replaced the boot.

Yazzie didn't bother with any posturing, he merely scowled and said, "I do all of my own gunsmithing."

Marcus rolled the smooth cylinder over his left forearm. He closed his eyes and listened to the perfection and precision of Yazzie's work. He said, "You're an artist. The way you have the gun modified, and as fast as you are, makes me wonder if you were ever in any of those cowboy fast draw competitions."

"Not any of the legal ones. Those are just about trophies and bragging rights. The illegal ones are about money. I'd rather have money than a bunch of strangers stroking my ego."

Marcus had heard about illegal fast draw competitions where men and women wore ballistic vests and then went head-to-head with opponents in an Old West style showdown. Instead of shooting targets with wax bullets, as they did in legitimate fast draw competitions, the underground players shot real people with real bullets. The dangers were obvious, and you could bet on it; which was a perfect combination for clandestine bloodsport.

Yazzie said, "Listen, Agent Williams, we're on the same side here—"

Marcus cut the statement short with a little quick-draw

of his own. He snatched the Ka-Bar knife from his belt and, with practiced speed and precision, stabbed the tip into Yazzie's leg at approximately the same spot where Yazzie had cut him earlier. Then, just as quickly as he had pulled and thrust the knife, Marcus ripped the blade free and replaced it in his holster. Yazzie cried out in pain both as the blade entered and exited his body.

Marcus said, "Sorry, I just needed to feel like we were on equal footing during this discussion. Although, I do still owe you a scorpion sting. Harvey? You still skittering around here?"

Breathing hard, his words coming out in short bursts, Yazzie said, "Let's get to your point. I'm not a real cop. I'm more of a security guard. Not employed by the Navajo Nation. I'm employed by John Canyon. Just like everyone else in this valley."

"Your employer's about to have a real bad day, which means that there's going to be a lot of people out of work tomorrow. Or worse."

"I wouldn't be so sure. John's a resourceful man."

"Yeah, I've noticed that. In fact, the more I think about this case, the more I think that the man Maggie came here looking for isn't necessarily the one who ended up taking her. All she had to do was come up here asking questions about John Canyon and what kind of operation he was running. Maybe what he was doing twenty years ago? That's all it would take. A federal agent asking questions. Guy like Canyon might kill her first and ask his questions later. So, right now, I don't care about the old case she was digging into. I don't care about justice. I don't care about Canyon and his drugs. All that matters to me is finding Maggie. So that's what I want to know. Do you know where she is or what happened to her?"

"Canyon may be a killer, and he may have his men kill for him. But I don't kill for him. I may not be righteous enough to be considered law enforcement by a belegana like you, but I do my best to keep the peace under inherently crappy circumstances. And don't forget that there are a lot of people who have good lives here, better lives than they could have ever hoped for. Maybe you should consider them for a second before you go pissing in the oasis that Canyon's built."

Marcus felt his muscles involuntarily tensing as his rage rose. "You don't seem to be understanding me. I don't care about any of that. All I care about right now is finding Maggie. When I set my mind on something, I'm kind of like a bullet fired from a high-powered rifle. I don't go veering off course. I don't get distracted with other stuff I find along the way. I just fly straight and true and hit my target, shredding anything that gets in my way. Now, I'm going to ask you one more time… Where is Maggie Carlisle?"

Yazzie replied, "I've already told the feds and your partner, that I have never even seen this woman. And I can't tell you where she is now."

Marcus punched Yazzie square in the jaw and said, "Every time that you lie to me, I'm going to hurt you. Do you understand me? My partner likes to do a lot of talking in situations like this or use some type of elaborate torture device that hasn't been in fashion since the 1600s, but I'm more of a straightforward kind of guy. If I need information out of you, I'll get it out the old-fashioned way. With a pair of brass knuckles and a hammer. I'll start with the knuckles and beat you to a bloody pulp. And then, if you're not in a coma yet, we'll move on to the bonus round and bust out that hammer. I'll start with your toes and keep going until I've broken every bone in your body. I love doing the little toes first. Those things pop just like a cherry tomatoes."

With blood in his teeth, Yazzie said, "I've never met the woman."

"I know that you're lying, Captain. I know that she was in your office. Now, I understand that Canyon may have ordered you to maintain that lie, but your cards are on the table now, so you might as well drop the act."

Yazzie hesitated, trying to save the lie, trying to figure out how Marcus knew. But Marcus didn't give him the chance to think, he struck him again using his father's old brass knuckles. He had to remember to keep his swing at less than 50%, way less, or the crack about putting the police captain in a coma might come true.

He had inherited the brass knuckles from his father. Not the serial killer one who went by the name Thomas White, but his adopted father, an NYPD Detective

In a way, Marcus hated using the brass knuckles that his stepfather may have used in much the same way. But when he and Maggie had gone back to New York recently during an investigation, he had picked up a few things from a storage locker there and had once again come across the brass knuckles. Transporting them was not a problem, since the FBI had loaned them a private jet, and so Marcus had decided to take them along for the ride. He never knew when a weapon might come in handy. And he had always lived by the condom principle: That he would rather have something and not need it, then need something and not have it.

Now, as he wielded his father's weapons, he couldn't help but feel a part of the man's spirit with him as well.

After the blow, Yazzie didn't spit blood on the floor or cry out or curse. He merely swallowed his own plasma, shook off the attack, and said, "Fine, you win. I surrender. She was in my office. She came in asking a lot of questions about Mr. Canyon and his activities and about a string of serial murders that have been occurring for years in New Mexico and Arizona. I basically told her the official line on John and that I knew nothing about any serial killings. All that was way outside of my jurisdiction. She left, and I never saw her again."

Marcus considered this. It did seem to gel with the information that Ackerman had overheard and Officer Pitka had confirmed. But Marcus knew that there was more Yazzie wasn't saying. "And the second she was out of your door, you called John Canyon and told him that a federal agent was there asking questions about him. Maybe she even told you where she was staying. Probably at the casino. So Canyon would've had Maggie on a property that he owned, staying in his hotel. And you led him right to her."

"I was just doing my job. If you want to stand there with blood all over your hands and preach to me, that's fine, but we both know what it's like to take orders. What kind of a security guard would I be if I didn't tell my boss that a federal agent had just come in and was asking about him."

Marcus replied, "So hypothetically speaking, let's say that

I believe you. And that is a pretty big leap even hypothetically speaking. But if that story's true, you're still not telling me everything. Because if you fast-forward up to earlier tonight, I'm sure that after my brother busted his way, literally, out of your police station, I'm positive that a smart guy like you would've asked your friend John Canyon what he did with the information you gave him. So this is your one chance before I get the hammer. You see, I'm a little worried that these brass knuckles may actually give you permanent brain damage, and if that happens, then you can't answer my questions. But I can work on your toes for hours without damaging the knowledge you have up top. So what did Canyon tell you he did with the agent you called him about? This is the last time I ask nicely."

Yazzie grimaced back at him and said, "You seem to be pretty comfortable with torture for someone who's supposed to be a righteous law enforcement officer."

"Let's just say I'm no stranger to coloring outside the lines. And like you said, there is no law around here, except for the law that Canyon writes."

Yazzie said, "I've been riding John Canyon's coattails since high school. I always saw the potential in him. He was a smart, charismatic man with a dream. One that, most of the time, I respected. I guess what I'm saying is, why would I betray my friend, a man who's trying to save our people? Why would I rat him out to a representative of the same government that has wanted nothing but to subjugate and steal my people's heritage for centuries now? Why would I give up my career and my home? Those seem like pretty good causes to die for."

Leaning forward, Marcus whispered, "I thought I made

those reasons abundantly clear with the whole hammer and smashing toes like ripe grapes thing."

"I thought it was cherry tomatoes."

"Thanks for paying attention. So yeah, all that. I also saw some nice butchering instruments out in one of Canyon's buildings. Maybe I'll grab a few of those on the way to pick out a hammer? And let's get something else clear, Captain Yazzie, your career and your life are already over. Nobody's just walking away from today. Canyon and his whole operation are through. You're providing security for a sinking ship. The only question left is whether you're going to be one who makes it onto a life raft or one that goes down with the boat. Maybe you can still walk away from this. Tell me where she is and everything that you know, and maybe we can work something out."

Yazzie remained as stone.

Marcus added, "You talk about friends and family, about your people. Well, Maggie is not just my friend or coworker, she's the love of my life. And I've pretty much done nothing but screw things up with her from the first moment we met. So I want you to understand. I want this to be perfectly clear. There is nothing I won't do to get her back. I may not enjoy it like my partner would, but that doesn't mean I'm not any good at it."

Yazzie laughed. "And you think your partner—or is he your actual brother as you mentioned—" Marcus had noticed when he misspoke in the heat of the moment, but he had tried to cover and keep going with the hope that Yazzie hadn't heard. "—You really think that the two of you are going to take on Canyon and a whole army of men?"

"I think my brother and I could take down just about

anyone. And from what I've seen, Canyon doesn't have more than a couple dozen guys. That's hardly an army."

Yazzie shook his head. "That was before he called in for reinforcements from Mr. Alvarez. You see, he's the one whose shipment you disrupted. He wants the drugs back more than we do. And I'm afraid that, when his emissaries arrive, they may employ more of a scorched earth policy and just kill everyone. Except for you and your brother. Perhaps they'll turn some of these interrogation techniques around on you, until you tell them what you did with their merchandise."

"All the more reason for you to tell me everything you know before they get here."

"I don't track your logic."

"The way I see it, I have nothing to lose. And if you're right, and an unstoppable force is about to sweep down on this valley. Then all that does is tell me that I need to find Maggie even faster. But even if all that's true, and this Alvarez is on the way, Canyon's whole operation is still going down after today. We have friends who'll have the FBI crawling all over this place by this time tomorrow. No matter how tough Canyon is. He might be able to kill me and my partner. But can he kill the whole U.S. government? That's what's coming down on him. Cartel thugs or not."

Marcus could plainly see the police captain's wheels turning as he chewed on this information. Yazzie said, "Okay, I'll tell you everything I know. But before I do, I want the promise of immunity when Canyon goes down."

Marcus replied, "Fine, you may have to testify. But as long as what you've been telling me is true, then I can make that deal."

"Even if you're not able to get your missing agent back alive? Would I still have a deal then?"

The question and the tone in which it was asked made Marcus's heart feel like it was trapped in a vise. Since all this began, since Maggie went missing, from the moment she had taken off, he had never truly felt that he wouldn't get her back. They had been through so much. They had fought so much. He just couldn't imagine a world without her. He asked, through clenched teeth, "What are you getting at?"

Yazzie wouldn't meet Marcus's gaze but said, "I'm just worried that you're not going to like what I have to tell you."

Marcus felt the rage building. The cloud of red was falling across his vision like a shade. His heart pounded so hard that he couldn't hear himself think. He felt himself losing control. He had been worried about what Ackerman might do, if they were to find evidence that Maggie had been killed, but he had never allowed himself to consider what he would do. And from the way he felt right now, he couldn't imagine that there were any dark secrets or ancient wisdom or knowledge of medieval torture devices that his brother could bring to the table that would be able to compare with the violence Marcus was contemplating.

Before he fully knew what he was doing, he was on his feet, nose to nose with Yazzie, his hands on each side of the captain's head. As if in a dream, he felt himself squeezing Yazzie's skull and screaming, "Tell me where she is!"

Grimacing in pain, Yazzie replied, "Okay, okay, I promise! I'll tell you everything I know!"

62

One week earlier…

The Houston FBI field office sat off to itself on a lot enclosed by white pillars and a black rod-iron fence. It was as long as it was tall, and a grid of mirrored windows covered its entire front. Special Agent Victoria Vasques's office was on the fourth floor against the south wall, overlooking a room full of agents working away at cubicles. The whole place smelled of fast food and Pine-sol.

The young agent who had escorted Maggie from the front door excused herself. Vasques stood and moved to meet Maggie. They exchanged an awkward handshake, and then the FBI agent directed her to a chair in front of her desk.

Maggie immediately said, "Isn't this place a carbon copy of your office in Chicago?"

Vasques shrugged. "You know the FBI. They have a leaning toward uniformity. So, Maggie how is everything?"

"Everything's great," Maggie lied.

Opening up a drawer in her desk, Vicky Vasques pulled out a foot-long meatball sub sandwich and asked with her eyes if it was okay for her to eat. Maggie replied, "By all means. I know how busy you are. I appreciate you taking the time to meet with me and potentially help on the case."

Vasques smiled. "After what you and your team did for

me in Chicago, I definitely owe you one. Speaking of your team," Vasques said as she unwrapped her sandwich. Then preparing to take a bite, she completed her statement, "How is Marcus doing?" The agent punctuated her sentence with what Maggie felt was an overly sensuous bite of the footlong.

Maggie wasn't sure if Vasques was naturally territorial around other women or if she established dominance like this with everyone, but Maggie also wasn't above bowing down a bit in order to get the information she needed. Maggie maintained her smile, but she wasn't sure if she kept the look of offense from her eyes as she said, "We're still together, if that's what you're asking."

Vasques laughed. "Good for you, girl. You know, he may be the…hardest man I've ever known."

"I'm not sure what you mean. Is that a euphemism for 'he's an asshole?'"

"No, I was actually thinking physically. We only kissed once, but I don't believe I've ever been that close to a man who was quite so muscular. Not in a bodybuilder sense, but more that every inch of him was firm."

Vicky took a bite of her sandwich and seemed to consider this.

Maggie, considering whether she would be able to shoot Vicky in the chest and then make it out of the building, said, "If you don't mind, I'd rather not discuss you feeling up my man."

Vasques seemed to shake herself awake and replied, "Of course. I'm sorry. I've been awake for seventy-two hours on a sting, trying to find a semi-truck full of kids coming across the border. They're all meant for a life of prostitution in some US city. We haven't found them yet, but anyway. Why don't I chew and you talk and tell me why you're here?"

Biting back her pride, Maggie explained from the beginning about her brother, some of which Vasques already knew. But the main thing that Maggie wanted the FBI agent's help with was identifying the people in the photograph that she had received in the mail, the one that seemed to show her brother only slightly older than when he had been taken. She had run the print through facial recognition, but the databases she had access to without Stan's help weren't anything she wanted to rely on. Her hope was that Vasques, through her human trafficking work, may have firsthand or even tangential knowledge of the people shown.

Removing the photograph and sliding it across the desk to Vasques, Maggie said, "I received this picture in the mail a few months ago, and it's sort of thrown my whole world into a tailspin."

Vasques had put down her sandwich as soon as Maggie had told her that this wasn't about a normal case, but about her brother. Maggie had to admit that after she had revealed that information, the agent's demeanor had changed greatly.

Vasques closely examined the photo for a moment, and then Maggie saw the recognition pass over her face. She said, "Well, he's much younger in this picture, but the initials you have here on the back would match up with who I believe this to be."

"You noticed that? I hoped that it was initials, as you said, and that maybe it could help with a positive ID."

Vasques turned the photograph over again and examined the back. "The JC you have here matches up with a man I know named John Canyon. And when I say, I 'know,' I mean that I've seen the surveillance reports. He runs pretty much the biggest criminal organization in the northern half of the Navajo Nation. But he's smart. No one exactly knows how he fits into the larger picture."

Maggie had already been scribbling notes in her notebook and verified the spelling on that name.

Vasques said, "I'll have someone here in my office pull his file for you. The RC in your picture, that's Reyna Canyon, John's wife."

The beautiful Hispanic agent was about to hand the photograph back but then spent another moment examining it and asked, "The initials that match up to JR, who do you think that is in the photograph?"

Maggie hated herself for the tear that fell down her cheek as she said, "It appears to be my younger brother, Tommy. His hair is long there, as if it was taken several months after he was taken."

Still keeping hold of the photo, Vasques looked to the last initial in the code. The one merely marked as 'X.' The face on the other side was obscured by white, black, and red paint and a massive headdress of feathers, several of which shot down in front of the face. The person in the photograph also appeared to have closed their eyes from the flash.

Vasques asked, "What are you thinking about the last one here?"

Maggie shrugged. "I'm not sure. It's hard to even see any of his face, and the way each one of them had two initials and that one's just an X makes me wonder if it was just one of the dancers that they had taken a picture with and that was the way that whoever took the photograph with used to identify a stranger."

Vasques nodded. "Makes sense. Would you like me to run it through the facial database, or have some of our computer guys look at it anyway."

"How sure are you that the two people there are John and Reyna Canyon?"

Vasques hesitated a second but then said, "This isn't something that holds up in court, but to my eyes and with the initials matching, I don't have any doubt that the two people you're after from this photo are John and Reyna Canyon."

Maggie picked up the photograph and slid it back into the pocket of her suit jacket. She stood and said, "Well, that's really all I needed."

Vasques didn't seem convinced. "Maggie, you shouldn't be going after this guy by yourself. You have backup, right?"

She smiled and said, "We might not have as much money as the FBI, but we make do."

Vasques stood and offered, "Well, if you need anything, you let me know."

Maggie smiled and shook Vasques's hand. She was about to turn toward the door when abruptly she looked back and said, "Can I give you two pieces of advice, Vicky?"

Vasques cocked a half-smile and said, "I'd love to hear it."

"The first piece of advice is that you go get some sleep. You look like shit. The second is that you should really quit smoking. If I recall, the last time we met you had switched from being a nicotine addict to a chewing gum addict, but apparently, that didn't last."

Vasques looked genuinely confused now and, scanning her desk for a stray pack or lighter, asked, "How did you know that I'm still smoking?"

Allowing just a little bit of malice to creep into her smile, Maggie winked and said, "Easy, dear. You have an odor."

63

Liana involuntarily glanced at Frank in confusion but then quickly returned her gaze to the two armed men in front of her, sighting at them down the barrel of the MP5 she had snatched from one of the trading post's tables. She surely hadn't heard him correctly. The two men armed with 9mm Berettas also seemed perplexed by the proposal.

Frank said, "Or if you prefer you could take your chances with me, but it is my belief that Miss Liana would easily trump the both of you little girls in hand-to-hand combat."

The gangbanger in the bandanna, the one who was obviously in command of his counterpart, said, "This is over, man. Just tell your girl to stand down."

Liana's aim didn't waiver from the man's head as he spoke, but out of the corner of her eye, she saw a flash of movement. At first, she thought that another threat had joined the fray, but then she realized that it was Frank who had moved, despite his frail condition. With a quick flick of his wrist, he sent the Bowie knife spinning through the air. It came to rest beside the gangbanger's foot, embedding itself into the plank flooring.

The banger jumped back and screamed, "What the hell!"

Frank laughed and replied, "I want you to understand something, boy. Do not think for a second that you are alive for any other reason than because I will it to be so. With a tiny change in the way I just flicked my wrist, I could've embedded that knife into your crotch. I'm not allowing you choices. I'm giving you one option where you may have a favorable outcome. I suggest you take it. But I want to be clear on the fact that taking us in any other way is completely off the table. Now, I'm going to drop my gun, and I suggest that you accept my perhaps overly gracious offer and put down your weapons."

The two gunman glanced at one another with obvious unease, but neither complied. Frank continued, "I can quickly analyze a person—their movements, demeanor, posture, eyes, etc—and accurately determine whether that person is predator or prey. The two of you stink of prey. You're no different than the sheep that Canyon packs down with drugs and ships out across the country. You're nothing but livestock. But my associate, Officer Liana, on the other hand, she has the potential to be a real predator. Personally, I'm itching to see her in action."

The banger said, "You are batshit crazy, man."

Frank glanced at Liana and winked. "Why are people always saying that?"

Leona looked down at the Bowie knife that was embedded into the floor at a perfect 90 degree angle in a spot right where do rag's foot had been. She said, "Maybe it's because you're always trying to stab or hit someone."

The banger said, "Fine, you put your guns down first."

"I'll drop mine now, but I suggest that you and Liana put your guns down at the same time just to be sure that everyone is adhering to the rules of the game. What should we call this little exhibition? How about 'Last Lady Standing.'"

"We aren't putting down our guns."

Liana quickly added, "And neither am I. We have the two of you. Don't make this any harder than it needs to be. Put your guns down, and I'll let you walk out front and join your friends."

A loud thud made every muscle in Liana's body tense up. Frank had dropped the Glock to the plank flooring. He said, "I'll give the three of you ten seconds to make the right decision before I intervene. Come on, boys, do you really believe about yourselves what I believe about you? Because I think that Liana will take down the two of you without either of you landing a single blow. I think you're nothing more than a couple of little girl sheep. Baa baa."

The gangbanger said, "Shut up."

The other of Canyon's minions, who had been relatively quiet, said, "I'm sick of this. You gonna let him talk to us like that?"

"Everyone shut up," the main banger said. "Okay. The two of us versus the little lady. And she ties you up to make sure that you're not going to interfere."

Frank said, "Excellent, then we have an agreement."

It seemed to Liana that the longer she was in proximity to Frank, the more surreal her world became. She considered Frank's words about him seeing a predator in her. But in her heart, she had felt like she had always been nothing but prey. She wondered if that was really how Frank saw her, or if it was all just a ruse to disarm their opponents. He could have easily been lying to them, just as he had lied to her when they had first met and he told her that the batons were glued to his hands.

Either way, he somehow expected her to best these two armed men, who—if they are anything like Canyon's other recruits—had been trained by the United States military. She didn't recognize the two men, but Canyon had a sort of rotation between the ranch and his other endeavors, and so it wasn't uncommon to see a lot of new faces in Roanhorse, New Mexico.

Moving behind Frank but keeping the MP5 trained on the gunmen, she crouched down behind his chair and with her left hand began to secure his hands using some of the zip ties that he had apparently brought with him. All the while, she kept the MP5 submachine gun trained on the men with her right hand. She whispered to him, "What the hell are you thinking?"

He whispered back, "Just roll with me, darling, I'll take you everywhere you need to go."

She stood up and returned to her original position, still covering the two gunmen. They both had their weapons trained on her now, completely ignoring Frank. Was that his plan all along?

The banger said, "Okay, we put them down at the same time."

But Liana didn't want to put her gun down. In fact, that was just about the last thing she wanted to do.

She couldn't imagine how she was expected to best these military-trained, athletic young men with her bare hands. But Frank's words came to mind, when he told her to use her resources and had implied that she should cheat in any way she could. So what were her resources? And how could she possibly cheat her way out of this.

As the gunmen slowly bent their knees and prepared to lay down their firearms, Liana followed suit. As she moved, she wracked her brain to think of what resources were at hand. Her best resource was the gun she was about to surrender. What else did she have at her disposal? There was the knife that Frank had thrown into floor. Was he expecting her to use that? Was he referring to her wits or intelligence as the resources she should be using?

She wondered if the two men would allow her the first strike out of some sort of gesture of chivalry or would they immediately charge at her once the weapons were on the ground?

And then, the answer came to her. When it did, she wasn't sure what she had been thinking before. She was a police officer and was wearing her body armor and uniform, which included a utility belt which held her pistol and handcuffs among other tools of the trade.

As she was about to place the gun on the ground, she felt confident that these were the resources to which Frank had referred, and using them in this instance would definitely be considering cheating. Which didn't concern her in the least.

Once they all had their weapons on the ground and all had slowly stood up to full height, the two men raised their fists. The main banger motioned for her to attack. So she did. Liana, using her left hand, snatched the Taser, which she kept in a holster in the small of her back, and discharged the weapon into the gunman on the left. He jerked and screamed as fifty thousand volts coursed through his body. She kept the trigger depressed as her right hand moved to the small pouch just in front of where her Glock normally rested.

The main banger was already charging at her with fire in his eyes. Fingers fumbling over the pouch, trying to remain calm, Liana pulled out her pepper spray. The second gunman was three feet away when she unloaded the small canister into his face.

His hands shot to his eyes, and he screamed, but Liana wasn't done yet. She proceeded to kick him three times in the crotch, and then, using the pepper spray as a fist pack, she punched the main gangbanger squarely in the temple.

The extra momentum and power added by the fist pack caused her blow to be an instant knockout.

The other gunman was on the floor but trying to push himself up, and so she squeezed the trigger of the Taser again to encourage him to stay down.

She looked over at Frank and found him smiling from ear to ear. He said, "You are poetry in motion, my dear. I couldn't have handled that any better myself."

She felt a strange sense of pride swell up in her, and she asked, "What we do with them now?"

"We take their pants off, put them on their heads, and send them back out to their leader."

"What's your deal with putting their pants on their heads?"

Frank replied, "No reason in particular. I just find it hilarious. You truly must learn to appreciate the little things in life."

64

Marcus felt hollow, like a trap door had opened up inside of him and everything that he was had fallen out. He felt like an empty shell. Ever since Maggie had gone missing, he had been walking through a nightmare that kept getting worse and worse. But he couldn't imagine possibly feeling any more broken than he did now. Even his rage couldn't seem to claw its way to top of the bottomless pit that had taken residence inside of him. His soul had been murdered so many times, but he feared that this was the final break, the moment from which he would have nothing left inside but a cold hollow void.

Marcus had positioned himself in the back seat behind Yazzie, as the captain occupied the driver's seat of his Ford Explorer patrol vehicle. The main reason he had chosen to sit directly behind Yazzie was that he didn't want the his captive to see him crying.

He would never truly be satisfied that she was gone until he saw a body, but after what Yazzie had told him in the basement of the ranch, he felt that seeing the corpse with his own eyes was merely a formality now.

Yazzie had explained how he had confronted Canyon about the whereabouts of the missing agent. Canyon simply replied that he had taken her up into the hills and disposed of her. He'd gone on to say that she had warned him that "The Brothers" would be coming for him. At the time, Canyon hadn't considered much of the threat. But then a crazy man had walked into his police station covered in blood.

Marcus still wasn't sure he could trust the police captain, but there was something about the story that rang true. Maybe it was that he had always known. Or maybe it was the warning she had allegedly given Canyon about brothers, a phrase she often used to refer to Ackerman and himself. But whatever it was, until he learned different, Marcus believed Yazzie's story.

With a submachine gun sitting across his lap and tears in his eyes, he watched the desert landscape, lit by a slowly waking sun, fly past.

From the front seat, Yazzie said, "May I ask you a question, Agent Williams?"

In Marcus's head, Yazzie's voice carried a strange dream-like quality. He responded, "Keep your mouth shut and drive."

Ignoring him, Yazzie asked, "You didn't mention my eyes. You didn't even seem to notice."

Of course he had noticed. Marcus noticed everything. But why would he say anything? Yazzie obviously was born with partial ocular albinism, which Marcus knew to mean that one of his eyes lacked normal pigment. He was familiar with several eye conditions like this that he had researched because of his own abnormality called sectoral heterochromia, in which one eye contains two different colors. Of course, he didn't care to share all that information with Yazzie. He merely replied, "Why would I?"

"I don't know, I guess it just seems to make people uneasy. Always has. That's why I wear the glasses all the time now or colored contacts if I know that I'm going to be in a situation where I have to take them off. But when you had me tied to that chair, my glasses were off and you were looking right into my eyes. You didn't even flinch. It's actually been a very long time since any man has looked me in the eyes. My real eyes."

"Is there a point to any of this?"

"I'm just trying to say that I appreciate that you didn't make anything out of it. I was bullied a lot when I was a kid because of what they called my 'ghost eyes,' and it wasn't until I was a teenager and started working for John that I was able to afford colored contacts."

Marcus could definitely understand that. He had experienced the effects of bullying and psychological abuse firsthand, and he knew the kind of scars that such trauma could leave on one's psyche. He said, "Being bullied isn't an excuse for becoming a bully yourself."

"Maybe you're right, but I learned early on that you are either meat for the grinder or the butcher doing the grinding."

Marcus said nothing.

Yazzie continued, "It seems pretty strange to me that your Agent Carlisle would come out here all by herself. Is conducting an investigation without any kind of backup typical for you feds?"

"Just shut up and drive."

Yazzie said, "I'm sorry about your friend."

"If you say another word, I'm going to hogtie you to the luggage rack."

65

Staying far enough in the shadows and back from the broken front window to avoid snipers, Ackerman watched the two interlopers descend the stairs and begin the long walk of shame down to their comrades waiting at the base the bluff. He said, "I still think we should have removed their pants."

Standing beside him, watching the reaction of their enemies through the binoculars, Liana said, "That's just juvenile. If anything we should have kept them as hostages. Now they're going to be down there holding two more guns pointed up at us."

"It doesn't matter how many guns they have or how many hands. And we have more hostages than we know what to do with," Ackerman replied, as he pulled open the foil packaging of a MRE and began to eat, hoping to regain his strength. He had already downed several full bottles of water.

"I see you're getting your appetite back. That's a good sign."

Ackerman said, "Did you know that insects retain the pathways required for cells to differentiate and reorganize at the site of a wound. It's a trait that we humans have nearly lost over the millennia. Most insects are able to lose whole limbs and regenerate them without even losing much volition. While I don't inherently have the same ability, I feel that I have gained certain traits through my various trials that would set me at the pinnacle of human evolution in regard to regeneration."

"Please don't tell me you think you can re-grow a limb like a spider."

"Of course not. I'm merely observing that I don't feel pain or fear in any way that your neurotypical brain can understand. Reality is what we will it to be, my dear. And I have a strong will."

Liana responded, "If you're not careful, those wounds are going to re-open, you'll lose what little blood you have left, and you will die. That's reality."

"I've survived much worse. These are paper cuts in comparison to what I've endured in the past. The issue was blood loss, which caused my operational efficiency to fall below one hundred percent."

"Is that so, Dr. Roboto? Here's my diagnosis: If those wounds re-open, your blood reserves will be at zero percent." Putting the binoculars down, Liana added, "Canyon looks like a tick that's ready to pop."

"Good, maybe he'll finally realize to abandon this idiot's pursuit and focus his energies on finding Agent Carlisle before his time runs out."

"You were serious about that deadline you gave him?"

"I'm always serious."

"What happens when time's up?"

"I feel that's self-explanatory. Time is the one attribute of reality we can't escape. When your time is up, there's nothing you can do to change that."

Liana cocked an eyebrow and replied, "I sure did my best to give you more time. What do you think would've happened to you if I hadn't showed up here?"

"I'm grateful for your assistance, but I'm also confident that I would've been able to handle the situation on my own. That being said, I've been continually impressed with how you've handled yourself throughout this evening's events."

"Was that a compliment?"

"An honest observation, and I'm not easily impressed." He then reached out and laid a hand on her shoulder, allowing the briefest caress of her smooth skin, the pigment of which seemed to be a blend of the colors of sandstone canyons and buttes that marked her ancestral lands. He whispered, "Please don't misunderstand me. You've performed admirably, and I thank you, Officer Nakai."

Satisfied that their guests had been shown off properly, Ackerman turned his thoughts to the next phase of the operation. With that in mind, he made his way through the shadows to where they had assembled all of the weapons and armament cases on a series of countertops attached to one wall of the old storefront. Snatching up one of the tactical backpacks they had also brought along, he began removing grenades from the foam housing of one case and dropping them into the backpack. Liana, coming up beside him, asked, "What are you doing?"

He smiled. "I'm merely preparing for when Mr. Canyon's time inevitably runs out."

Marcus had procured three different types of grenades, each labeled in their own cases and coming in a slightly different shape than their counterparts. The first type was a smoke grenade. The second, a flash bang. And the third, a frag grenade. Only one of them would kill by itself, but they were all useful tools in their own ways.

Removing one of the ball-shaped frag grenades from the case, he unscrewed its cap in order to get at the internal workings of the device.

Liana hovered over his shoulder, probably brimming with more questions that he didn't feel needed explanations. He supposed it was natural that she look to him as a rock to lean on. Unfortunately, the situation was fluid, and he had little to offer in way of assurances. She'd only known him a short while and was unaware of all of the other times that he had been the underdog and had still come out on top, an outcome that he mostly equated to his inability to feel fear. As she hovered beside him, he knew that a question was hanging on her lips. Although he wasn't sure what that question was. Most likely something about the next step in his plan and all of its contingencies.

When she finally opened her mouth, the question she asked surprised him. Ackerman was not easily impressed, but it was only on the rarest of occasion when he felt true bewilderment.

She said, "Who is Itzel? You kept saying that name over and over while you are passed out."

Itzel…a name he hadn't heard aloud for many, many years. The name of his Mayan princess, his rainbow goddess.

He hesitated, unsure of what to say and how much to share. He had never felt the therapeutic results of talking about his problems or the pains of the past. But as he turned and stared down into Liana's large brown eyes, which reminded him so much of those that had belonged to Itzel, he said, "She was a Mayan girl I met along the road to Cancún. She was the love of my life."

66

John Canyon felt the blood pooling in his face as he watched his two climbers being sent back to him. All his muscles were tensed, and his jaw clenched. His head throbbed, and his brain ached. He wanted to break something. He wanted to hurt someone. But the person that he really wanted to hurt—the stranger, the man calling himself Frankenstein—always seemed to remain just out of reach.

The two men he had sent in as a surprise attack from the rear were walking down the long sloping driveway toward him. Not limping. And they still had their pants where they belonged. So, apparently, these two had fared a bit better against Frank and his new acolyte than the original two scouts.

Not wanting to think about it any longer, Canyon put down his binoculars and turned away from the trading post, heading to the rear of the siege camp at the bottom of the bluff. He'd also sent a few men around to the rear, to make sure that their quarry didn't try to escape down the cliff face. He had twenty-four men in all on-site, a good size for a unit. They had positioned their vehicles along the roadway as barricades to make sure that the stranger didn't try to make a run for it. Seeing his men with their rifles aimed up at the trading post or waiting at the ready behind cover made him think about his time in the first Gulf War.

Master Sergeant John Canyon had a lot of good

memories of his brother Marines and the camaraderie, but his thoughts always seemed to turn to the negative side of things, to past mistakes and past sins. He thought of times when command had screwed the pooch and nearly gotten them all killed. Once, they had even sent the wrong uniforms, jungle instead of desert, which resulted in he and his men looking like a bunch of mulberry bushes marching across the sand. Other memories flashed through his mind. He recalled coming across an Iraqi encampment full of corpses sitting around the ashes of their fire, tin coffee cups still in their hands or on the ground nearby, cups identical to the ones he and his men used every morning.

With the enemy he had faced in the Persian Gulf, Canyon had recognized his common humanity. That wasn't the case with Frank. He and the stranger were not of the same species.

Canyon stopped short as he noticed that three men were present who weren't supposed to be. He had instructed his right-hand man, Todd Todacheeney, to take Ramirez and Slim, his original two scouts, back to the ranch for medical attention. As he passed by, he motioned for Toad to join him at the back. Waiting until a few feet separated them from the men, Canyon said, "I thought I told you to get those two idiots out of my sight."

Toad was a barrel chested little man with no neck, dressed in camouflage fatigues and looking the part of a trained operator. Although, Canyon knew that Toad had never actually served a day in the military because of his flat feet and poor test scores. Having known Todacheeney from back in their gangland days, Canyon could spot all of his underlings mannerisms and their meanings, and Toad now displayed his nervous habit of rolling his neck and head back and forth, almost like an owl, when he was avoiding a question.

Toad finally said, "Ramirez refused to go. He's a tough kid. He ended up patching himself up with glue and duct tape. He's looking to prove himself."

"If he wants to prove himself to me, he can start by following orders and completing missions."

"I know, I know. But he can't do either of those things if he's back at the ranch in bed."

Canyon whispered, "I wasn't only sending you back because of them. I was also thinking that you could check in with Yazzie."

"You don't think he has the ranch covered?"

"No, it's not that. It's more that I'm not sure how much I trust our good captain anymore."

Toad's eyes went wide, and he immediately said, "Isn't Yazzie family? He's your brother-in-law."

"You know, Toad, you may be the only person in this world I trust these days. I'm not so sure about my wife or her brother at this point."

"What makes you say this?"

"There are signs, but mostly a feeling. A shift in the winds. Monsters and madmen have their places, old friend. But the thing about working with either of them is that at some point you have to expect the monster to be what it is and the madman to show his true colors."

"And which of these is Yazzie?"

Canyon laughed. "Yazzie?... He's both."

Toad shook his head. "But I've known Xavier for almost as long as you have. I've never seen this from him."

"You haven't known him like I've known him. You haven't seen the things that he's done. The people he's killed. The aftermath of his interrogations. You haven't mopped up the blood. And I'm beginning to wonder if our real enemy is one that has been here all along."

67

Ackerman had never shared Itzel's story with anyone, including his brother and his now-former therapist, Emily Morgan. He wasn't sure why he had chosen to share it with Liana. Perhaps it was a slight resemblance between the two. The dark hair, the big brown eyes, and the same impetuous nature of a free spirit. Ackerman noticed, not for the first time, that both Itzel and Liana were rare and beautiful flowers, ones yet to bloom and reach their full potential. Itzel never had the chance. But he was sure Liana would.

He wondered if a better question was why he had never shared the story of his first love with anyone else. As he thought back on several recent interactions, he realized that he actually had tried sharing her story with his brother and Maggie, but neither seemed interested once he started in on the gory details. But Liana didn't need to know any of that. She didn't need to hear about Itzel's murder or their crime spree together prior to her death. Or his revenge. All she needed to know was the story of their love.

Liana asked, "What happened to her?"

"She was prematurely taken from this world."

"I'm sorry."

"It was a long time ago."

"Itzel is a very beautiful name. Where was she from?"

"She was of Mayan heritage. We met in the Yucatan. That's the culture from which her name originates. It means

'Rainbow Goddess.' The first time I saw her she wore a rainbow-colored dress with little fringy things at the bottom and looked exactly as her name implied. She possessed a radiant beauty that I found utterly captivating. I was only seventeen or eighteen at the time. I spent some time in her village and got to know her and her family. The two of us had an instant connection. She spoke a little English, and I spoke a little more Spanish. But we didn't need words to communicate. There was this strange electricity between us. One where she knew what I was thinking, and I knew what she was thinking. The only thing close to that connection I've experienced over the years is when my brother and I are fighting side-by-side."

"She sounds amazing. I'm sorry you lost her."

"You keep saying that, but there's really nothing for you to be sorry about. Events played out exactly as they were meant to. We can't change the past, and I'm not one to do much contemplation of those circumstances over which I have no control. They are gone from this world, and there's not a single thing I can do to change that.

"They?"

"Yes, I didn't find out until later, after she was gone, but Itzel was pregnant with my child."

Liana's hand covered her mouth, and her eyes grew wide and wet. Realizing that he was also on the verge of tears at the raw memory, he decided it was perhaps time to change the subject. "Well, regardless, it was all a long time ago, in another life. I suppose in many ways it was a very different person from myself who loved and lost the Rainbow Goddess. I do know this. She was the only woman I've ever loved, or at the very least, the only one who's ever loved me back. I'm sorry. I don't know why I'm telling you all this. Sometimes, I have trouble where I think that I'm saying something in my head, but I'm actually saying it out loud. Let's move on with the—"

Liana surprised him again by reaching out and encircling her small arms around his waist. She laid her head upon his chest and squeezed him tightly. At first, he had no idea how to react. His arms hung in the air like a strange marionette whose master was either drunk or distracted. But then, he wrapped his own arms around her and returned the embrace. After a few seconds, they parted, and he asked, "What was that for?"

"It was a hug. Something we humans do from time to time when we're showing positive emotion toward one another."

"Funny you say that because it was my relationship with Itzel that taught me I would never be one of you. I would never be normal. No matter how hard I tried. No matter how bad I wanted to pretend I was. There's no escaping yourself. No matter where you go; there you are."

She asked, "How do you define what's normal?"

He smiled. "You would've liked Itzel. She was a lot like you. Both free spirits. And 'normal' depends on your perspective. As do a great many other elements of reality. But I think we can both safely agree that no one would ever consider me to be normal."

"There's nothing wrong with being extraordinary."

"And there's also nothing 'wrong' with being ordinary." Then, with a little wink, as he zipped up his backpack full of grenades, he added, "Maybe it's better that Itzel wasn't long in this world. She was certainly extraordinary, but she was also even crazier than me."

68

25 years earlier…

Xavier remembered feeling that it was unnaturally hot in the area surrounding the temple. The canopy above shaded them from the sun, but warm winds must have found a path through the canyon below and bombarded the spot with heat.

One of the only happy memories he had from his childhood was one summer when Momma and Uncle Red had taken him and Reyna to the beach at Lea Lake near Roswell, New Mexico. The lake was part of the bottomless Lake State Park, which took its name from nine deep cenotes formed from collapsed limestone caves. The day they had chosen to visit Lea Lake happened to be the same day that a local festival was taking place. He remembered the carnival games, cotton candy, and jugglers. But what he remembered the most, and what had fascinated him at the time, was the artist who had created an intricate sandcastle out on Lea Lake's shore. He had been fascinated by the details, the small windows, the amazing way that the sand packed together.

As he had stared up at the temple on that day, Xavier was reminded of the sandcastle. He had seen many ruins of the Old Ones. The cities looked like a giant had carved them into the sand. But this place was different. The structures here were larger and seemed to be made more for some type of congregation or meeting. He could tell that this was a revered and public space.

A part of Xavier hated to desecrate the memory of the ancient people, but a will to survive and greed far overpowered any sense of sentimentality he had for the long-lost people of the high places.

Rubbing his hands together and giving a wink to Reyna, he said, "Let's get started. This tomb ain't gonna raid itself."

As they went to work, the others seemed quiet and apprehensive. Even Xavier had to admit that there was some kind of oppressive feeling just from being in the place, like the weight of the ages had increased the gravity within the temple. It was as if the air had changed. It was hot, but it was also somehow dead. The inner temple, which was farther back in the rock inside a natural cavern, was basically five rooms set up like the spokes of a wheel. In the center, there was a large open space. The walls were covered from the floor all the way around the domed ceiling of the round center room with strange symbols and pictographs. They were reminiscent of others he had seen at Anasazi archaeological sites, but they were also somehow different. These were darker. More frightening and violent. The center room was empty of everything but symbols, but the offshoots contained a treasure trove of artifacts.

Eugene, swallowing hard, his massive Adam's apple moving up and down like the arm of an oil derrick, said, "I don't like this place. There's something wrong about it."

Reyna quickly added, "Let's just forget this. If we tell some of the dirt diggers about this place, we might even get a reward. It's going to be getting dark soon. We should get back."

But Xavier wasn't about to be deterred from reaping his rewards by old ghosts, real or imagined. He softly said, "Nobody leaves here until the job is done." Then he directed each of them to an area where they could wrap up and pack away various artifacts. He had already researched the most valuable pieces to grab.

Before any of the pillaging began, however, Xavier removed a disposable camera that he had purchased from a local drugstore. He at least wanted to document his discovery. He told the others to get to work and then went from room to room snapping pictures until the small camera was filled up. Then he had set to work himself on loading his pack down with artifacts from the past that would provide a future for him and his sister.

They had been working for some time and were nearly ready to go, having gathered everything in the center room, when Xavier first heard the cracking sound. He locked eyes with Eugene, who was standing a few feet away, and knew they were thinking the same thing. Then the floor fell out from beneath them.

69

Sound traveled strangely in the desert, and so Canyon suggested that they continue the conversation at Toad's home. Canyon wouldn't have entertained the idea of leaving a hostage situation where the hostage was his own son under other circumstances, but considering that Toad's house was parked less than twenty feet away, along the side of the road, he agreed to have a drink with his old friend in order to calm his nerves.

Now, sitting on the small couch inside Todd Todacheeney's motorhome, John Canyon sipped his whiskey and laid out his story. Toad had come to work for him after Canyon had returned from the Persian Gulf, during the time when he organized the various gang factions in northern New Mexico into a cohesive unit under his control. But he had known Xavier Yazzie for much longer than that. And when he had come back and saw that a brutal display of strength would allow them to take power, he had called up the most brutal person he knew: Xavier Yazzie.

Not sure of where to begin, Canyon took a sip of the dark liquid and ran a hand over his now graying hair as he leaned back and said the first thing that came to mind. "Did I ever tell you how I met Reyna?"

Toad shook his head, leaning forward in his barcalounger and gripping his glass with both hands.

"Xavier was actually the one who introduced us. He

caught me looking at her and made the comment that if I would like a date with her, he could arrange it. I told him that she could speak for herself and I could get my own dates. He shrugged it off, but I got to thinking about it later, and I guess my attraction to Reyna won out over my aversion to her brother. I had him set me up with her. A year later, we were married. I never really thought much about all that at the time, until I heard about the way they had grown up. Reyna didn't talk about it much, but I'd heard it from others. Then I started to wonder, on that night when he offered to set me up with his sister, was he meaning that he could set me up on a date like a friend, or was he saying that he would give me a free night with her if I wanted?"

Toad didn't comment. The thick man merely nodded and sipped from his glass.

Canyon continued, "After we were married, I always made sure that I had a place in my operation for my brother-in-law. And he was an expert at certain kinds of work. When I ordered Yazzie to eliminate out rival gang leaders, he would usually take them out into the desert to dispose of the bodies. I don't know what he did to them out there, but what was left of them looked like they had been eaten by animals. The few that were discovered were found naked and staked to the ground with their limps splayed out in an X."

At the description of the way the bodies were found, Toad's brow furrowed, and he said, "That sounds just like something I saw on—"

"Right, all the belagana prostitutes who have been getting snatched and murdered around the border towns. The work of a serial killer who has been operating for years, killing in every major town from Cortez all the way down to Flagstaff. They've only recently starting connecting the cases with the use of some new database. "

"And you think Yazzie is the one doing all that?"

"I don't know what to think. Not completely. But a few months ago, I found that there was money missing at the casino from a lockbox that only a few people have access to. One of those people is my wife."

"And Yazzie?" Toad asked.

"No, Reyna seemed to be the only real possibility. I confronted her about it. I thought she was using again. She swore to me that she wasn't. And she got so angry at the accusation that she moved out of the ranch and has been staying in the penthouse ever since."

"But you think that she stole the money?"

"I think that Yazzie made her steal it for some reason. I've suspected for a while that there's been another man in her life, but every time that I think I'm going to catch her with a lover, she's with her brother."

Toad's eyes went so wide now that they were almost comical, and although Todacheeney hadn't earned his nickname because of his physical features, Canyon couldn't help but think that he now had the look of an amphibian. Toad said, "You think that… Your wife, Reyna… And her brother, Xavier… Are what? Stirring the Kool-Aid, so to speak?"

"If I knew anything for sure, I'd have already done something about it Toad. I only have a lot of suspicions and questions. But I know that Yazzie is up to something, and I don't trust him because I know what he is. He's a monster. He has no loyalty because he has no love for anything but himself. He is an expert manipulator, and he always plays the long game. He's a dangerous man, and I think I failed to notice just how dangerous until now."

Toad leaned back in his chair and stared off into space. He said, "That's unbelievable. I can't imagine that Reyna would allow that to go on for all these years. She always seemed like such a strong woman."

"You never know what kind of battles are being fought inside someone else's head. This could've been something that's happened since they were kids. I always got a weird vibe when they were together, like they were a little too close for brother and sister. But how do you tell your wife that she and her brother love each other too much?"

"Why are you telling me this now?" Toad asked.

Canyon answered the question with another. "Did you know that Yazzie is also the Director of Security at the casino?

Toad shook his head. "No, I thought that Begay girl was in charge."

"Ramona Begay is the Chief Security Officer, but Yazzie made me put him as an executive director. He explained that it would help in the long run if any of our illegal dealings were uncovered, and would help in the short term for him to do his job as a cop. I didn't think much about it at the time, but a man in his position could have been skimming a lot of money over the years, and he also would've had the access to have taken the missing agent right out of her room without anyone ever knowing."

"But why would he want to kill an agent and bring the heat down on us?"

"I don't know that either. I've known since we built the casino that he had some ulterior motive going. The south tower was constructed under his direct supervision, but he didn't really care about any of the rest of the hotel or casino. I thought that perhaps he was going to try and start up a brothel out of there, like he did when we were kids. Then I thought maybe he was selling drugs."

"So what was he doing?"

"I'm not sure."

Toad took a deep breath and sighed. He said, "No offense, boss, but it doesn't sound like you know a whole hell of a lot. If you would have come to me sooner, maybe I could have—"

"I'm telling you this, because I don't want any more surprises from my manipulative psychopath of a brother-in-law. I want you to get back to the ranch and keep an eye on him. Stick to him like glue throughout the rest of this ordeal. That clear enough."

Toad nodded as he dropped his empty glass onto a counter of the claustrophobic motorhome and shot to his feet. "You don't have to worry about a thing, boss. I'm on it."

Canyon smiled as he stood and headed for the door, but he wasn't able to reach it before it flew open and Ramirez poked his head in to say, "Sir, you need to see this."

As they headed outside, he expected some surprise coming from the trading post, but Ramirez gestured in the opposite direction where a single red streak divided the pre-dawn sky. A flare. A message of some sort, and it either had to be the boys from the cartel announcing their arrival, or it was Frank's partner. Turning to Todacheeney, Canyon asked, "How long has it been since we've heard from Yazzie at the ranch?"

"Too long," was Toad's reply, "I'll try to raise them."

To Ramirez, Canyon said, "Radio our friends from south of the border. Find out if they sent up that flare. If not, have them go check it out on their way in."

"How do I reach them?" Ramirez asked.

"Find Ahiga. He has the frequency."

Before Ramirez could walk away, Canyon grabbed him by the shoulder and whispered, "I'm only asking you to do this because you were standing the closest. You fail me again, and no amount of glue and duct tape will be able to put you back together. Do you understand me, boy?"

"Yes, sir."

"Good. Then make sure your bootstraps are tied up tight and let the rest of the boys know as well. War isn't coming. It's here."

70

After discharging the flare gun into the air three times, for good measure, Marcus climbed back into Yazzie's Ford Explorer and dropped the keys on the console beside the police captain. Picking them up and restarting the vehicle, Yazzie asked, "You couldn't think of a better way to talk to your brother and tell him you're coming? Canyon and all of his men will have seen that too."

"It won't matter whether they know we're coming or not. Whether there's twenty of them or a hundred. My brother and I are like the biblical plagues. We're cursed. And now so are all of you."

He sat back against the leather seat and laid the MP5 across his lap.

Yazzie asked, "What now?"

"We wait."

"Wait for what?"

"We wait quietly."

Looking to where the sunrise was just beginning to show over the distant red rock mountains, Marcus was briefly in awe of the colors, of the beauty, of all the swirling molecules combining into a tapestry elegantly stroked by the Creator's brush. He wished he had spent more time doing things like this with Maggie, just experiencing life and seeing the world in all of its wonder. Thinking of Maggie brought back the emptiness, but there was another part of him, the stronger part, that was too stubborn to accept defeat. He knew that he would never give up hope until he had seen her body. Even if there was a one-in-a-million chance of her still being out there somewhere alive, he would never stop searching. He would never give up hope, he would never stop...

And suddenly, he realized how blind he had been. The way he was feeling now, the sense of urgent panic and crushing loss, was the way Maggie had felt her whole life. How horrible it must have been for her, wondering if her brother was out there living a life of pain. Maggie was even more stubborn than he was, which meant that, just like he would never stop searching for her, she would have never stopped fighting to locate her brother and the people who took him. He should've recognized the depth of her desire before now. He should've supported her sooner. Unfortunately, he had always been too wrapped up with his own problems, his own struggles and demons.

He was almost glad for the distraction when Yazzie said, "We have company."

Looking over his shoulder, Marcus saw that the captain was right. There was a set of headlights headed their direction, and they appeared to be attached to a rather large vehicle—a semi-truck, dump truck, farm implement, or the like.

Marcus said, "Start it up and whip around to face them. Put the engine block between us and—"

"I know how to set up cover, kid," Yazzie said as he twisted the wheel and pressed the accelerator, filling the desert air with dust and gravel.

71

Ackerman stared down the scope of the .50 caliber rifle and wondered how fast he could blow apart the brain cases of each man he sighted in on. He watched Canyon and the squat man who seemed to be his second enter an old Ford motorhome that they had parked along the back of their perimeter. He supposed that some forward-thinking member of their group realized that during an extended siege, they may need restroom facilities.

The implication of that to Ackerman was that Canyon had never really taken his threats seriously. He had given an ultimatum and a deadline. He wasn't used to being ignored, and there was something about the affront that made his hackles rise and the wolf inside want to rip out of his flesh and take control.

How easy it would be to adjust his aim from one target to the next. Squeeze. Splatter. Readjust. He could certainly have some fun imagining which series of timings would provide the best outcome in terms of how many of Canyon's men he could kill before they were able to reach cover. Canyon was smart enough to realize the kind of devastation that he could rain down on them from this position. Maybe all of his men were blissfully unaware. But Canyon knew.

It seemed that without the fear of death, people just didn't want to listen.

Over his shoulder, Thomas White whispered, "Just do it. Pull the trigger. Those men would kill you in a second if they had the opportunity. And they're all probably going to get the chance here shortly. Why not even things up a bit? At least put a little fear into them."

Trying to ignore his father's voice in his head, Ackerman turned to Liana, who hadn't strayed more than three or four feet away from him since the last attack, and said, "Seven. In case you were also wondering."

She cocked her head in confusion and asked, "Wondering what?"

"Oh, I thought perhaps you were also wondering how many of them we could kill with the .50 cal before they could reach cover."

"No, I wasn't wondering that at all. And it looks to me like most of them are behind cover right now."

He laughed. "You're adorable. So tell me about Liana. And don't worry, you can share anything with me. Your darkest secret. Your deepest desire. Innermost fantasies. I promise not to judge, and you'll find that I'm a student of people, a sort of cultural anthropologist."

Liana still had that perplexed look on her face, but people always seemed to stare at him like that. She finally said, "I'm not sure that this is the best time to play get to know you."

"That's the funny thing about time, Officer Liana. Time is always moving forward, unrelenting in its efficiency and its dedication to destruction. So, for all of us who are bound by the laws of space and time, there truly can be no other moment but right now. We, of course, should learn from the past and plan for the future, but we must strive always to live in the present. Because right now and right here may be the only time we have left."

Liana replied, "That's easier said than done. When your present circumstance sucks, it's a lot easier to look toward the hope of the future."

"Sounds like you just need to learn to make the best of your present circumstances. Trust me, there's nothing you've ever been through, nothing you've ever seen or done or experienced or feared or felt, that I haven't also went through and overcame." He noticed her look down at his scars, that were now covered with a long-sleeved black shirt, but he sensed she could still picture his disfigurements plainly. She said nothing.

Repeating his inquiry, he said, "So tell me about yourself. There's nothing better we can do at this moment."

"There's really not much to tell. I grew up down in the southern part of the Rez. I got out, went to one of your people's schools out east. Ended up coming back to take care of my grandmother when she got sick, took this job to pay the bills. There's not much to me."

Now, it was his turn to look at her in confusion. With a little shake of his head, he said, "You just listed a series of things that you've done or that have happened to you. While I can certainly make some judgments based upon this information, it doesn't really tell me about you."

"You're going to have to be more specific."

Ackerman asked, "What do you love?"

"That's also a pretty vague question," she said with a little laugh and a diversion of her eyes. "Are you asking if I'm seeing anyone?"

Again, she had confounded him. That wasn't at all what

he was asking. He wondered why she would make such a leap in logic. He replied, "No I was merely—"

His sentence was cut short by a red light that suddenly appeared in the sky beyond their enemies' place of encampment. It was father down the road, heading toward the town of Roanhorse. Perhaps a mile or two away. Ackerman, of course, recognized it instantly as Marcus's signal on what to do for the next phase of their plan.

He and his brother had planned for a few different outcomes of the recon of the ranch and had established a different signal for each. The red flare was not the one Ackerman had wanted to see.

Beside him, also noticing the signal against the predawn sky, Liana asked, "Is that your partner? You said he would send us different signals. What does this one mean?"

Pulling away from the rifle, Ackerman found a place against a wall and allowed himself to slide down it to the plank flooring. As he did so, he absently replied, "That's the signal that Maggie's dead, and now we're going to kill them all."

72

Three days ago…

The name-tag on the young woman's shirt read, Officer Nakai. She opened the door for Maggie and said, "He's on the phone, but he'll be done in a second."

Maggie stepped into the small office at the back of the remote police outpost. The floor creaked beneath her feet, and the walls appeared paper-thin. Maggie took a seat in an old but sturdy-looking metal chair in front of the captain's desk. His back was turned to her, a Stetson cowboy hat hung on a hook behind him. All she could see was his long black and gray hair pulled into a ponytail. He was speaking on the phone to someone who seemed to be a city alderman or tribal leader. Without turning around, he held up a finger to tell her it would be just one moment.

Her plan was to slow-play Canyon into a trap, but she needed to know whether the local law enforcement had been paid off or whether she could rely on them as allies. So, her first step was to introduce herself to the highest-ranking local law enforcement officer and see if he could be trusted.

Maggie was glad for the moment to survey Yazzie's desk and the small room which he called home. The walls were mostly bare, a few pictures, a few rusty old handguns mounted to the wall. Besides the photos, there were a few

American Indian artifacts and feathers. Then, among the plumage, Maggie spotted a photo that caused her to take note. It was of a young man dressed in an outfit very similar to the one worn by "X" from her mystery picture.

As her mind raced through the possibilities, she scanned the rest of the wall and noted younger photos of the woman Vasques had told her was Reyna Canyon, another of those displayed in her mystery photo.

And then, she saw a photo tucked in among the others that stopped her racing heart dead. It was a photo of a young man looking directly into the camera, a scowl on his face, and Maggie instantly knew she was no longer here investigating John Canyon.

The man with the black eyes, the real Taker, was right before her.

She was in the lion's den, the belly of the beast. She considered going for her gun right there, but a feeling from a picture seen across the room and a memory that was a quarter of a century old wasn't enough to condemn a man, and definitely not something that Maggie could explain to a "righteous shooting" board of inquiry.

She couldn't be sure at all, but somehow, she knew. She considered the X on the photograph. Could that have been some nickname that Reyna had for her brother, or was that perhaps his first initial?

She scanned the desk, but all the name placard said was "Captain Yazzie." She tried to scan the rest of the room, looking for anything that might have his name, but there were no diplomas, no awards.

She was interrupted by Yazzie hanging up the phone and standing to shake her hand. The captain wore small oval glasses that were heavily tinted and completely hid his eyes. She knew there was no medical condition that would cause a person to have jet black eyes, but the little girl in her wondered if beneath Yazzie's glasses were a pair of black orbs that provided a view straight into the darkness of hell.

Yazzie said, "So, Agent, to what do I owe the pleasure of a visit from the Department of Justice. I don't believe I've ever met one of you before. Sounds very official."

Some part of Maggie that wasn't scared out of her mind stood up, smiled, shook Yazzie's hand, and said, "Actually, the Department of Justice encompasses several different agencies. I work for a think-tank known as the Shepherd Organization."

Yazzie smiled and said, "That's funny. We have one of the biggest sheep operations in the Southwest right here in our little town of Roanhorse."

Maggie sat back down in her chair as Yazzie took his own. She tried to remember the story she had carefully composed when she planned to meet with the local police captain. The lies wouldn't come to her. Her brain was completely blank, and all of her work on her cover story and her plan to manipulate the locals had been erased by fear.

She smiled and laughed nervously. "I just wanted to stop in for a moment. I don't want to take up much of your time."

She noticed that Yazzie still seemed to be sitting up and poised for movement. He said, "It's no bother. What are you investigating?"

Fighting for a response, she said, "I'm not at liberty to discuss those details, but I'll tell you this. It's mainly down at the casino and so…it might involve employees who live in your district. I just wanted to give you the courtesy heads-up and introduce myself in case something pops up."

She supposed that, all things considered, she had handled the improvisational cover story pretty well. All she needed to do was get the heck out of there and make a phone call that would reveal to the world the true identity of her lifelong tormentor.

Yazzie cocked his head in surprise and said, "Really? I hadn't heard anything about any investigations at the casino. Have you spoken to all of the proper security personnel there?"

"No, it's hush-hush, and I would appreciate it if you didn't mention this to anyone. I'm only trusting you because you're a fellow law enforcement officer. I don't put much stock in private security people."

"I know the folks over there well. They're quite good at their jobs. I'd be happy to put you in contact."

She smiled in response and stood. "I appreciate that, but it won't be necessary. I'm hoping to be out of here soon anyway. I really don't expect the need to involve them. If things pan out, I'll be back to have a discussion with you about the resident in question, but at this point, only a courtesy call. So, I'll just let myself out."

She moved toward the door to his paper-thin office, and she felt him stand and step up behind her.

He said, "Whoa, little lady. I'm happy to give you insight and assistance. Why don't you share the details of your investigation, and we can go from there?"

She replied, "I'm sorry, but I can't discuss the details of an active investigation with non-Department of Justice personnel. I'll be in contact soon. Thank you so much for your hospitality, Captain."

"The pleasure was all mine, and…I'm sorry, I didn't get your name."

She nodded and said, "Thanks again. It's Agent Carlisle."

"I meant first name. Mine is Xavier. I've never really liked it. A lot of people don't know how to pronounce it."

Her terrified mind searched frantically for a response, but all she could manage was the truth. "Maggie," she said. "My first name is Maggie."

She could smell gun oil and chewing tobacco on him as he winked and said, "I once knew a little girl named Maggie." Her heart caught in her throat, and she considered whether she could actually vomit on him as a distraction for escape. She said, "Nice to meet you, Xavier. Now, if you would excuse me, I'm not feeling so well, and I'm dead tired. I'd like to get back to my hotel room."

"By all means. I'm here when you need me."

Maggie nodded to the young female officer on her way out. Nakai asked, "Are you okay, ma'am?"

Maggie mumbled, "Yes, thank you," as she stepped from the tiny Navajo Nation Police outpost.

Her rental car was only ten feet away, but it seemed like a distance of miles. She fumbled with her keys as she walked toward the door. She pressed the button and dropped into the car, shutting it and locking the doors.

Her heart hammered. She couldn't breathe. Xavier. He was the "X" from the photograph. He was the variable she had been searching for. Captain Xavier Yazzie of the Navajo Nation Police was the real Taker.

As she recalled the recent encounter, other memories that

were once blurry now came into focus. She remembered seeing him at the pow-wow her family had visited, and she more vividly remembered that day and the face of the man with the black eyes.

She started the car. As she did, she pulled out her burner phone and started to call Marcus, ready to burst with the information that she had just learned and afraid that her boogeyman would be coming for her. She kept her eyes on the door to the station, but no one came out. No one perused her. Her hand reached toward the gear shift to put the car into reverse, when a knock on her window startled the phone right out of her hand.

She turned to see the smiling face of Captain Xavier Yazzie.

Her terrified mind searched for the answer of how he had gotten out of the station without her noticing. There had to have been a back door, but she hadn't seen one. She reached out for the switch to roll down the window—as he was motioning for her to do on the other side of the glass—but her right hand strayed toward her gun. If he made any move, she was prepared to pull the weapon and fire.

Her teeth almost chattering, she awkwardly asked, "Did I forget something?"

Yazzie laughed. "No, no. I don't think you've forgotten a thing. And neither have I."

Then, with a blur of movement, she saw a tubular object appear in his hand and felt the wet spray in her face and eyes.

Her training kicking in, Maggie instantly punched out and connected with Yazzie's chest, pushing him back from the window. She couldn't see anything. The world was going dark. She went for her gun. She wondered what he had sprayed her with. She had been sprayed with pepper and mace in the past, but this was something different. She pulled the gun from her holster but didn't have the strength to hold it. Just before the darkness took her, she recognized the sweet smell as sevoflurane—a potent anesthetic that Ackerman had once introduced to her.

PART 4

73

Although Liana had only known Frank for a matter of hours, she felt strangely at home by his side. During their time together, Frank had been shot at, cut, burned, and nearly bled to death. Through it all, Liana never witnessed him show even a hint of concern. But now, as he sat on the plank flooring, slumped against a wall, he looked deeply troubled. The thought of something that could bother Frank even a little filled her with panic.

Liana knelt down in front of him and asked, "What does that signal really mean?"

He looked up at her, and she saw that his cheeks were soaked with tears. "It means that my little sister is dead. And John Canyon is the man behind it. It means that Marcus and I will now initiate Plan C."

"What's Plan C?"

"The whole point of this standoff was to distract Canyon while my brother searched the ranch and wherever else he needed to. My job here was to keep all the little bees busy while Marcus snuck into the hive to see if they had stolen our queen."

Liana wondered why Frank always seemed to talk in riddles and analogies, and she wasn't sure what it said about her that she was starting to understand them.

He continued, "The red flare indicates that my brother

either found her body for some other evidence that tells him that Canyon is responsible for her disappearance."

"I'm sorry about your friend."

"So am I."

"What now?"

Frank said, "As I already indicated, we move forward with Plan C."

"But what is Plan C?"

"The one that comes after Plan B."

She growled in frustration and said, "Can you give me the details?"

"I'll get close to Canyon and his men using one of the hostages. While I will distract them with a little talk, my brother will attack from the other side."

"Won't they be expecting that with the flare going up?"

Ackerman smiled. "Don't worry. My brother and I are pretty good in a fight, and although every situation is fluid, we have several tricks up our sleeves."

"What about me? What do I do?"

"You lay low and hope that my brother and I don't get ourselves killed. If we do, you'll have the other four hostages for leverage, but after I take Tobias out with me, I'm not sure how much leverage they'll be."

"I'm not going to do nothing while the two of you take on a whole platoon. What about the .50 cal rifle? How much ammo do we have for that?"

Frank shook his head. "I won't allow it."

"I can make my own decisions, thank you."

Looking deep into her eyes, his still glistening with the tears of a lost loved one, he asked, "Have you ever killed anyone, Liana?"

"No, I haven't."

"How many times have you drawn your weapon?"

"Only a few. But I think I've proven that I can handle myself tonight."

"It's not about handling yourself. I'm telling you this to protect you. If you've never taken a life, there's no reason to start now."

"What about you? I don't think they're going to roll over and play dead for you."

"I'm going to do what I have to do because my brother will also be down there and the same men that will be shooting at me will also be shooting at him. I'll do my best only to maim them, but I have a feeling that there may be some casualties this evening. However, that's beside the point. This isn't my first rodeo. With the number of people that I've killed, a couple more ghosts on my conscience isn't going to make a difference one way or another. But it would start you on a road that you don't want to go down."

"Those men out there are killers, every one of them. Some of them might be young, but trust me, I've seen the things that those boys will do to women. I've seen the hatred in their eyes. Right now, they're camped out there with illegal weapons threatening to kill an officer of the law and federal agents, and as far as I'm concerned, that justifies anything that we have to do in order to protect ourselves and any innocents that might get in the way."

"Have you seen what a .50 BMG caliber bullet will do to a human being, Liana? It shreds them. It doesn't put a hole in them; it blows them apart. As if you walked up and stuffed a grenade down someone's throat. And don't be so quick to dismiss those boys out there. There is no one, and

I mean no one, who is beyond redemption. By taking their lives, we are interfering with a beautiful story that has yet to be told."

Standing firm, she said, "I know what I'm doing. I don't want to take a life or hurt anyone, but I also won't stand by and let men like John Canyon take away the things I care about and believe in. I'm going to fight, whether you like it or not, so you might as well tell me how I can help. As far as I'm concerned, by going up against the law in the first place and threatening our lives, every one of those men out there is trying to commit suicide by cop."

He laughed. "I'm the furthest thing from a cop, but Suicide by Ackerman does have a certain ring to it."

Liana's eyes went wide as her brain caught on that name. Ackerman. The name of one of the most notorious murderers in American history. She looked down where his scars were now covered, and everything made sense. There was a sort of awe in her voice when she proclaimed, "You're Francis Ackerman Jr."

With a wink, he said, "Pleasure to meet you, Officer Liana Nakai. But don't go spreading that around, it's classified information. And this only serves to reiterate my point. Remember, when you're sighting in with that life-ending rifle, that there was no one in history whoever deserved redemption less than me. Yet, here I stand."

74

After fitting Liana with a radio earpiece and giving her a crash course on the 50 BMG caliber rifle, Ackerman picked up a grenade from the table and walked over to Tobias Canyon, who was tied and gagged in the corner of the room.

With duct tape in one hand and a frag grenade in the other, Ackerman smiled down at the wide-eyed Canyon youth and said, "I like to call this game: Kissing the Pineapple. Because typically frag grenades have a sort of bumpy pineapple shape. You have to use your imagination in this case, since these fragmentation grenades are actually round, but I still like the imagery. Anyway, pucker up."

After he had finished taping the grenade to Tobias Canyon's face, with the pin and trigger release still accessible, he proceeded to cut the fishing line from Tobias's hands, feet, and chest. He then rewrapped the young man's hands and attached another grenade to the back of Tobias's belt.

With his preparations complete, Ackerman shoved Tobias toward the door and said, "It's time to take the long walk, kid."

Liana stood by the door leading onto the covered porch and front steps of the trading post. The sight of her waiting there like an expectant wife ready to hand him his thermos and give him a kiss on the cheek before he headed off to work made Ackerman's heart flutter in a strange way that he had seldom felt. He gave her a genuine smile and asked, "Do I get a kiss goodbye?"

She replied, "I wish I had never met you."

"Well, that's not a very nice thing to say. Especially to someone marching off into the lion's den."

"Let me finish. My life was a hell of a lot simpler before you barged into it, but that doesn't mean that I want to see you get killed now. Why don't you put on some of this body armor and take one of the Berettas?"

"I have my push daggers. And I've never been one to use body armor, it's restrictive, and it always felt like cheating."

"I thought you were in favor of cheating."

"I'm in favor of winning when it comes to life and death circumstances because winning equates to surviving. But I also love a challenge, and bad things seem to happen when I use guns."

"Then put on one of the vests."

Beneath his frag grenade gag, Tobias Canyon mumbled something. Ackerman replied, "You don't need a vest. No one's going to shoot you. And I prefer freedom of movement over extra armor."

"I'm not letting you out this door without you putting on a vest and strapping on one of these Berettas."

He found the look on her face quite adorable. She reminded him of a little girl ordering a parent to put on a coat for risk catching cold. With a roll of his eyes, he said, "Fine, I'll wear the vest and take the gun."

She seemed surprised. "Really?"

"Yes, I'm not sure how you intend to stop me from going if I don't adhere to your demands, but considering the time it takes to argue and our escalated timetable, it's easier to merely acquiesce."

Liana didn't say anything more, but she had a little grin on her face as she strapped on his body armor and stuck one of the procured 9mm Berettas in the back of his waistband. Just before he stepped through the doorway, he turned back to her, winked, and said, "Don't worry, darling. This is what I do." Then he shoved Tobias Canyon down the front steps of the old trading post and began the long walk toward the awaiting army of enemies.

75

A small dagger of pain stabbed his side with every step. He suspected that there was an infection brewing, as happens sometimes when cauterizing wounds. But that was something to worry about hours from now. There were plenty of things that could be killing him within the next few seconds that were of more pressing concern.

Ackerman had made it halfway down the lane without any interruptions, and he had to admit that he welcomed the quiet respite. Nothing but the rain smells of creosote and sage and the fragrance of fear from his captive. Sometimes, he could only handle so much of the normals chattering before he needed to retreat to solitude. Luckily, his only companion on this walk was gagged with a fragmentation grenade.

But then, the beautiful silence was broken by his father's voice and the apparition of the man appearing beside him saying, "You know I've been thinking…"

Ackerman tried not to show any reaction.

Thomas White continued, "As I'm evaluating your options here, tallying up all the variables so to speak, I've come to the conclusion that we will be seventy-three percent more likely to survive if you allow me to take control."

Rolling his eyes, Ackerman replied, "But did you know that sixty-three percent of all statistics are just made up on the spot?"

In his ear, a voice said, "What was that?" But it wasn't the voice of his father. It was Officer Liana Nakai.

Ackerman replied, "Sorry about that. I forgot that I had this communicator in my ear. But since I have your attention now, I'll take a sit-rep."

Over the small wireless receiver and transmitter in his ear, Liana said, "They're hunkering down like a nest of rattlesnakes. I don't see any sign of your brother, but they have a few new barricades and men facing that direction, away from us."

"Good. All to be expected."

"Frank, can I ask you a kind of personal question?"

With a cock of his eyebrow, he said, "You can ask me anything, but I'm afraid that I might not have ample time to reply."

He kept moving, pushing the Canyon boy along in front of him, while keeping his ring finger in the pin of the grenade attached to the young man's mouth. If any of Canyon's lackeys had any inkling to take a shot, they would quickly change their minds when they saw that any attempt to take him down would result in the detonation of young Tobias's head. What they may or may not have seen was that there was another grenade taped to Tobias's back, and Ackerman was ready to pull that pin at any point as well.

After a few seconds, Liana said, "Earlier when you saw that red flare go up, there was a sadness that came over you. I understand that you're worried that you may have lost your friend. But there was something else. An expression that seemed so alien on you. It looked like you were... afraid."

"I'm afraid that you must have misinterpreted my reaction. I'm neurologically incapable of fear."

"Everyone is afraid of something. Maybe you just haven't found out what scares you yet. But I definitely saw fear on your face when that flare went up."

Ackerman hadn't taken the time to fully consider his feelings on the matter, but he supposed that Liana was right. He had experienced some strange fleeting moment of what normals called fear. He replied, "Because of the damage to my brain, I'm incapable of fear in the way that you are, and I'm also addicted to pain, which is actually pleasurable for me. I'm also not afraid to die. I'm not afraid to be paralyzed or go blind or suffer any kind of indignity or torture. But what does scare me is going back to the way that I was. Losing control and returning to my old self. The dark wind that occupied my years of bloodlust. The scary part is that right now I'm stepping into a situation where I may be forced to kill again. And during the dark years, I wasn't only addicted to pain. I was addicted to death. I suppose I'm just looking down this long dirt lane at all of these potential victims and wondering, like an alcoholic stepping into the bar and trying to have just one drink, if I wouldn't be better off allowing them to kill me."

"Don't say that."

"Because if I ever returned to the way that I was. The world would be much better off if I was dead."

She asked, "So what changed you? How did you go from being addicted to death to a protector of life?"

He had never thought of himself as a protector. Marcus was a protector. He was always more of a destroyer.

"In a way, I suppose it was meeting my brother. From the

moment I first laid eyes on him, I knew there was something different, a connection that I had with him that I have with no one else. At first, I didn't know what to think of it. Later, I realized that it was my brother's resemblance to our father which caused me to latch hold of him. Even before I knew that we were siblings. But deeper than that, I guess what changed me was the epiphany that everything happens for a reason. There is a grand design to the universe, and we're all part of that design. Every pain I suffered, every life I've taken, every drop of blood I've extracted or shed, it was all for a reason. It was all leading me along the path to this moment and every moment after. Sometimes, you can't see the hand of God until you look back on events from down the road. Weeks or months or even years later. When I met my brother, I looked back at my life, and I saw beautiful narrative. I saw my path not heading toward destruction and oblivion, but toward redemption."

Liana said, "Has that changed for some reason? Do you ever want to follow that path of oblivion again?"

"No."

"Then why are you worried about going back to the person that you were? It seems to me that this epiphany you've had isn't something you can forget and just go back to who you were before you had it. It's changed you, and you can no more go back to your old self than the coyote can catch the moon."

Her words lifted a weight from his chest and filled him with warmth. With their adversaries growing closer, he only had time for one more exchange, and so Ackerman asked, "If we make it out of this alive...would it be improper of me to ask you for a kiss?"

The reply that came a few seconds later made his heart flutter in some strange and uncomfortable way.

Liana said, "No...I'd like that."

76

As Ackerman approached, he was pleased to see that John Canyon was waiting to meet him in front of the barricades, acting as the tip of the spear. They had placed two massive pickup trucks with their beds angled toward the trading post. The resulting V formation reminded Ackerman of the paddles in a pinball machine. He had never been allowed to play games such as that when he was a boy, and when he was a man, he had much better things to play with. Still, he was familiar with the concept and design.

Between the two trucks, they had backed up a panel van, the type that normally carried the name of someone's plumbing business stenciled on its side. The rear doors of the van were open to two men with AK-47s trained on Ackerman. From various points, all along the barricade, there were other guns of other calibers pointed in his direction. A lot of fingers on a lot of triggers, but he wasn't worried, and not only because he was incapable. Behind each of the angled pickup trucks were additional vehicles and additional men. Then, far back to the left, away from the action, was the motorhome that Ackerman presumed to be their command post and outhouse.

It was a good little roadblock. It would've been difficult to ram a vehicle through it and escape.

He was pleased to see that Canyon had positioned his resources in much the same way that Ackerman had imagined he would. Although he had never played Battleship as a child, at the moment, he felt a bit like he had just won a giant iteration of the popular board game.

Stopping ten feet short of the barricade, Ackerman waited his finger held tight against the ring attached to the safety pan attached to the release mechanism of the grenade, which was then attached to Tobias Canyon's face. To the young man's father, he said, "I know that you were wanting to see your boy, and my associate informed me that you had wished to come up to the trading post and speak face-to-face. But I figured what kind of a host would I be if I didn't come out to meet and greet all of you myself."

Stepping forward, the elder Canyon said, "Cut the crap. Let's talk deal. I want my son back, and I want my truck back. And I'm sure that you and your little girlfriend would like to walk out of here with your lives. So let's talk. How much is it going to cost me?"

Ackerman cocked his head and replied, "My apologies, John. I appear to have somehow been imprecise or unclear with my demands. You were to bring me Agent Carlisle by a certain time, or I told you that I would destroy you and your little kingdom. Am I speaking with a dialect or an accent that makes it difficult for you to comprehend. I would be happy to restate in a manner that would—"

"How are you operating under the assumption that you have any room to dictate terms to me? Look around! I have you completely surrounded, outmanned and outgunned. The only thing keeping you alive is the fact that I need information from you. And fortunately for me, you aren't the only one who possesses that information. I don't care where it comes from. You or your brother. I expect him to be along shortly."

Ackerman felt an eye twitch at the use of the word "brother" and laughed to cover the gesture. "Yes, I expect Marcus to be along soon as well, but I'm not sure that you'll enjoy his company. He's not nearly as much fun as I am. He kind of just cuts straight to the point without all the embellishment. But what you refuse to comprehend, my dear Mr. Canyon, is that we are in the exact same situation that we were in earlier. With you sitting in a position of weakness and believing yourself in the seat of power. It's sad really."

"You are completely out of your mind. I have no idea where your friend is. I think it's time that you had a reality check." Turning to one of his subordinates, he gave a nod, and a short barrel-chested man picked up a radio receiver and said, "Come on in."

Ackerman had no idea to whom this man was speaking or why it would have a bearing on their current discussion, but he didn't like surprises, unless he was the one doing the surprising.

He said, "I wouldn't try anything reckless, John. I will not hesitate to separate your son's head from his body. Well, I guess 'separate' is a bit imprecise—there won't be much head or body left—but you get the idea."

Canyon had a little smirk on his face. "Just watch, my friend." Ackerman stepped to the side of the van in order to see the approaching vehicle. It started as a pair of headlights and became a pair of headlights attached to a massive dark shape. Then it emerged as the biggest, blackest, armored narco tank that Ackerman had ever seen. The armored truck stopped, and Ackerman watched as his brother dropped down from the back with his hands raised in surrender.

77

Special Agent Marcus Williams felt like his whole world was falling down around him. Five men armed with silenced MAC-10 submachine guns had pulled up to him and Yazzie in the equivalent of a ghetto tank. With no other choice, he had surrendered. Now, with his hands raised and his weapons stripped from him—the MP5 and all his ordnance remained with Yazzie's patrol vehicle, and his brass knuckles had ended up in the pockets of the Mexican gentlemen currently jamming a MAC-10 into the small of his back. The ornate Colt Peacemaker, they had given back to Yazzie, as the southern crew of cartel thugs seemed to be thoroughly acquainted with the police captain.

They shoved Marcus forward to the point where he could see his brother over the top of the back of the pickup trucks. Canyon stood just in front of Ackerman, while Frank had hold of the wannabe king's son. In order to hold back the blind rage he felt, Marcus used an old technique he had learned to keep from hitting someone when he really wanted to. He flexed his bicep muscles, while keeping the expression on his face neutral. He felt like a heat seeking-missile. He wanted to zero in on Canyon and pull the truth out of him by any means necessary. But the twenty-something of Canyon's men armed with assault rifles and the cartel members armed with the submachine guns made it difficult for him to reach Canyon without being torn to shreds. So no matter how much he wanted to, now wasn't the time. Still, he had trouble keeping himself from spinning on the man behind him, taking the submachine gun, and mowing down everyone who got in his way. Over the top of the truck bed, Ackerman smiled and said, "Good to see you, brother. Although, you've looked a hell of a lot better."

"And I've looked a hell of a lot worse too."

"Not by much," Ackerman said. "What did you find out there?"

Canyon stepped into view and proclaimed, "I'm the one in charge here, and I'll be the one asking the questions." Turning to Captain Yazzie, he added, "Xavier, I thought you had this one under control?"

The police captain remained characteristically stoic and unreadable behind his small oval-shaped glasses and Stetson hat. Yazzie replied, "They're a slippery pair."

Marcus moved closer and felt half of the guns follow him, while half remained on his brother. His biceps felt like balloons about to pop. Unable to contain himself any longer, Marcus snarled, "What did you do with Maggie Carlisle?"

As he asked the question, his gaze bore directly into the gang leader's eyes.

With a shake of his head, Canyon replied, "Why does everyone keep asking me that? I don't know where your missing agent run off to. How can you be so certain that she was even here?"

"According to your police captain," Marcus said, "You killed her and disposed of the body somewhere up in the hills."

Canyon tried to keep the emotion out of his face, but his gaze flicked to Yazzie with suspicion and hatred swirling in his eyes.

The police captain seemed about as concerned as Ackerman would have been. He merely shrugged and said, "He's lying to save his own ass, trying to pit us against one another. A pretty obvious attempt to manipulate us."

Marcus looked at Canyon and asked, "May I pull my phone out of my pants pocket?"

With a nod of approval, he retrieved his phone from a pouch on the front left of his tactical pants. After a series of swipes and taps, a voice came over the device's small speaker. Turning the volume all the way up, her directed the speaker toward Canyon.

The recording was of Yazzie's previous confession at the ranch: "When I confronted him about it, Canyon told me that he had taken her up into the hills and disposed of her. I do my best to keep the peace around here, but it's hard when you work for a monster like John Canyon. What was I supposed to do? He has the feds on his payroll. I was scared for my life."

John Canyon quivered with rage, and his eyes burned with fire at the police captain. He yelled some curses or obscenities at Yazzie in a language that Marcus didn't understand.

For the first time, Yazzie—from whatever words Canyon had spoken—seemed visibly affected, a small crack in the man's gargoyle mask. But then without saying another word, Yazzie turned to one of the cartel members and gave a nod. The four Mexican gentleman who were pointing their submachine guns at Marcus instead turned their weapons toward Canyon and his men. But that wasn't all, Marcus also noted some of Canyon's own number who redirected their weapons, apparently turned by Yazzie and betraying their brethren.

Gritting his teeth, rage eclipsing fear, Canyon asked, "What in the hell is going on here, Yaz?"

"I've been in conversation with Mr. Alvarez, and while we feel that this is a good business model, we're in agreement that the operation is in need of new management."

Canyon spit on the ground and said, "You've been slithering through the grass a long time waiting for this moment, haven't you, old friend?"

"No," Yazzie said, "I'm a lamprey, not a shark. I was perfectly happy playing the roles we were in, but someone has to go down for all of this. The feds have the truck. They have evidence that could take down your entire operation. And they've already sent one of their own out to bypass your communication blockade."

Seizing the moment, Marcus stepped forward and added, "In fact, I received a phone call on the way here. Your Officer Pitka was kind enough to disable the cellular block you had on the valley. I spoke with some of my associates at the Department of Justice. Within a few hours, this whole place is going to be swarming with federal agents. This isn't a negotiation or a battle. I don't give a shit about your family baggage or your little power struggle. This is me, giving you one last chance to surrender and maybe make it through this night alive. If you kill us, you had better run as fast as you can, because the long arm of the United States government will find you wherever you go."

Canyon locked gazes with Marcus for a few seconds as silence hung over the whole encampment. Then the drug kingpin of northern New Mexico nodded and said, "Fine, let's make a deal, Agent Williams. I'll tell you everything I know."

78

They were all one itchy trigger finger away from a bloodbath. At the moment, Marcus didn't care. Canyon had information about whether or not Maggie was still alive. And Marcus would do whatever it took, including dying, to find out what happened to her. And, of course, there was always a chance. There was always hope that she was still alive.

Canyon, turning to his men, proclaimed, "Do any of you know the kinds of things our great police captain has done? Yazzie used to steal children and then every year on the anniversary of the adoption, he would send out a piece of their clothing or hair, just to torture the families. He did all that up until a couple years ago when I found out about it and put a stop to it. He's sick in the head."

Yazzie laughed, "That's interesting coming from a man like you. And, if memory serves, you are the one who brokered the sale of those same children and profited from it. I sent the families those items because it was a custom of our ancestors when a prisoner was taken, to send a piece of their clothing or hair every year in order to let their family know that they were still alive and well. Of course, that was in a time when we treated even prisoners better than we do today."

"It doesn't matter what insanity you use to justify it, Yazzie. What about all the girls? All those belegana women who have went missing. All of the women who've then turned up staked out in the desert after having been eaten alive."

Yazzie merely looked to his cartel friends and shrugged. He said, "Those are all things that my new business partners value in an associate. You see, John, you're done. You're dried up and over with. Your little kingdom is crumbling down around you, and you see that. He's telling the truth about getting the call and Officer Pitka disabling the cellular blocking. The only choice any of us have now is to run."

"Bullshit," Canyon snapped. "This can all be cleaned up. We buy off the right white men, and it goes away. That's how this world works. The only evidence is these two agents, your little turncoat deputy, and the missing truck."

Marcus, although he didn't seem to be in any position to demand anything, asked again, "What happened to Maggie Carlisle?"

Canyon looked from Ackerman to Marcus and said, "Like I've been telling you all night, I had nothing to do with her disappearance! Yazzie is a pathological liar. I'm not sure he even knows what's true anymore, everything that he said on that recording was a lie. He never called me about any agent because she wasn't here looking for me. She was here looking for the Taker. The man who had stolen her brother all those years ago. One of the missing children. I never told him that I did anything with your Agent Carlisle because I don't know what happened to her."

Marcus considered all that Canyon had revealed, and a few things started clicking into place. He said, "Captain Yazzie…the girls found staked out in the desert, by the time they were found so many animals had eaten on them that it was impossible to tell, but you used rat torture to kill them?"

For the first time since Marcus had met him, Yazzie seemed to show a genuine emotion as his face split into a wide grin.

Marcus added, "That's why you did the little experiment with the scorpion and your lighter, it was a smaller version of what you did to those girls. Everything Canyon is saying is true, isn't it?"

Over the top of the truck bed Canyon asked, "What in the world is 'rat torture'?"

Looking to his brother, Marcus gave a nod. With an almost gleeful excitement, Ackerman said, "Rat torture, also known as rat excitation. The methodology varies from age to age, but it's been a common practice throughout history. It basically involves encouraging a rat to eat its way through a person's body. The most common iteration is accomplished by placing a bucket over the abdomen of a naked victim and then heating the bucket in some way to encourage the rats—fleeing from the fire, following their natural instinct—to gnaw their way down through the person and then continue to do so until they find a way out. Needless to say, this doesn't end very well for the person being eaten. Rat torture has also been featured in the works of Orwell, Easton Ellis, and R. R. Martin. One of the earliest cases on record being used for purposes of extracting information was during the Dutch revolt by Diederik Sonay, an ally of William the Silent. It also appears in a famous case study by Sigmund Freud about a patient being obsessed that his father and a friend would subjected to this torture. Also, on a personal level, I once employed a similar form of torture where I cut someone open, and using a tube, I inserted a rat and sewed the victim back up, in order for—"

"Thanks, Frank. We get the idea." Then, turning to Yazzie, Marcus said, "Enough games. Did you do that to Maggie? Or is she still alive?"

The captain seemed to consider that a moment and then replied, "No, she was too special to merely be food for the desert rats. I don't see what difference it makes now, so I will tell you that, when I last saw your friend, she was alive. That very well could have changed between then and now."

"What the hell did you do with her?"

"You wouldn't understand if I told you. I think it's time that we end this."

Ackerman cleared his throat in a loud and facetious manner and loudly exclaimed, "I agree. Remember me, I'm the guy who has killed more people than cancer and is currently holding a grenade to a person's face. I think this has been great. See, we all came to the table, and talked this thing out. Now, we know that Yazzie is our man, which some of us may have suspected for a while, but we couldn't be sure who had actually taken Maggie. Now that we have established that Mr. Yazzie is in possession of the knowledge we need," Ackerman turned to Canyon and continued, "we would be willing to trade all of the current hostages for your police captain. I would think this would be something that even if we were playing it by the book would be something everyone could agree upon, that the leader of the police force of any community would be willing to trade himself in such a manner."

Yazzie laughed. "You don't have any bargaining power left. I'm about three seconds from telling my associates—both those who have come from south of the border and pledged their alliance and those in Canyon's employment who think that he is coming to an end here—to start killing all of you. I don't care about Tobias or his friends. As far as I'm concerned, you have no hostages. Kill him, if you like."

Canyon screamed, "£eechaa'itsa'ii biyaazh! You're his uncle!"

Ignoring Canyon, Yazzie continued, "The only thing keeping you and your brother alive is that we would still like to recover the truck. But it has also been deemed an acceptable loss, if we are unable to locate it. However, considering that Mr. Alvarez has offered me a cut of the money to recover your truck, I would love for you boys to reveal it's location without too much drama. If that's not on your agenda, then I'm happy to kill all of you and sort out the details later."

Ackerman merely smiled and said, "Oh now, Captain, you're not the shoot first and ask questions later kind of guy. You're a player of the long game. But you are right about one thing. What we have here is essentially a war for knowledge. You want the location of a product worth millions of dollars. My brother and I want to know the whereabouts of my little sister. This is information which holds no value to you from a monetary standpoint. In a perfect and rational world, one would think that we would be able to come to some sort of agreement where all parties involved can get what they want."

Canyon was first to add, "This is far from a perfect world."

"Yes," Ackerman continued, "this entire situation has been clouded by doubt. We each doubt that the other party would give up that info no matter what. Even at the threat of torture and death. But then we also doubt that, if we were to exchange this information in some way, the other party would tell the truth and would not, in the end, try to screw us over in one way or another."

Yazzie asked, "Was there a reason in there as to why I shouldn't just kill all of you?"

Ackerman rolled his eyes. "Come now, you haven't gotten to be your age by having a death wish. Again, you doubt that you would make it out of such a battle alive. You don't want to fight."

"I don't see any other solution, but I'm up for a quick suggestion, before we just see who's left standing."

"Well, I do have one thought. When in doubt…blow something up." With the last word, Ackerman pulled the pin on the frag grenade duct taped to Tobias Canyon's face and shoved the boy toward his father.

79

After pulling the pin on both grenades—the frag grenade duct taped over Tobias's mouth and the smoke grenade taped to his lower back—Ackerman dived to the side and, knowing that there were still a lot of gun barrels pointed in his direction, rolled and came up beside the back tire of one of the angled pickup trucks. This positioned him to where no one could possibly have a clear shot, except for maybe Canyon, who was busy at the moment.

Grabbing for his backpack full of explosives, Ackerman pulled out multiple smoke grenades and tossed them over his shoulders to land in the midst of the encampment.

The next item he pulled from his bag of tricks was the detonator for the C-4, which he and Marcus had strategically buried earlier in the evening. Although his brother was still in the danger zone, Ackerman had to merely pray that Marcus remembered where the bombs had been buried and wouldn't be hit with any flying debris. They had buried the C-4 in the spots where they expected Canyon and his men to park, and then Ackerman had stopped the caravan in approximately the correct places using the Barrett sniper rifle. The plan and placement had worked like a charm.

Flipping open the tiny plastic guard on top of the detonator, Ackerman closed his eyes and smiled as he pressed the red button and unleashed hell.

80

25 years earlier…

Xavier's first recollection of the fall was his stomach flipping like he was on a carnival ride, then pure terror, then the pain of landing on a pile of jagged rocks. At least, he thought they were rocks, at first, until he rolled over and came face to face with a petrified human skull. Xavier didn't scream or cry out, he merely tried to stand up, only to fall back to the pile of bones. He looked down at his ruined leg. He could see the bone sticking out from one side. Oddly, he couldn't feel it at all. Shock and adrenaline, he supposed.

Light shined in from the chamber above, and in the pale glow, Xavier could see Eugene laying among the bones across the chamber. He wasn't moving. Crawling over to the older boy, Xavier flipped him over to examine his wounds.

With the movement, Eugene came awake and screamed his lungs out. Xavier supposed that Eugene didn't have as good of a system as he did for handling critical shock. Eugene had what looked like a femur, or at least the broken end of one, embedded in his side.

Xavier cursed under his breath, grabbed one of the skulls, and threw it against the sandstone wall. The pit was perhaps twenty feet deep and shaped like a teardrop. He had read about such chambers in Anasazi culture. Called a kiva, it was usually a place reserved for religious ceremonies.

Looking to the opening of the pit, where they had fallen from, Xavier saw Reyna looking down at them. He screamed, "Go get help! We're both hurt pretty bad."

But his sister merely stared at him. He matched her gaze, and in her eyes, he saw her working it all out. They hadn't told anyone where they would be that day. There was no way that either Xavier or Eugene would be able to pull themselves out from pit. They were totally reliant on her.

In the split second when he saw her realize this, his beloved sister Reyna smiled and then turned and walked away.

81

John Canyon knew that there was nothing he could do for his son. He knew that because he had been standing there asking that very question for the past few moments. He had ran the scenarios in his head. Duct tape was tough stuff, and the grenade had been thoroughly wrapped. His only hope of getting it off Tobias's face in time would've been to perhaps slice it with a knife, and then grab it and throw it. Trying to pull it off would have been working against all of those little fibers of the tape and its glue. He probably could have slipped his fingers underneath and ripped it off the boy's head, but he doubted that he could do it within the three to five seconds he would have before the grenade detonated. He knew that no matter what he did, those little glue fibers would always beat him in the race. There was strength in numbers, and the numbers were against him.

Not to mention, that was only the grenade on Toby's face. He was almost certain that Frank had hold of another behind the boy's back.

So John Canyon did the only thing that he could think to do when he saw his son coming at him and the release mechanism of the grenade falling away. He didn't bother trying to help the boy, instead he dove for cover.

John Canyon, war veteran and leader of his own small crime syndicate, fell to the ground and shielded his head with his arms, hoping to survive the blast, if for no other reason than to avenge his son's unavoidable demise.

Eruptions of gunfire had followed the second that Frank was clear of his hostage, and the shots continued now.

But after six seconds, Canyon still hadn't heard the detonation of a grenade. He looked up to see Tobias fighting with his restraints and coughing, the grenades still taped in place on his mouth and back. The frag grenade was apparently a dud, and the other spewed smoke.

Then the explosion came.

82

Marcus knew what was coming, but there was no real way to prepare for it. The moment that Frank made his move, chaos overtook the small encampment. No one seemed to know what to do or where to aim their guns for a split second. Several of Canyon's men who were standing close, opened fire on Frank as he dove away, but Marcus knew that none of them would be quick enough.

And, at the moment, he was only concerned about the cartel thug standing behind him pointing a Mac-10 submachine gun at his back. After Frank sprang into action, Marcus waited a few seconds keeping his hands raised and his shoulders hunched in a nonthreatening way. He wanted to make sure that the cartel thug's attention had been drawn away before he made his own move.

Seeing the proper reaction in his periphery, Marcus spun on his captor. Grabbing the Mac-10 by the long black suppressor threaded over its barrel and then, using leverage and a forearm to snap the wrist, Marcus pulled the weapon away from the cartel henchman, who seemed to be barely over the age of eighteen. Although, it seemed the older Marcus became, the younger everyone else looked. He swung the submachine gun like a club, smashing the metal into the side of young man's face. Gunfire was erupting all around them now, and Marcus knew that he only had a few seconds before Frank detonated the C-4.

So, instead of merely disarming and dispatching the young cartel member, Marcus had other plans for him. He grabbed the disoriented man around the neck and then, throwing his weight forward, he pulled the disoriented thug down to the ground with them. Holding him in place with a chokehold, Marcus rolled his new human shield over.

The woman who had provided him with the C-4, at the Director's request, had told him the bombs were shaped charges that would blow straight out, meaning that the bombs should cause more confusion and distraction than destruction. Still, Marcus knew the power of such devices, and most of the small buried packages were now resting beneath the vehicles of Canyon's blockade.

He was still in the process of rolling the cartel thug over when the bombs detonated. The concussion wave took his breath away. The heat was overwhelming. Dust and smoke consumed the air. He heard the sounds of screeching metal as vehicles were torn apart, exploded, flipped, and crunched into one another. Then he heard nothing but a high-pitched ringing. The sand and grit assaulted his eyes, and so he couldn't see all of the destruction, but he could hear the screams. The air was filled with an acrid smoke that smelled of burning plastic and gasoline.

Unfortunately, most of his equipment was back in Yazzie's patrol vehicle, and so he didn't have the mask and breathing apparatus that he had planned to wear during this part of the plan. Nevertheless, he would have to make do. Despite the ringing in his ears, the spinning of the world around him, and the disorientation that he felt, he knew that he had to act. This was their chance.

He knew that using a gun within this haze would be

firing blindly, and so he instead opted for the pair of brass knuckles that had belonged to his father and had been shoved into the pants pockets of the young cartel member. Retrieving his weapons, he shoved his bleeding captor off and pushed himself to his feet. He stumbled at first, but soon found his footing and began his search for Captain Xavier Yazzie.

83

Two days ago…

Before tossing her into the pit of bones, Yazzie had graciously provided her with two items: a watch and a wind-up flashlight. One to see how much time she had left and one to illuminate her nightmare surroundings. After awakening in the pit, Maggie had used the flashlight to search every inch of what Yazzie had called a "Kiva" and concluded that there was no way out. Then she had set to work on a weapon, which hadn't taken long. There was already a piece of bone from a recent victim that had snapped from the fall and was almost knife-like to begin with. She had sharpened it on other larger bones in order to hone its edge.

After some time, she had grown accustomed to the smell, but the sound of the beetles that would soon be devouring her was impossible to tune out. She knew that her only hope now was to preserve her energy and wait for rescue, or for Yazzie to get tired of this game and want to play another.

With that in mind, she had done little more than sleep and project thoughts into the darkness for days now. Winding the flashlight or looking at the time wasn't worth her energy and only served to erode her confidence and nurture her despair.

When light flooded the tear-shaped kiva of death, it stung Maggie's eyes, and she raised an arm to protect herself against the glare. She heard the woman falling before she saw her. The woman's screams filled the pit until she smashed into the pile of bones below. Then she started rolling back and forth and crying in anguish. The newcomer wore a tight-fitting cocktail dress and too much makeup. Maggie wondered if the woman was a prostitute—a typical victim of Yazzie's, and serial killers the world over.

As Maggie's eyes adjusted to the new light source, she saw Yazzie standing over them in the ring of the kiva's entrance. He said, "I found you a playmate, little girl."

Maggie found the energy to go to the woman and check her for wounds, but she was surprised to find that the working girl was relatively unscathed. Still, the pit's newest occupant appeared in a daze, as if she were highly sedated.

Leaning down to the woman, Maggie said, "I'm a federal agent. Don't worry. I'm going to get you out of here. Everything's going to be okay."

From above, Yazzie laughed and sat down with his feet dangling into the opening. "Let me tell you a story, little girl. This one goes back to when I was young. I discovered this place and decided I would make some money by looting the Old Ones, but He Who Devours had other plans for me. An associate and I fell into this very kiva, and during our time there, He Who Devours came to me in a vision and supplied me with the strength to survive. The strength to work for him and help him to rise again."

Maggie wondered if there was a point to the story other than displaying his madness to people who were already judging him and couldn't do anything about it. But she didn't waste the energy on a smartass comment.

He continued, "The only way I survived was that I had the strength to kill my friend and to drink his blood and consume his flesh. In that way, I was able to sustain myself until they were able to rescue me. So, I figured that it was only fair that I give you the same opportunity. If you choose to drink Carol here—who as I'm sure you deduced is a prostitute and drug addict, a drain on your belegana society—you'll survive long enough to make it out of this pit."

Maggie asked, "What does your insane god want from us?"

Yazzie laughed as he slid the metal cover over his personal pit of death. As a parting gift, he called out, "And Carol, if you can hear me, this offer also goes to you. If you kill Maggie and drink her, then you should have the reserves to survive as well."

She heard him chuckling as darkness consumed the pit once again.

Using the wind-up flashlight to fill the macabre kiva with light, she attempted to further examine the woman, Carol. But her new companion still appeared to be mostly out of her head. She looked up at Maggie with tears in her eyes.

Maggie reiterated her earlier statements and, with a smile, added, "Don't worry, I'm not going to eat you."

Before she knew what was happening, Carol had grabbed a loose bone and was swinging it feebly up at her, screaming, "I'll eat you, bitch!"

Maggie easily pulled the bone from Carol's grasp and dropped her with a single blow. After Maggie landed the punch, she said, "I don't see that happening, kitten, but I respect your life choices."

Letting Carol rest where she had fallen among the dead, Maggie went back to her own bed of bones and waited for rescue.

84

Standing in the front room of the old trading post and looking out the now-broken front window, Liana watched the scene play out using the pair of field binoculars. She supposed that she should've been looking down the scope of the enormous black rifle, but the powerful machine scared her. She was, of course, qualified in handguns, assault rifles, and shotguns, but the power of a .50 BMG caliber sniper rifle was a whole other world than what she had experienced. The recoil of an AR-15 was almost nonexistent, but the Barrett kicked like a professional soccer player was practicing on her shoulder, almost dislocating it with her earlier shot. Still, with the situation escalating, the time was coming when she would have no choice but to slide in behind the scope.

As Frank moved closer to John Canyon, she had also moved closer to the Barrett rifle. She wondered if it was possible for this thing to tear her arm completely off. Could it break her collarbone? The concussion wave had given her a headache after one shot.

The rifle smelled of gun oil and the remnants of packing grease now cleaned away.

When, still looking through the binoculars, she saw Frank pull the pin on Tobias's grenade and then leap to the side, Liana didn't hesitate. She tucked the butt of the rifle tightly into her shoulder pocket and sighted down the scope. One of Canyon's thugs was starting to head around the truck toward Frank. She sighted in on a place in front of the young man, and having no more time to consider broken collarbones or dislocated shoulders, she squeezed the trigger and unleashed one of the massive bullets into the truck bed just in front of the young thug. He fell back in fear as the truck seemed to have been smote by the hand of God.

Then, within the blink of an eye, the spot where the blockade had stood became a rolling mushroom cloud of fire, smoke, and dust. Taking her eyes away from the scope, she saw vehicles flipping over as they were blown upward like they weighed nothing. As the dust settled, the fire gave way to clouds of smoke. She couldn't see much of what was going on even when looking down the powerful scope.

A part of her was glad that she couldn't see what was happening. Not only for the fact that she didn't want to see Frank bleeding out or unconscious, but also because she really didn't want to have to use the Barrett against anyone down there. They were mostly kids. Kids from her community.

But then she supposed that most of them were actually her age or older. She was certainly capable of making her own choices, and so were they. She thought about what Frank had told her regarding ghosts coming back to haunt you. The Diné people believed that, when a person died, all of the bad things they had done could be left behind in the form of what they called a chindi. It was a tragedy to have someone die in a home, as the hogan would need to be torn down, and most Diné were hesitant to be in the presence of a corpse under any circumstance. For fear of the chindi following them home.

She wondered if the ghosts Frank had warned her about were the chindi of all the people he had killed, following and tormenting him. She didn't want that for herself, but she also wasn't about to sit out this fight. This was as much her battle as it was Frank's. Perhaps even more her battle. John Canyon might've done a lot of good for their community and created a lot of new jobs for the reservation, but he also corrupted and twisted people through the business he conducted, his real business, the transporting of drugs that would be a blight upon the youth of the belagana and the Diné alike. He was a criminal, and she was a cop. It was her responsibility to do something.

But what could she do. She scanned the area through the scope of the rifle, but she could only make out vague shapes moving within the fog.

She needed to do something. She needed to get down there. Frank could be hurt. He could be dying. But this was also the opportunity to turn the tide, and Frank and his brother needed all the help they could get. After a few seconds of trying to find a target through the scope and seeing nothing but a cloud of smoke that only seemed to be getting thicker, she screamed aloud in frustration. Dropping the rifle, she paced the floor a few times to get her brain working. Think Liana, she told herself. But in the end, all she could really come up with was to grab one of the AK-47s they had procured from Canyon's men and run down the long drive as fast as she could. The more she thought of that idea, the more she didn't like it. She would be exposed for a long time, and by the time she reached the blockade, the fight would have been over.

She needed a faster way to get down from the top of the bluff, where the old trading post sat, to the base, where Canyon had erected his barricade. She needed something that could traverse that distance fast, something with wheels.

85

As he pressed the red button with his right hand, Ackerman slipped the fireman's mask over his face with the left. He knew that the mask was state-of-the-art technology for firefighters, having received a crash course on the device's operation from his brother. It was a full-face respirator mask—minus the air tank that a true fireman would wear—and was equipped with a small camera on its side. The camera captured digital thermal images and then displayed the results through a nine-inch holographic projection on the inside of the glass face plate. The technology was called Sight, which made Ackerman think more of clairvoyance than thermal imaging, but to each their own. It basically allowed firefighters to see through the smoke, fire, and debris in order to find and rescue victims caught in the blaze.

Ackerman, however, had different plans with the victims he located with the device.

He had just slipped the mask into place when the concussion wave knocked him off his feet. The force of the blast, and its proximity surprised him. Laying on the ground, the backpack full of grenades poking into his ribs, Ackerman turned back to the carnage just in time to see the truck next to which he had been hiding flipping end over end and coming straight down on him. Having no time to regain his feet, he rolled furiously, trying to get out of the way before he was crushed beneath several tons of metal and fiberglass.

He cleared the danger zone a second before the truck came smashing down beside him, but he was not completely unscathed. He felt the cauterization of his side wound pulling free with every movement.

As he caught his breath, Ackerman surveyed the damage. Unfortunately, he could hardly see a thing through the haze of smoke and dust. Still, he knew that the cover wouldn't last long, and so he unloaded the rest of the smoke grenades that he held in the backpack into the center of the now-burning barricade of vehicles.

Then, he activated the thermal imaging technology equipped in his mask and, discarding the backpack, retrieved the push daggers from the bottom of the bag. The small daggers fit perfectly in his fists and protruded out between his ring and middle finger. The blades were only two inches long, but he knew that he could easily penetrate deep enough to kill with them. Although, he only planned to inflict debilitating but non-fatal wounds upon the men now coughing within of the smoke.

Before stepping into the fray and dispatching their would-be attackers, Ackerman was reminded of the Beretta 9mm that Liana had forced him take. It was still tucked into the back of his tactical cargo pants. He pulled it out now, examined the weapon, and dropped it onto the gravel of the driveway.

Then, looking toward the billowing clouds of smoke, where others would see nothing, he saw the shapes of targets within the thermal imaging of his helmet. He squeezed the push daggers tightly in each fist and poised his muscles to spring into action. Ackerman half-expected Thomas White's voice to whisper something in his ear, but the old man was silent. That silence reminded him that, despite him now thinking of the delusion as a person of its own, the old man and his bloodlust were a part of him.

And he hated to admit it, even to himself, but he knew that he was going to enjoy what came next.

86

When Liana realized how she could get down the lane faster, she felt like a fool. Her patrol vehicle was only a few feet away and only needed the battery reconnected. On her way to the back door, she snatched up an AK-47. She was halfway down the back steps before she remembered that she would also need the battery. Feeling like a fool again, she ran back into the old trading post, retrieved the battery, and rushed over to the old shed.

Working as quickly as possible, Liana dropped the battery into the compartment, hooked up the cables, and threw open a rickety old garage door that seemed ready to fall in at any second.

Before climbing in behind the wheel, she readied the AK-47, checked her Glock, and pulled her tactical shotgun from its mount. Then, ready to go to war, she turned the key and was rewarded with a buzz and a click.

She screamed "No!" and punched the steering wheel before trying to turn the key again. This time the buzz and click were even weaker. Apparently, the electromagnet had completely drained the battery.

With a frustrated scream and a few curses under her breath, Liana grabbed her guns and prepared to find another way down to the battle.

87

Xavier Yazzie had been standing by the edge of where the road split between the lane, which led up to the open trading post, and another dirt road that wound its way up into the hills and eventually behind the trading post and down into the canyons. When the explosion rocked the world, Yazzie was thrown into the air and—for a few seconds—didn't realize what had happened. But then, as he felt himself flying, time seemed to slow, and he realized that he had once again fallen into one of the brothers' traps. He hoped it was merely the compression wave that had blown him off his feet, as opposed to discovering that he no longer had legs. He didn't feel any pain in the lower extremities, but he also knew that, when sustaining devastating wounds, the body often shut down the flow of sensory information to the brain.

The dust cloud engulfed him. He felt himself falling. And then he felt a bone-crushing impact. He didn't know where he was. He rolled around on the ground trying to get his bearings. His eyes were full of sand and smoke and only the spirits knew what else. He coughed and tried to clear his vision, but as his eyes regained focus, he could see little of what was happening back on the main roadway.

He found himself lying on the dirt road which led up into the hills. The smells of gasoline and burned debris were overwhelming. He felt like the dust had been blown into every pore of his body. He tried to sit up, but pain lanced through his thigh. Realizing that he still had both of his legs, Yazzie was almost hesitant to search for the source of the pain and the trauma.

When he finally worked up the courage to look, he discovered that the wound was due to a piece of metal, likely from one of the vehicles, that had imbedded itself into the meaty part of his thigh. It didn't seem to be too deep, but there was always the fear that when he pulled it free, the wound would start spurting blood, having hit some vital blood flow tributary.

Yazzie, more worried about the two brothers who seemed to be possessed by some dark wind than he was worried about the metal having hit anything major, pulled the piece of shrapnel free and tossed it aside. Then he retrieved the tourniquet that he always carried when on duty from his TQ911 tourniquet holster and applied it to his wounded leg.

With his injuries tended to and only a few seconds of time wasted, Yazzie shakily pulled himself to his feet and limped over to a spot where he could see the smoke-filled encampment, but where he was still partially obscured by the dip in the roadway. Along the way, he scanned the area for his hat and glasses, but they were nowhere to be found. Checking his holster, he also realized that he had lost his weapon, the pearl handled Colt Peacemaker that he had been holding in his right hand when the bombs had gone off. Luckily, he saw a glint of the flames reflecting off of the silver a few feet away. He felt much better with the gun back in his hand. It seemed to strengthen him and bring the world back into focus.

He checked the barrel and spun the cylinder. Finding it in working order, he slid it back into his holster.

Looking over the top of the roadway, Yazzie could see less than fifteen feet in front of him. The rest of the blockade was completely obscured by the smoke. Within the clouds, he heard gunfire and screaming.

88

Francis Ackerman Jr. had recently begun keeping a diary, after being turned onto the idea by Baxter Kincaid, a private detective and blogger from the San Francisco area with whom they had worked with to capture the Gladiator and take down the crime lord known as Mr. King. Kincaid actually made a good living peddling his musings, but Ackerman would never be able to share his journals with anyone, at least not while he was still alive. But he still felt it good measure to preserve his thoughts for study by future generations.

As such, throughout the day, he had taken to thinking about the diary entries and what he would write later on.

He wondered what he would note about this situation. How did he feel? That was often difficult for him to describe to the normals, since he didn't feel emotions in the same way that they did. His first thought was that his current experience in the smoke would be likened to a prima ballerina on opening night. On further consideration, he decided that wasn't quite right. The idea implied a certain level of anxiety and fear, or at least he supposed it did, and that was where the analogy broke down. So what imagery could he use to describe his feeling in this moment in a way someone like his brother or Officer Liana would understand?

All of these considerations were, of course, made in the

back of Ackerman's mind as he waded into battle and began to dispatch enemies. He almost felt bad for them. They had assault rifles and a desire to kill, while he had only a pair of push daggers. But that didn't take into account the thermal imaging displayed on the inside of his mask. Canyon's thugs and the cartel mercenaries were all trapped in a suffocating world of smoke and tear gas, which Ackerman had added for good measure. While his enemies contended with the acrid fumes coming from so many sources, he was safely tucked away under his mask, watching all of them groping around in the dark through thermal imaging.

Suddenly, he realized what he would write about in his journal.

This situation was much like that film his brother loved so much...Predator, Ackerman believed it was called. Like the titular alien of the film, Ackerman was now able to see where others were blind. A part of him felt badly that his brother—who was such a fan of the film, while Ackerman had only seen glimpses that Marcus had forced upon him—wouldn't be able to enjoy the experience.

Ackerman used the first target he came to as a guinea pig. He needed to determine the distance at which he was invisible to his prey. The young man—whom he saw mostly as different shades of red, orange, and yellow through the thermal imaging system—was crouched beside the wreckage of a pickup truck with his assault rifle, another AK-47, up and at the ready. Of course, the weapon was aimed in the opposite direction from which Ackerman was coming.

He then initiated a series of movements, testing to see how the young man would react. Once satisfied with his experiment, he plunged both push daggers into the flesh of the unsuspecting young man. Ackerman's right fist punched the pistol grip of the assault rifle, puncturing straight through the young man's left hand. At the same time, Ackerman struck the bicep of the man's right arm with his left hand.

The trauma had the desired result, and the young victim instantly dropped his weapon and fell back clutching his wounds. And the injuries had been inflicted in such a way that Ackerman doubted the man would be picking up any other weapon for a very long time.

He felt the bloodlust building now as he pushed forward and started to hack, punch, and slash his way through the sea of potential victims. He couldn't remember the last time he felt so alive. He felt euphoric. He was soaring.

In his ear came the voice he had expected earlier.

"You're a bird, now fly," said Thomas White.

And so he did.

He floated through the smoke like the spirit of retribution and death itself, a dark wind of divine wrath.

He dove and pirouetted and rolled and zigzagged his way through the throng of men. He felt like he was on top of the world. Soaring now, high above the mortals. He was a bird, and he could fly. Why would a bird choose to remain on the ground? He punched one man in the side of the face with a right hook, the push dagger puncturing the side wall of the man's cheek and likely knocking out a few of his teeth. Another victim he stabbed in both thighs before punching up beneath the man's jaw, just hard enough to puncture the skin. With a slightly longer knife, the blow would have gone up into the man's brain, killing him instantly. Ackerman knew that his blow would only leave a scar.

But still, he was staying on the ground. He wanted to fly. He wanted to let go.

Instead of fighting every second of every day to keep the darkness inside of him at bay, he longed to merely relax and let go and allow the himself to fulfill all the desires of the monster living inside of him. He longed for release. Leaping into the air, he punched the push daggers into both shoulders of one gunman. Another, he drove his right fist into the inner side of the man's right knee and followed by driving the blade in his left hand into the man's right pectoral muscle, hoping that he had pulled back on the punch enough to make sure that the blade didn't puncture the young man's lung. But he was heading toward takeoff now and such things were becoming of less concern. These men were in his way. All of them wanted to kill him and his brother and would do so in a second. Why not let go? Why not have a little fun with them? Why not be the bird of prey that he was meant to be?

Why not let go?

89

Liana supposed she had always had a bit of a thing for dangerous men. There had been the Todacheeney kid in high school. He had been her first real love, and a cousin to John Canyon's operations manager. He had been a bit of a daredevil: a BMX racer, skater, and freestyle rock climber. He had amazed her with his ability to scale a rock wall like he was Spider-Man or some kind of Skinwalker. She supposed now, that she would've ended up marrying him, if not for the fact that he had died young. Then, college for her had been a revolving door of bad decisions. Still, falling for a self-proclaimed serial killer would probably take the cake.

And now, she was considering risking her life to help that man. She already regretted her decision, but the continued sound of gunfire spurred her into action.

As Liana had walked out of the garage and looked down the lane toward the point where sloping rock met flat road, she realized it was at least a hundred meters farther than she had previously thought. She could try to run it, but there was virtually no cover along the way, so if the smoke cleared and Canyon and his men emerged, she would be a sitting duck.

An idea came in a flash as she stepped out of the garage and imprinted on a memory from her childhood of watching the Little Rascals build a pinewood derby car. The lane which Canyon and his men had blocked off was a long, straight slope, and there was only one other thing on wheels at the trading post: the cast iron bathtub. The old man must have built in on a rolling cart so that he could pull it out into the sun and warm his bath water, but it also made the tub a passable entry for the pinewood derby.

Pushing on the bathtub and getting its attached wheels rolling, Liana steered as best she could along the side of the building and through the small parking area where the lane began to angle down. From this viewpoint, she could see that the road wasn't perfectly straight. Instead, it contained a few slight curves. A sense of vertigo now assaulted her as she looked down the steep slope. Maybe this wasn't such a great idea.

The sound of gunshots clanging off metal and screams of pain spurred her forward. She needed to get down there and help Frank. She needed to fight.

So, with the shotgun and the assault rifle both inside the tub, Liana pushed her makeshift vehicle far enough to get it rolling on its own. Running behind the tub, to make sure that it picked up enough momentum, Liana pushed until she was sure and then leaped up and into the tub herself. As the rolling bathtub picked up speed, she tried to see if she had any steering at all by shifting her weight or pulling a certain way. She found that she could affect a little of the tub's direction by throwing her body weight around, but it was also picking up speed a lot faster then she had anticipated.

The momentum and the swirling smells of gun oil, mold and moss flourishing inside the tub, and fire and death wafting up the hill threatened to make her sick.

She hit the first jog in the road too fast and nearly lost control, but the extra speed helped and she was able to jump back on after the wheels slid off the roadway into the dirt. The next small curve she was ready for and made without issue, the maneuver only requiring minimal course correction. She was getting close now. Realizing, she had hadn't breathed since she had hopped up into the tub, Liana began gasping in greedy mouthfuls of air.

Then she heard a strange sound. Something was tinking off the front of the tub. And it didn't sound like rocks. Looking ahead, she saw one of the cartel thugs had stumbled out of the haze of smoke and had apparently found a target in the form of a police uniform riding down the hill at him in a bathtub.

The man started running up the hill toward her, screaming and squeezing the trigger of his Mac 10. A sound suppressor had been threaded over the gun's barrel, and so all she heard were little thump-pings as he opened fire.

Luckily, the old tub was built to last and seemed almost impervious to the gunfire. She kept her head down, only peeking over the edge to see where she was headed.

Then, in a flash of realization, Liana recognized that her plan didn't include how she was going to stop.

Only having a couple of seconds to react, Liana raised the AK-47 to her shoulder, took aim, and squeezed the trigger. The gunmen jerked back, having been hit at least once. Figuring that was much as she could ask, she dove off the side of the runaway bathtub, trying not to break her neck in the process.

The gravel came up to meet her with surprising force, the hundreds of small rocks feeling like they had been shot from a cannon. As she pulled herself to her feet, retrieved her assault rifle, and looked back to where the cartel gunman had been, she discovered that her shooting had been more than effective. The man was dead, sprawled out across the gravel like a child preparing to make an angel in the snow.

The runaway bathtub had missed the debris of the first and second trucks from the barricade and had disappeared into the smoke. She heard it crash into something, but she had no idea what it had hit. Thankfully, there had been no screams connected directly to the collision.

Staring into the black cloud of smoke, she now wished that she would've grabbed for the shotgun rather than the assault rifle. The shotgun with its wide dispersal pattern would be more effective where she was going. But it was too late to change now, the shotgun having traveled along with the bathtub into the void. Tucking the butt of the rifle into her shoulder and aiming into the swirling mist in front of her, Liana moved toward the fight.

90

From the moment Maggie went missing, Marcus had felt like a homing missile without a target, and now that he had a target, he could barely see two feet in front of his face. His left leg had gone numb, and he still felt woozy from the scorpion sting. At least, the ringing in his ears had subsided, so that he could now hear his enemies before he saw them.

With his adoptive father's brass knuckles held tightly in each fist, dragging his left leg, Marcus pushed forward in the direction that he had last seen Yazzie. From the moment he had pulled himself from the ground after the explosion he had been stumbling around blind with everything he bumped into trying to kill him, but he still hadn't found his target. The original plan had been that Ackerman would be in position at the front and detonate the bombs. After which, Marcus would come in from the opposite side, with both of them using thermal imaging to easily subdue Canyon and all of his men. Marcus hadn't liked the plan from the moment of its conception. He had killed in the past, but it wasn't something that he ever wanted to do again. But war had casualties, at least that's what he told himself. Not to mention the fact that he had never intended for events to escalate to this point, but situations had a way of spiraling out of control. At least, they did around him and his brother.

Within ten steps of stumbling through the smoke, he had

encountered and brutally knocked unconscious one of the cartel members and two of Canyon's men. Canyon's men had been noisy and disoriented, but the cartel thug had put up a bit of a fight. Still, Marcus had overpowered the shooter with strength of will.

The next two he encountered were on Canyon's crew, both armed with AK-47s. Since assault rifles were ineffective in close-quarters combat, he was able to see the barrel of their gun moving ahead of them like a beacon. The two had been working together, both unharmed from the explosion.

Marcus grabbed the stock of the first man's rifle and pushed it back up, slamming the barrel into the gunman's face. The second man turned to fire but Marcus stepped forward, caught the stock, and dispatched him with a blow to the side of head from the brass knuckles. He wasn't sure how hard he was hitting them and whether or not they were unconscious or dead, and he hated to admit it, but in that moment, he didn't really care one way or another. All he could think about was finding Yazzie and, by extension, saving Maggie.

He heard the next group of attackers before he saw them. Dropping low to the ground, he waited for the closest man to pass, then positioning himself just right, he remained still and quiet until he had a clear shot at a shinbone. Cocking his arm back like a crossbow ready to fire, Marcus punched the gunman in the shin so hard that he felt bone snap from the impact

Crying out in agony, the gunman toppled over, but as he did so, he squeezed back the trigger of his AK-47, spraying his two companions with lead.

Marcus supposed that he wasn't directly responsible—why

in the hell did the kid have his finger on the trigger like that?—but he still felt the weight of their deaths being added onto his shoulders. The next attacker he encountered appeared to have suffered some burns and was more than a little disoriented. Marcus disarmed him, and wrapping one of his arms around the man's neck, he applied pressure, his bicep and forearm tensed like a coiled anaconda, until the burned man was safely unconscious.

He continued on in this way for what felt like a mile. A mile of stumbling and coughing on acrid smoke and fumes and punching and grappling through the throng of Canyon's men. His eyes burned, and his nose ran; Frank must have thrown in a few teargas canisters. Still, he had to fight his way forward. He had to find Yazzie.

He felt like he should've broken free of the smog by now and hoped that he hadn't been stumbling around in a circle. Still, like a shark, he kept swimming.

He heard the next danger a second before it killed him. At first, he wasn't sure what to make of the sound, but he could tell that whatever it was, it was on collision course. Diving out of the way just before being run down, Marcus landed against the debris of one of Canyon's truck. The metal was hot and seared his shoulder. He turned back in time to see that what had nearly ended the battle for him appeared to be a runaway bathtub.

Suspecting that he may have a concussion or some other injury that was causing visual and auditory hallucinations, Marcus pushed himself to his feet and continued forward. Luckily, he only had to push on for another few feet before he was rewarded with the smell of clean air and the gradual dissipation of the haze. Gulping in greedy lungfuls of air and trying to wipe the teargas from his eyes, Marcus was finally able to look up and see a police officer, who he assumed to be Officer Liana Nakai, about twenty feet up the road. The young officer was headed toward him, an assault rifle at her shoulder.

Marcus kept his hands raised as he lumbered forward, but as he closed the gap, he saw a man creeping up behind her. Captain Xavier Yazzie already had his arm reared back to pistol-whip Liana across the back of the head.

Marcus, dragging his left leg and motioning frantically for Liana to look behind her, tried to speak but broke into a coughing fit instead.

Nevertheless, his game of charades had apparently been effective because Liana turned back toward her attacker. But not in time to avoid the blow.

Now—standing beyond the cover of the veil of smoke and staring face-to-face with an armed man who knew exactly what would happen when Marcus got ahold of him—he really wished that he had picked up one of those AK-47s.

Liana was still falling when Yazzie took aim at Marcus with his Colt Peacemaker and, slapping down on the hammer of the single-action revolver like an old west cowboy, he fired off three shots in quick succession.

Marcus felt all three hit him in the chest, driving him backward, once again into the rolling clouds of smoke.

91

After knocking his former deputy unconscious and shooting the big fed in the chest, Xavier Yazzie decided it was time that he made a quiet exit from the party. The smoke was now clearing enough that he could make out the van which Canyon had parked in the center of the roadway between his two pickup trucks. Estimating that the van, which appeared to be relatively unscathed by the explosive attack, would be the best transportation away from this mess, he picked up Liana, throwing her over his shoulder in a fireman's carry, and then headed toward the back of the van.

The rear doors were closed. With his right hand, he pulled them free and snatched the Peacemaker from his holster in the same motion. Two men with semiautomatic pistols hid inside the back of the panel van.

The man on the left raised his hands and said, "Whoa, Uncle Xavier, don't shoot! It's me."

The other skinny little man who had always been Jamie Ramirez's sidekick since they were boys followed suit and lowered his weapon. Slipping the Peacemaker back into his holster, Yazzie said, "I didn't recognize you Jamie, with all that blood and dust all over you. What are you two doing in here?"

Both men had fear in their eyes. Ramirez answered, "El Diablo was out there walking in the fire. And laughing."

Xavier Yazzie kept his face stone, but inside he snorted a laugh. El Diablo, that was rich. Obviously, these two had had another run-in with Frank out there as they were stumbling blindly through the smoke. Or perhaps they had heard or seen the aftermath of what happened to someone else who had come across the killer, who had more than earned Yazzie's respect.

Yazzie said, "Help me get her inside the van, and we'll get out before the devil even knows we're here." He laughed internally about their foolish fears, but seeing that both men were still shaken, he added, "Just stick with me and shoot where I shoot. We'll be fine."

With that he climbed inside, closed the doors, and slipped in behind the wheel.

He hesitated a moment, fearing that the vehicle wouldn't start or that there was some kind of a leak in the gas tank that would cause it to explode. But he also knew that to stay here was to court death.

With a twist of the key in the ignition, the van fired right away and without exploding.

Ramirez dropped into the passenger seat, gun in hand, and asked, "Where are we going?"

Yazzie replied, "We're headed to the casino and then we're getting the hell out of here. Don't worry, kid. Just stick with me and do what I say. If you do exactly what I tell you, you may even escape this valley as a rich man."

92

One of the cartel thugs—a man with long black hair slicked back into a pony tail wearing a leather vest over a white T-shirt—had decided to get fancy and was wielding a Mac 10 in each hand, waving them around and popping off random shots into the smoke.

But Ackerman could plainly see that this gentleman was not versed in proper akimbo dual wielding techniques.

He rolled three times on the ground, staying low and out of the line of the man's sporadic fire. On the last roll, Ackerman popped up like a jack-in-the-box and drove the push daggers into the bottom of Ponytail's forearms. He followed by slashing Ponytail across the abdomen and then driving the push daggers forward beside the man's head, piercing both blades through the man's ears.

Ponytail screamed in agony as Ackerman manipulated him like a marionette.

Ackerman found the whole thing rather humorous. If it hadn't been for the thermal imaging mask, he would've given Ponytail a kiss on the forehead. Since that wasn't an option, he instead pulled his arms straight back out and whipped his elbow against Ponytail's temple. The man dropped, instantly unconscious.

Ackerman moved to lick the blades of the push daggers clean but again realized that the mask prohibited him from doing so. Which was probably for the best. Who knew where these guys had been.

He now felt like the Thunderbird, a massive predatory avian of legend, as he soared over the battlefield. He was the top of the food chain. He was the lion, the eagle, the great white shark. And it felt good to be king.

But the experience was interrupted by the sound of screeching tires and tearing metal. He turned to see the panel van that Canyon had emerged from earlier speeding toward him.

The van collided with the burning husk of one of Canyon's farm trucks and spun the wreckage in his direction.

With nowhere to go and a couple tons of burning metal spinning his way, Ackerman jumped forward and landed atop the charred husk. He grabbed hold of what had once been the truck's axle and gas tank and held on for his life as the wreckage nearly spun a circle from the van's impact.

Luckily, there were plenty of handholds on the truck's bottom. Unfortunately, those same pieces were extremely hot. He felt his flesh melting, not an unpleasant experience for Ackerman, but he still pulled his arms free as soon as possible, leaving skin and hair from his forearms behind. The pain sent electric shivers through his body.

Looking toward the path that the van had cut through the ruined barricade, Ackerman hoped that the vehicle had only contained a few scared mercenaries finally making a wise decision. But intuition told him that he wasn't going to like it when he found out who the vehicle's occupants were.

Turning away, another electric shot of ecstasy pulsed up his side from where the metal shrapnel had been removed earlier. He supposed he had torn loose the effects of the cauterization and was again bleeding from whatever part of the circulatory system he had damaged.

He needed to re-treat the wounds.

Lifting up his shirt, Ackerman leaned against the charred and smoking husk of the pickup truck once more, this time pressing his side into the metal and rolling it back-and-forth to melt the wounds closed. He knew all of this cauterization would soon result in infection that would ultimately be as dangerous as the original wounds, but that was a problem for another time. And he could properly tend to the injuries later. Right now, he only needed a temporary fix, and burning himself was his approximation of a Band-Aid.

As his flesh touched the metal and began to sear and smoke, the familiar sent of burning human meat filled his nostrils. The maelstrom of smells and sensations caused his head to swim, and he realized that he was again going to lose consciousness.

As he fell back onto the gravel road, Ackerman recalled hearing shots from a 45 long Colt caliber pistol while he had been dealing with Ponytail. He wondered, as darkness took him, who Yazzie had been shooting at.

93

Ackerman awakened at the sound of crunching gravel. He rolled to his feet, the push daggers still in his fists, and came face to face with Tobias Canyon.

Although he had a blade pressed to each side of his throat, Tobias didn't flinch. He looked Ackerman in the eyes and said, "We need your help. You said that you didn't want anyone to die. Someone is about to."

Ackerman pushed the boy back and scanned him to make sure that he was unarmed. Then he said, "Lead the way."

The smoke had cleared enough now that it was more of an annoyance than a blinding force. Ackerman flipped his mask up and sat it aside as they reached the site Tobias had been describing.

Surveying the now utterly devastated roadblock, Ackerman saw the aftermath of his rampage along the right side of the road. He saw a string of unconscious and bleeding men, many sprawled out, many rolling back and forth or clutching at wounds. Looking to the other side of the road, he saw in the now-shifting winds that Marcus's side of the battle contained men sprawled out and either completely unconscious or dead. The whole scene brought a smile to Ackerman's face. Perhaps it was wrong to find pride such destruction, but he and his brother truly were forces to be reckoned with.

Tobias led him around a truck that had flipped over on

its side, and Ackerman was pleased to see Marcus already on the scene.

His brother had stripped out of his tactical gear and body armor and now wore only an A-frame shirt stained black with blood and soot. Marcus was turned around, gripping the bed of the truck and pushing his back against the wreckage, trying to lift a three-quarter ton pickup truck by himself in order free someone pinned beneath. As he came closer, Ackerman saw that the trapped victim was John Canyon.

Seeing him approach, Marcus yelled, "Help me with this, Frank!"

Moving to his brother's side, Ackerman examined where the truck had landed on the drug smuggler. After using his trained eye to survey the wounds, Ackerman locked gazes with his brother and shook his head in the negative. Marcus's face fell.

Canyon's son must've registered the change in their moods and asked, "What are you doing? Why did you stop?"

Standing up to full height and matching the boy's gaze, Ackerman replied, "I'm sorry, kid. The truck is sitting above his waistline. Even if we could move it, he'd be dead in less than a minute."

"So what do we do? How can we help him?"

"My brother will be calling an ambulance for him and the rest of your fallen comrades, but if he were my father, I would take this opportunity to say goodbye."

The young man looked to the ground, his jaw clenched, and said, "You did this. You killed him."

Ackerman replied, "Yes, I did."

Neither of them moved or spoke for a moment.

Marcus was already on the phone calling for ambulances and using his federal credentials to put a rush on things.

To Tobias, Ackerman said, "Your father lived by the sword, by the law of tooth and claw. That path has only one end. I suggest that you choose a different one." He could see tears forming in Tobias's eyes and added, "Go to your father. He needs you now more than ever."

Under his breath, Tobias Canyon said, "This isn't over. You'll pay for what happened here."

He admired the boy's spirit. "Well, kid, if you're up for taking a shot at the title, I accept all challengers. It won't end well for you. Many have tried to traverse that trail, and many have discovered that it only leads to self-destruction. Regardless of all that, you have more important concerns at the moment. The cost of revenge is something I suggest you weigh out for yourself with fear and trembling, but not today."

Without another word of protest, Tobias Canyon moved to where his father was pinned beneath the wreckage.

94

John Canyon wasn't in any pain. In fact, he felt almost euphoric, but he knew that he was dying. It was never a good sign when a person couldn't feel anything beneath his or her naval.

Tobias was on his knees beside him, and in the new dawn light and the flickering illumination of the flames, Canyon could see a little bit of himself in his son. He had always thought that the boy took after his mother, but when he looked up now he saw his own eyes looking back. The same fire, but one he had never taken the time to notice.

Tobias said, "An ambulance is on the way. We're gonna get you help. You'll be okay. Just lay still."

Canyon snorted a laugh and felt something tear inside of him as he did. He said, "I always could tell when you were lying, boy."

"I'm sorry that I allowed myself to be captured, Father."

"You don't have anything to be sorry for. I'm the one who's sorry. I've been so busy trying to build a legacy for our people that I forgot the best way I could do that was through you. I should've had you working beside me a long time ago."

Tears streamed down Tobias's cheeks, and he said, "I would've fought you every step of the way."

"But at least we would've been together. I love you, and I'm proud of you. Go be a better man than I was." Canyon coughed up blood before finishing, "Tell your mother that I love her and that I should have been a protector for her."

Sobbing and his words barely audible, Tobias said, "I can't believe this is happening. Maybe we can still do something. You should be telling her that yourself."

"Most people in my line of work, son, get their ticket punched without any warning. A bullet to the back of the head or a random chance death, wrong side of a deal gone bad. I'm just thankful that I've been given a moment to say goodbye."

Leaning over and crying on his father's chest, Tobias whispered, "I'm going to kill him for this. I'll avenge you, Father. I'll make him pay."

Canyon asked, "Who are you talking about?"

"The stranger... Francis Ackerman Jr. I heard him tell Liana. That's his real name."

Canyon used what strength he had left to grab the boy by the shirt and pull him close. He said, "You stay as far away from that man as you possibly can. He's filled with the spirit of Coyote, an ancient force that you cannot fight. Tell him to come over here."

"But Father—"

"I don't have much time or strength left. The real one who is responsible for this is your Uncle Xavier. And right now, the only way I'm going to get my vengeance against him is by helping the enemy of my enemy."

With a nod and a wipe of his tears, Tobias stood and went to fetch the stranger. A moment later Frank knelt by his side. He looked much different than he had before the bombs had gone off. He was now covered by layers of dust, soot, and blood. And there was something else. Something in his eyes that frightened Canyon beyond reason. Feeling himself slipping away and his cognitive reasoning slowing by the moment, John Canyon proclaimed, "Please kill him for me, Coyote. I recognize you now."

Frank said, "Where has Yazzie taken her?"

"The casino. He'll try to take Reyna with him. And he has cash there. If you don't stop him now, he'll disappear into Mexico."

Frank replied, "It has been some time since I've taken a trip south of the border, but considering that my friends probably don't have that long to live, I am completely open to your suggestions."

"Once, he took me up into the hills north of Roanhorse. I couldn't tell you where now. It was years ago, when we were kids. Way up in the cliffs, hidden, there was temple of the Old Ones. Undiscovered by the belegana dirt diggers. They had a kiva up there filled with bones. He showed it to me once and told me about a spirit that visited him when he had fallen into the pit. He called it He Who Devours the World. Yazzie always was out of his mind, to believe in such nonsense. But he does believe it, and I've heard him talk about He Who Devours several times over the years. I think he worships whatever it is as some kind of god. That's where he's taken your friend."

"I appreciate the information," Frank said, "but if you don't know where this temple of the Old Ones is located, that's not much help to me. How are we supposed to find it?"

Canyon shook his head. "Only Yazzie can tell you that. He'll be in the penthouse of the south tower. Thirteenth floor. And he doesn't think that I know about it, but there's a back way into the south tower that allows you to take the service elevator up to the penthouse. It's how he's been sneaking up to visit my wife. Just promise me that you'll kill him for me, Coyote."

Frank smiled and replied, "Consider it done."

95

Marcus was tired to the point that laying down in the dirt and sleeping from sheer exhaustion sounded like a good option. He, however, had no time the rest. He and Ackerman had begun searching the wrecked vehicles for any that were still usable. Worst case scenario, Marcus knew they could walk back to where he had left Yazzie's patrol vehicle. But time was not on their side.

His leg was completely numb now, and nausea was still on the attack. Noticing him dragging the leg, Ackerman asked, "What happened there?"

Marcus replied, "Yazzie introduced me to an Arizona bark scorpion. I named him Harvey."

"Sounds like fun."

"Oh yeah, you'd have loved it. I'll get you one for Christmas."

"That would be very exciting. I've never received a Christmas present before."

The smoke was still clearing out, the wind increasing and helping things along. As they walked, Ackerman noticed the crashed bathtub and asked, "How in the world did that find its way down here?"

Marcus said, "Your new friend, Officer Nakai, used it like a bobsled and rolled down the hill."

At the mention of her name, Ackerman's expression went dark. He said, "She has spunk, but I was just going to put the dynamite in there. Even I'm not crazy enough to take it for a ride. She should have stayed up at the trading post, as I instructed."

"We'll get her back. We'll get them both back."

Ackerman nodded in reply, and Marcus noticed a strange an alien expression on his brother's face. At the mention of Liana, Ackerman almost seemed to show the physical markers of fear. Perhaps the fear of losing his new friend? Or being responsible for her death? Marcus had been watching with amazement in recent months as his brother—whose ability to feel fear had been stripped from him by invasive brain surgery—had begun to exhibit signs of the emotional response as Ackerman discovered things that he loved and didn't want to lose.

Marcus was about to suggest that they run back to Yazzie's Explorer when, at the back of the now-destroyed line of cars, he saw what he'd been looking for. Emerging from the smoke like some sort of mythic beast was the narco tank, also known in Spanish as "monstruo" for their hulking size. Marcus had read about vehicles like this one, extensively manufactured and operated by drug cartels and other gangs involved in the Mexican Drug Wars. They were often modified semi-trucks, SUVs, dump trucks, or other large consumer or commercial vehicles that were converted into military grade weapons with varying levels of defensive and offensive capabilities. Even the smallest narco tanks, however, were plated with multiple inches of steel armor, and the black monstrosity emerging from the smoke looked like it could survive an attack from a real tank.

Upon further examination, Marcus realized that thought

was probably accurate, since one of the C-4 explosives had gone off beneath the Narco tank and it seemed relatively unscathed.

Glancing over at his brother, Marcus smiled for the first time in a in a long time and said, "You think the keys are in it?"

96

Having dropped off Ramirez and his scrawny partner with the keys to his patrol vehicle, Xavier Yazzie wheeled the panel van into a spot on the lowest level of the casino's parking garage and used an access tunnel to wind his way up to the service elevator of the south tower. He typically used this entrance to sneak up to his sister's penthouse, but today being clandestine was even more important, considering that he was carrying a woman, bound and gagged, over his shoulder.

Liana had, unfortunately, awakened halfway between the trading post and the casino and had required rope and a gag before proceeding. He had never imagined such things coming out of the mouth of his sweet, little subordinate.

She bucked and fought with every step, anything to make it more difficult for him. She didn't realize, however, that he liked it rough. The thought conjured mental pictures, which brought a smile to his face, but first, he needed to collect his sister and his nest egg before Frank found his way here.

The service elevator smelled like fresh linens. The maids must've already delivered Reyna's fresh towels and sheets. He didn't expect his sister to be awake at this hour. Still, she—just like their mother—was accustomed to being up all night.

The service elevator opened into a long pantry behind the penthouse's kitchen. With Liana still over his shoulder,

Xavier made his way through the kitchen and into the great room. It was an open floor plan, twelve foot ceilings with exposed rafters. The interior stucco walls were various shades of tans and warm reds, and the outer walls were lined with massive windows. The place spoke of opulence and smelled of creosote and sage, like the desert after a rain.

Xavier knew, however, that none of this beauty was because of his sister's good housekeeping or taste. Instead, it was interior decorators and maids who deserved the real credit. Or perhaps himself for providing her with a lifestyle like this. It was a far cry from the pervasive scents of sweat, sex, and soiled sheets that had marked their childhood. Of course, she didn't appreciate all he'd given her. All she seemed to care about these days was her next fix and her bed.

Liana seemed to have given up fighting for the moment, likely realizing that it merely gave him the opportunity to grope her rear under the pretense of restraining her. Not that he needed pretense with his young beauty any longer. She was now his to do with whatever he desired, but he enjoyed the game.

With his free hand, he opened the French doors that led out onto the balcony of the 13th floor. He took a deep breath as he did. The air always smelled so clean here. Up high, away from the smells of man, where only the wind and the birds were supposed to live.

Kicking out one of the chairs from the balcony's stone patio set, Xavier dropped his prisoner into the chair. Liana looked up at him with contempt. He could almost read what she was thinking with that look alone. Something about betrayal and that she had trusted him and looked up to him and blah, blah, blah. He didn't really care to hear her admonishments, and so he left the gag and restraints in place.

Ignoring her piercing gaze, he looked out over his land one more time. He didn't own any of it. After all, no man could truly own the land and the sky, but he controlled it all. John Canyon—as he had slaved away on his farm with his neck deep in sheep shit—had believed that he ruled this kingdom, but like other hidden figures throughout history, Xavier was the one who truly had the control and reaped all of the rewards. Like a good figurehead, Canyon would play his part perfectly. If he lived through the debacle at the trading post, he would still have to answer to federal authorities regarding his drug smuggling business. While Yazzie escaped south of the border with Canyon's wife and their money.

Turning away from the view, he noticed Reyna standing by the door and staring wide-eyed at the bound police woman in the chair. Meeting his gaze, his sister asked, "What is this?"

She looked beautiful, even though the two-hundred dollars a day that she snorted up her nose had started to cause her features to go slack and gaunt.

He said, "I'm glad you're up. Was it an all-nighter or did you just hear us come in?"

She merely looked at him with the same question in her eyes.

"Doesn't matter. You need to get the essentials packed right now. We're getting out of here."

"I'm not going anywhere with you."

"You'll do as I say, just like you always have, just like you always will."

"I'm not going anywhere without my son."

Xavier rolled his eyes. "He's fine. He's safe. He's not the one who's going to be in trouble. There are a couple of federal agents coming here."

She snapped back, "What have you done?"

"Once we get where we're going, I can buy you a new wardrobe and everything else you need. We're traveling light. Now. We have to hurry."

"I said that I'm not going anywhere with you."

"We can send for Tobias once we're safe."

"And who is this girl?"

"You know her. Liana, one of my deputies. And now, I suppose she's our insurance policy."

"Insurance against what?"

"In case the devil comes calling."

"The only devil I see is you, Xavier."

"I would choose my words carefully if I were you, sister. You can either do as I say, or I can knock you out and take you with me by force. Your choice, but think quick. We don't have much time."

Her bloodshot eyes bore holes into him, and her breath smelled of whiskey. She reminded him so much of their mother.

She said, "I hate you. I wish that I would've let you die all those years ago. When you fell into that pit, I knew exactly how to get back to those ruins. I know this land better than you ever will. The true spirit of this land. I took them around and pretended to be lost because I didn't want to find you. But I guess I'm not like you. My conscience got the better of me, and eventually, I led them up there. I saved you, and it was the biggest mistake I've ever made."

Xavier took a long step forward and said, "Don't worry, little sister. You got your wish. Your brother died up there in that pit, surrounded by the spirits of the Old Ones. You didn't save anyone. Your brother died and something else climbed up out of the pit when your weakness got the better of you! Now, if family therapy is over, I'm going to tell you one last time. Do as I say, or I will make you very sorry."

With tears dripping from her beautiful brown eyes, she retreated in fear to do as he had commanded. Just as she had always done, since they were children.

As Reyna left, Liana began making noises in her throat to get his attention. With another roll of his eyes, he undid the gag and asked, "Yes?"

Her face was a mask of hatred and barely contained rage. She said, "He's coming for you. You know that. And hell's coming with him."

Yazzie's face remained like stone as he stuck the gag back in her mouth and stroked her cheek. He replied, "The trick to not getting dragged down to hell is to get out of town before the devil knows you're dead. Your boyfriend won't be able to find us once we're down south with our friends from the cartel."

Yazzie felt his phone vibrate against his leg. Pulling it out and looking at the screen, he saw that the call was coming from the casino's security chief. Pressing the button to answer, Yazzie said, "Speak."

The woman's voice sounded tinny and muffled over the phone's speaker. "We have an urgent situation."

"I'm listening."

"We just had someone call in a bomb threat, telling us that we have less than fifteen minutes to get everyone out of the building. What should we do? They said that they have enough explosives hidden to take down the whole place."

He, of course, knew exactly who had called in the supposed bomb threat, and it made perfect sense. Frank knew that more of Alvarez's men would be waiting at the casino, and he knew that's where Yazzie would be headed.

The security chief asked, "Sir?"

"Go ahead and evacuate everyone. We can't be too careful. Pull them back to a safe distance, and keep them there until I give the go-ahead."

"Yes, sir."

Turning to Liana, Yazzie said, "Speak of the devil. Your friend is closer than I thought. He thinks he's smart by getting all of the civilians out of the way in order to avoid casualties. But his little plan is going to work out perfectly for us. We'll let the cartel and the feds fight it out while we slip out the back and melt away into the crowd of evacuated guests."

The phone still in his hand, Yazzie dialed the number for Alvarez's lieutenant, who was waiting with his men in one of the casino's ballrooms. When the cartel team leader's voice came over the phone, he said, "They're coming. Get your men ready for war."

97

Just as Marcus had hoped, the parking lot of the Grand Canyon Hotel and Casino was a mass of humanity, a few thousand people awakened before breakfast and told that they were about to explode. Marcus supposed it to be a fitting use of the term "rude awakening."

The parking lot took up several more acres than was necessary, especially with the built-in parking structure, but it was definitely useful in situations like this. Marcus had stopped by the casino earlier and had been impressed by the extravagance of the place. It was comprised of several interconnected buildings of sandy-colored glass and concrete. The windows had been tinted with some kind of red reflective material, which gave the impression of a shimmering mirage. The most impressive feature Marcus had noticed, however, was the casino's version of the Grand Canyon. A circle had been cut in the ground and covered with reinforced plexiglass. A portion of the glass surface was inside the building and a portion beneath valet parking.

When Marcus had walked through the place earlier, he had taken the tour, which included a viewing area adorned with plaques that had been inscribed with the story of the building of the faux canyon.

Marcus had to admit that the effect was realistic and dizzying. The plaques had stated that their canyon was only fifty feet deep, but as a result of some excellent artistry, the area beneath the glass, incorporating shading and optical illusions, made it seem that you were standing over the actual Grand Canyon. He imagined it was quite the tourist attraction and draw for the casino. A fact that was confirmed by the number of people who had flooded into the resort's parking lot.

Marcus stayed back from the crowd, not wanting the Narco tank to draw too much attention. He wondered how in the hell the cartel members had gotten the thing across the border. But he supposed it was probably as simple as a few bribes to the right people to look the other way. Money had a way of opening doors, especially locked ones.

He pulled over to the side of the road leading up from the interstate after passing a gas station, fast food restaurants, and stores that had taken advantage of the influx of people the casino had brought with it. It was clearly a place that had sprung up from nothing, rather than a town that had benefited from an economic boost.

Marcus closed his eyes and pictured the pathway through the casino. He had walked the whole property earlier, just to get the lay of the land for future reference. So now, using his eidetic memory, Marcus traveled back in time and relived those moments, verifying the layout of the casino and his path through it.

He had no idea how many cartel gunmen were waiting for him, and he supposed it didn't really matter. He wasn't the kind of person that had ever enjoyed killing. He knew that every one of those men had a mother and a father, a family, a wife, kids. They were each someone's loved ones, no matter how evil they may have seemed when viewing them through the snapshot of a few moments of their lives.

But there were times in life when it was kill or be killed.

If it were merely his life on the line, maybe he would've looked at things differently, but it wasn't just his life. And he didn't have time for doubt or remorse. Whoever was left in that casino at this point—since he knew that there were no real police close enough to have responded yet—were either cartel members or Yazzie's men.

He was fine with both groups, as long as they didn't get in his way.

With the path through the casino laid out in his mind, Marcus pulled out onto the main thoroughfare heading up to the resort. Then he hit the accelerator and didn't intend to let off until he had rammed the Narco tank right down the Grand Canyon's throat.

What he was about to do reminded him of another incident at a hospital in Colorado Springs. At the time, he didn't even know that he had a brother, and Ackerman was the dragon he had come to slay. Instead, Frank had pulled him from the fire, and the pair had begun a journey that had taken them both to some very unexpected places. All he had wanted back then was to live a simple life somewhere quiet, but the Director of the Shepherd Organization had shoved his way into Marcus's life and altered it forever.

Now, the Director was dead, and the dragon he had come to slay in Colorado had become his brother and his best friend. He sometimes couldn't comprehend how easily life could turn one hundred and eighty degrees and change completely within the blink of an eye, with one choice.

But then again, he was about to make the same idiotic decision that he had all those years ago, so he supposed the things didn't change too much.

The steering wheel felt worn down against his palms. He

could relate. He gazed toward the building and calculated the path of least resistance. He laid on the horn to clear the crowd and braced himself for impact. The front entrance of the structure was a giant pillar of glass that rose up the entire height of the building. He didn't slow as the black beast broke through and rumbled into the building's interior.

Smashing through the glass, the shards falling like a waterfall of knives, he saw the first of the cartel members. They were armed with AK-47s and were already opening fire on the narco tank's tires. Marcus heard the bullets dinging off of the wheel wells, but he had also noticed earlier that both front and back wheels of the modified vehicle were protected by armor plating and equipped with dual wheels. Instead of having four tires, the narco tank rode on eight.

Shifting into a lower gear, Marcus plowed through the casino like a bull in a china shop. He pulled the emergency brake and yanked the wheel, sliding into the rows of slot machines that the cartel members were using as cover.

Following the path already laid out in his mind, Marcus plowed through the casino with reckless abandon, crushing everything and everyone in his path. He continued on this way until he reached the elevator for the south tower. Then he spun the tank in a tight circle, slamming into the high roller poker room, as he checked to make sure that he didn't have any remaining pursuers. Satisfied that the cartel members were all handled in one way or another, he threw open his armored door and stepped down from the black monstrosity.

With one last look over his shoulder, Marcus patted the side of the armor-plated behemoth and said, "Good girl. I'm probably going to prison after all this, but if somehow I don't, I'm gonna take you home with me."

98

Xavier Yazzie yelled across the penthouse, "We're leaving, Reyna." Then, moving back to the balcony, he bent down and looked Liana straight in the eyes. He had replaced his glasses and hat with an extra pair he kept there. He had always loved the fact that when he looked a person deep in the eyes, all they saw was his cold unfeeling expressions and their own fear reflected back in the mirror image on his glasses.

To Liana, he said, "If I take out the gag and remove the rope from your feet, do you promise to be a good girl?"

Her eyes still telling a tale of defiance, she nodded nonetheless. Removing her gag and restraints, he stood and was about to yell another warning at Reyna, when he heard a large and powerful engine roaring to life nearby. Moving to the railing—to the view from which he normally admired his land—he watched in horror as the narco tank plowed into his casino like a black bullet. Then he heard the breaking of glass and the echoes of destruction.

Turning to Liana, he said, "Time to go."

"I always knew you were a snake."

He stroked her cheek and said, "And I always wanted to get up inside of you, in more ways than one. Now, are you going to walk or do I need to carry you again? I have to admit that I enjoyed holding you."

Her eyes like daggers, she replied, "I'll walk."

99

Ackerman had always adored the shadows. In fact, if it were up to him, he would seize every opportunity to be bathed in the warm and comforting feeling of total darkness. It wasn't that a fear of the light or that he was ashamed and wanted to keep his dark deeds from the illumination of day. It was simply that darkness made it easier to block out the rest of the world and to go into his own mental universe. He had lived there most of his life, in one cage or another with nothing to occupy himself but his own mind. He had gradually begun to view the darkness as his friend. And now, he found it easier to see the light when he was in the darkness.

As he crouched within a niche in the service tunnel beside a series of electrical panels, Ackerman thought of something his brother had once said regarding darkness and light. That one could shine a light into the darkness but that the darkness could never shine itself into the light.

Even from his position at the very back of the casino, and on the lowest level, Ackerman plainly heard when his brother made his attack. He had to admit that he was a bit jealous that he hadn't been afforded the opportunity to play bumper cars with the makeshift tank. But he also knew how fast Yazzie was with the gun. Too fast for either him or his brother to take on in a quick draw situation, especially with innocent normals in the crossfire. Mostly fearing for

Liana's safety, Ackerman had petitioned to his brother to be the one who set the trap, and so Marcus and Ackerman had once again assembled the portable two-wheeled all-terrain vehicle, which Marcus had used earlier to scout the ranch in search of Maggie. Ackerman had then circled around through the desert, following Canyon's instructions, to find Yazzie's secret entrance into the casino. Now, with his brother serving as the distraction and driving their prey into the trap, all that was left was to wait for the service elevator doors to open.

As he waited, Ackerman considered a serial killer by the name of Harold Shipman, who had been a doctor believed to have killed over two-hundred and thirty-six people. Most of his victims were killed from intentional overdoses with no real motive as to why except for that Harold Shipman fancied himself a god. Many believed him to be the most prolific serial killer in history. That, of course, was adhering to the definition of a serial killer being a person who murders three or more people, in two or more separate events over a period of time, for primarily psychological reasons, which included historical figures such as Genghis Khan and Alexander the Great, each of whom was responsible for millions of deaths.

He had tried to count up his own number of victims on many separate occasions, but things like explosions and buildings he had burned to ash made it difficult to pin down the exact numbers. It also wasn't as if he specifically laid claim to each of his attacks, and so the authorities had no idea either.

Once upon a time, being the most prolific serial murderer in history had seemed like the only real goal he could ever attain. He had abandoned all hope of living in the light, and instead, he had chosen to embrace the darkness. What he'd found was that darkness was an illusion.

He was torn away from his mental thesis by the ding of an elevator and the whirring of its motors. He heard the doors part, but there was a hesitation before he heard any footsteps. He imagined that Yazzie was checking the corridor with his gun at the ready, just to be safe, but he also knew that Yazzie believed this exit to be one that they would never discover.

Ackerman waited in the shadows of his hiding place for a few seconds after hearing the eventual sound of three sets of feet exiting the elevator and moving down the corridor toward the parking structure. He then slipped out and without making a sound—utilizing a technique of walking heel to toe with light touches that he had actually learned from a book on American Indians—Ackerman moved up behind Yazzie, who was pushing the women along at gunpoint.

When he had closed the gap to ten feet, Ackerman said, "I have a shotgun pointed at your back, Captain. Do not turn around, but slowly place your weapon on the ground."

Yazzie became a statue. He didn't make any offensive movements, but neither did he do as he was told. The police captain and serial murderer said, "What are you going to do, Frank? Kill me? You wouldn't risk shooting me with a shotgun, when you still have no idea where your missing friend has been stashed away. Only I can save her, and only I know where she is. So give me one good reason I should put down my gun?"

"Well, Captain, this shotgun is loaded with special

home defense rounds, which would cause an exquisite level of damage from this distance. I wonder if I squeezed the trigger right now, with my aim on your legs, what would happen? Would you merely be peppered with lead, or do you think I could blow one of your legs completely off at the shin? You want a reason... How about this? I would love nothing more than to see what your insides look like as I start removing pieces of you."

Yazzie replied, "You wouldn't risk it. And even if you did, I would take the location to my grave. Even if you torture me, I'll just lead you on a wild goose chase. But if you let my sister and I walk out of here, I'll call you in two hours and tell you your friend's location."

Ackerman laughed. "I'm sorry, but this is just priceless. It's like the hyena dictating terms to the lion. I've already broken my no-murder streak today, so what difference does it make if I end you? I'm thinking of getting one of those signs that they hang up in factories and places where the work is especially dangerous. The kind of sign that displays information like the number of days without an accident. Only mine would say something like 'X number of days without the spilling of lifeblood.' And until I have a place to hang the aforementioned sign, I have a virtual version stored in my mental palace. If I killed you now, I wouldn't even have to worry about changing the sign."

"But you'd never find your friend."

"I wouldn't be so sure about that. Mr. Canyon had quite a bit to say about you after you left the party. He told some interesting stories about an undiscovered Anasazi temple hidden among the cliffs north of Roanhorse."

Ackerman had been studying Yazzie's every tiny muscle twitch, and at the mention of the temple of his ancestors, several of the captain's muscles stiffened. Yazzie said, "You would never find it without me."

Ackerman, unfortunately, knew that to be true. But he also took things one step at a time, and it always seemed that the universe provided.

As if right on cue, Reyna Canyon—John's wife and Yazzie's sister—said, "I can take you there."

Yazzie blurted, "Shut up, Reyna."

"No, Xavier," she said, and to Ackerman, "I can take you to the exact spot, but you have to do something for me."

"And that is?"

"You have to kill my brother. Right here. Right now. Pull that trigger and end him."

Ackerman, still watching for Yazzie's every twitch, recognized the slight sagging of the man's shoulders at his sister's betrayal.

With a small chuckle, Ackerman replied, "Deal. I can promise you that, where he's going, he'll never be able to hurt you again. So, now the only question is, Captain, would you like to die now or later?"

Reyna, her eyes going wide, said, "Kill him now! You don't know what he's capable of."

"You're right, my dear. I don't fully understand what your brother is capable of. But I know what I'm capable of. And lions don't fear hyenas."

Moving slowly, Yazzie laid his gun on the ground and said, "She would never be able to find it on her own. Not after all these years. You still need me."

Yazzie's last word was punctuated by another dinging

of the elevator. This time, Marcus emerged, an MP5 at his shoulder, and joined them in the service corridor.

Ackerman saw his brother marching toward their prisoner in his peripheral vision, and he honestly didn't know what Marcus would do to the man who had stolen Maggie. Without any warning, his brother raised the MP five and shot Yazzie in the meat of his left thigh, dropping the police captain to his knees. Then, sticking the warm barrel of the gun against the back of Yazzie's neck, Marcus snarled, "You're going to take us to Maggie. Right now. No tricks."

With a roll of his eyes, Ackerman said, "We've already been through this. Yazzie's sister, Reyna, is going to be so kind as to guide us to her brother's temple of the Old Ones."

Turning back to Ackerman, Marcus said, "Then what are we waiting for? Let's go get our girl."

100

Laying atop her bed of bones, Special Agent Maggie Carlisle fought to remain conscious. Intuition told her that to fall asleep now would mean to fall asleep forever. She had to be approaching the point of total dehydration, and without much ventilation in the pit, carbon dioxide poisoning was also a strong possibility.

Carol—her partner in the pit—had passed away in the night. Maggie had heard her stop breathing, and upon checking, she'd been unable to resuscitate.

Now, laying there thinking about how much longer she could possibly live without water, she thought of the blood coagulating in Carol's veins as she decayed. But still she refused the idea of cannibalism. It went against every fiber of her being.

Then again, she hadn't killed the woman. In fact, she had spared her when she had the chance. It just so happened that Carol must've been slightly more dehydrated than she had been at the onset of their ordeal. Maybe it wouldn't be so bad. But if she was going to do that, she should've done it at the beginning before the flesh had a chance to decay. She shoved the thoughts from her mind. She would rather die having been able to say that she had never eaten a person then the other way around.

She had tried to prepare herself for death as best she could, but she supposed that there was never really anyone who was completely ready. She still had things she wanted to see and do. Things she wanted to say. Most of all, she had never truly accomplished the goal she had set out to achieve. She may have found her brother's killer, but she still didn't know her brother's fate, and that bothered her immensely. Perhaps more than anything. She had to trust that Marcus would pick up the trail and finish what she had begun, but she had never been adept at trusting people.

Maggie felt like someone had attached thousand-pound weights to her eyelids and wondered how long it'd been since she'd slept. It felt like she had been trapped here for weeks, but she knew that it couldn't have been more than a few days. Otherwise, she would've already been dead of dehydration.

When a blinding light shined down from above and stung her eyes, even through her closed lids, Maggie thought that she had died and was being raised up to the next plane of existence. A part of her had been relieved it was over.

She heard the voices of two men.

Angels? she wondered.

Then, one of the men swore in Spanish, and the pair then started arguing about who is going to be the one to go down in the pit and retrieve her. Her foggy brain started making connections, and she realized that these men could be here to rescue her. Rolling over, she turned her face toward them and reached up. Her throat felt too dry to speak, and so she merely croaked deeper in her throat to get their attention.

In the dim light above, she could see the faces of the two men. One was a handsome bronze-skinned young man, well-built and clearly the leader of the two. The other was merely a pile of bones with skin stretched over it.

As Maggie raised her arm and moaned up at them, the skinny one said, "Zombie!"

The other man slapped him across the back of the head.

The handsome one said, "We're coming down, lady. We have water."

Those had been the sweetest words that Maggie had ever heard, and so she merely laid her head back onto her bed of bones and gently sobbed. Although, in her dehydrated state, she couldn't produce tears and felt like she'd been eating sandpaper, which made her cries sound like the wheezing of an asthmatic.

101

Marcus sat behind the wheel of the panel van Yazzie had commandeered from Canyon's roadblock, his foot pushed to the floor and his mind racing. All he could think about was getting there in time and seeing Maggie's face.

The drive up into the hills was mostly a quiet one. There had, of course, been the catching up conversations at the beginning: the tales of Liana's wild ride and his trip through the casino in the Narco tank and Ackerman had felt compelled to talk to them about a killer named Harold Shipman. The most difficult conversation by far, however, had been revealing to Reyna Canyon that her husband was dead. Although, after the fact, Marcus hadn't noticed much of the reaction one would expect from a grieving widow. She had insisted that they take her to her son, stating that she needed him there after John's death. But the brothers had quickly dismissed that idea, having no intention of trusting Yazzie to show them the way.

Temperatures in the valley were starting to rise along with the sun, even though the latter remained hidden behind dark storm clouds, which cast the desert landscape into shades of gray.

Marcus couldn't remember the last time he had slept, but he was far from tired now. He'd already pushed through that wall and was now going to see this race through to the end, even if it was the death of him.

Reyna directed him from the front passenger seat and led the way deep into the hills and canyons north of Roanhorse, to a place where all traces of modern life disappeared and the road came to an end. Marcus threw the van into park and cocked an eyebrow at his navigator. She said, "We're on foot from here."

102

The hike into the hills was long and arduous and none of them were really prepared for it. With every step, Ackerman felt as if tiny nails were being driven into his wounds. Not that he disliked the pain, but it had started to become a distraction within the first half mile. With most of them bleeding and having been awake for days, a hike into the wilderness was the last activity in which any of them wanted to partake.

Ackerman had suspected that it was Reyna Canyon who had sent Maggie the photograph for some time now, but his brother's brain worked differently. Marcus needed proof. He thought like a cop searching out a conviction, while Ackerman allowed his imagination to travel down the wildest of paths.

As they pushed forward for nearly an hour, several conversations popped up, all of them short and awkward. Marcus's intensity loomed over them all. His brother set the pace, and the others seemed almost too winded to speak. Ackerman, of course, had no problem keeping up. In fact, he had considered scouting ahead, but thought better of it, not wanting to let Yazzie out of his sight.

Liana showed him a few of the desert fauna along the way, plants with names like sagebrush, juniper, tamarisk, tree of heaven, blue mustard, and bull thistle. But each interaction seemed awkward in some way. He supposed that, since they had actually survived, she was reconsidering her invitation for a kiss. Not that Ackerman concerned himself either way. Things happened or they didn't. Unless one made those things happen on one's own, which usually resulted in adverse consequences.

Finally, Reyna stopped short and looked to her brother to reveal his own secrets. Yazzie—displaying what seemed to Ackerman a suspicious level of cooperation—hadn't really fought them at all since his capture at the casino. He moved aside some scrub brush and then swiped his hand across the sand to reveal a metal handle. Grasping it with both hands, he lifted off a piece of sheet metal, which covered a tunnel large enough for a person to comfortably slide down through hard-packed desert floor and into the rock below.

Ackerman asked, "You dug this?"

Yazzie shook his head. "It was always here. I found the opening on the other side and had to clear out many hundreds of years of dirt and disrepair. But this was a secret entrance to the temple, probably only used by the priests of the Old Ones."

Ackerman had read a few accounts of the Anasazi. Mainly the theories about how the group built their homes high in the cliffs with limited access to critical resources and then disappeared, which carried with it a myriad of speculation and conspiracy theories. Some of the more recent archaeological digs had also discovered irrefutable evidence of cannibalism in the form of fossilized human feces, known as coprolite.

Yazzie added, "The metal cover is a recent addition, of course. I wanted easy access so I could come out here to pray. I suppose I'm the priest of the temple now."

Through clenched teeth, Marcus said, "You ain't priest of jack or shit, but you'd better pray that Maggie's still alive down there."

The implication hung in the air until Marcus, taking a quick measure of the entrance, dropped down first in order to scout ahead and ensure that there were no traps. After a moment, he yelled back up to send Yazzie down.

Once they had all followed and gathered inside a small stone antechamber, Yazzie closed his eyes and took a deep breath. Addressing the group, he said, "Do you feel them? Can you feel their presence?"

Marcus shoved him forward and said, "Take us to Maggie or you're going to feel the presence of my foot up your ass."

Scowling at the disrespect of his heritage but not protesting, Yazzie led them through the corridors of stone and sand that the Anasazi had carved into the most inaccessible of places. They followed a narrow corridor into what seemed to be a natural cavern that the Anasazi had converted into their equivalent of the holiest of holies.

Ackerman asked, "Were you first one to discover this place, Yazzie?"

"No, most of these ruins, just like a large portion of all known remnants of my ancestors, have been pillaged. Either by people looking to sell the potsherds and artifacts or the belegana dirt diggers looking to carry them off to museums. Both of which are common thieves. I do, however, believe that I was the first to discover the lower kiva, a teardrop-shaped chamber beneath this temple where sacrifices were made to He Who Devours."

Ackerman, examining the stone altars, asked, "He Who Devours...Friend of yours?"

"He Who Devours the World. He is the darkness that will one day extinguish the fire of all existence. He's not my friend. He's my master. My god."

Ackerman nodded and replied, "I see. Reminds me of the story of a hen in Leeds, England that was believed to be heralding the end of days. It was laying eggs inscribed with the words 'Christ is Coming.' Whole thing turned out to be a fraud. They had used some sort of corrosive ink."

"Don't mock me!"

Cutting off the conversation, Marcus snapped, "I'm losing my cool here, Yazzie."

An angry snarl across his face, he said, "She's this way." Then he led them to where another metal sheet had been installed to conceal the entrance of what Yazzie had referred to as the lower kiva. As Yazzie pulled away the metal covering, he said, "This is where I saw her last."

Knocking the older man aside, Marcus threw the metal plate off like it weighed nothing and shined the beam of his Maglite down into the depths below. As the light licked at the darkness, Ackerman saw the mounds of skulls and bones and said, "This was some sort of sacrificial chamber. I've read articles that propose the Anasazi disappeared not because of invaders, but because of cannibalism and civil war within their own empire."

Yazzie chuckled for some reason known only to him. It was the first real moment that Ackerman detected the madness which lived inside the man.

Frantically shining the flashlight beam from one corner

of the chamber to the other, Marcus said, "What is this, Yazzie? Where is she? Where—"

The booming sound of a gunshot resounded across the cavern like thunder. Ackerman recognized it as the report of a high-powered rifle. Marcus looked over at his brother with a confused look on his face. Touching his side to reveal the blood, Marcus said, "Frank?" And then fell toward the sacrificial pit.

103

It didn't take Maggie long to figure out that the two men, who almost literally raised her from the dead, were more like ghetto commandos rather than paramedics or firemen. The skinny one even wore some sort of do-rag over his skeletal visage. Still, even if they were little green men, she didn't have the strength to fight back.

The next several moments flew by in a whirlwind, during which she phased in and out of consciousness. The fact that they were not rescue workers was further confirmed by the fact that they merely grabbed her beneath the arms and dragged her through the dirt of the cavern and up a small trail, to where natural stalagmite and stalagmite formations had formed a curtain of stone. The Hispanic-looking one carried a high-powered rifle with a scope, while his thinner partner carried an AK-47 assault rifle. The two men laid her in the niche and started setting up some sort of encampment.

"Water," she croaked.

The two men looked at each other, and the skinny one said, "You're in charge, Ramirez. What did your new boss tell you to do?"

"I do what I have to do to survive. And no one said that he's my boss."

The skinny one rolled his eyes and said, "Okay, Jamie, I didn't mean to—"

"Just get her some water."

The skinny one complied, and Maggie was thankful for the healthy gulps of H_2O as it poured down her throat. Maggie wanted to talk. She wanted to ask questions or figure out what the heck was going on. She wondered if this could be some sort of trap Canyon was setting for Captain Yazzie, but she really had no idea what was happening. For all she knew, this could've been an attack orchestrated by Marcus or his brother. But she supposed there wasn't much she could do about it either way, so she slipped off into a strange dreamland of scorpions and sand and old bones.

Still, her thoughts dwelled on the sharpened femur bone that she had hidden in her pant leg. It would be a useful tool, but she lacked the strength to wield it.

She wasn't sure how long she'd continued on that way, slipping in and out of consciousness, reality and dreams becoming so distorted that the world felt like the flipping of channels on an old TV set. Unfortunately, most of the channels seemed to be static.

But then she heard voices echoing through the cavernous chamber of the temple. Not just any voices, familiar voices. Her heart started racing. Adrenaline pumping. Her mind coming back into sharper focus. There were several voices, but two had stood out that she knew well. The voices of the love of her life, Marcus Williams, and his brother, whose voice she was also marginally happy to hear.

She tried to roll over without making too much sound or drawing the attention of her captors, which she now assumed these men to be. Dust and sand from the floor of the niche blew into her face and nose, but she didn't mind. Anything to overpower the stink of death that still clung to the inside of her nostrils.

The voices continued, coming closer. As they did, she prepared to move. Undoing her jeans, she slipped her hand behind the back of her thigh and removed the sharpened bone, a weapon she had been begun fashioning on her first day in the pit. She had intended it for the neck of Captain Xavier Yazzie, but it was always a good idea to field test a weapon before using it on one's primary target.

But even retrieving the weapon sapped her strength, and she began to doubt her ability to move against either of the men. The water had definitely helped, and she no longer felt the effects of the dehydration, but she was still weak from the ordeal, not to mention the damage to her leg and hand. Perhaps waiting would be a better idea, gathering her strength, clearing the fog from her brain. She had no idea what was actually going on, but she knew enough to know that attacking someone with the intention of killing them wasn't something you wanted to do unless you were sure. She was unsure in a lot of ways, and so she waited.

The two men conversed a few times in hushed tones. Maggie was close enough to hear them, but they spoke in Spanish, a language of which she only knew the basics.

The one whom the skinny one had referred to as Ramirez looked down the scope of his rifle and seemed to be making slight adjustments on his sights. The skinny one had propped himself on the ledge of the rock formation, ready to open fire with his AK-47.

As she tried to blink the cobwebs free from her eyes, which had been deprived of light for the past few days, Maggie recognized that Ramirez was military trained by the way that he moved and held the rifle. She could also tell that he was readying himself to fire, which meant it was now or never. Either she would make a move or not, because someone that she cared about could be on the wrong end of that rifle. She tried to lunge forward but was unable to push herself up on her arms. Her two captors were focused on their targets and ignoring her. She realized that, even if she was able to take out Ramirez and keep him from shooting, his skeletal little friend would simply turn the AK-47 on her. Pushing those thoughts aside, she told herself that her own life didn't matter. She just had to move.

But her muscles wouldn't cooperate. Her whole body tingled, and she felt like she had been sitting inside a dryer on spin cycle. She took several deep breaths, trying to psych herself up.

She rolled forward and pushed herself up onto one knee. From that angle, she now saw that Ramirez also had a side-arm, which answered the question of how she would handle his partner.

She heard Marcus's voice again, accompanied by others.

Ramirez, possibly aware of her presence but not considering her enough of a threat to take his eyes off his target, paid her no attention. The military-trained young man had underestimated her. A mistake that people had made about her for most of her life. Ramirez was about to pay for that mistake.

She lunged forward, her makeshift bone knife extended for the kill. But instead of connecting with her target, she stumbled and fell to the side, again ending up in the dirt. She remained there for second, the bone knife clutched to her abdomen, her left hand and knees supporting her.

And then Maggie felt the concussion wave of the rifle blast, followed a millisecond later by the sound of the shot.

104

It took Ackerman a fraction of a second to ascertain that they had walked into a trap and to take action. Having caught his brother beneath the arms before Marcus could topple head-first into the pit of bones, Ackerman carried him to a place of cover within the rock formation. As he made his first two steps toward safety, the cavern erupted with the sound of gunfire from a different caliber weapon. An assault rifle. It was difficult for Ackerman to determine the precise direction and angle of the shooters with the sound echoing all over the cavernous chamber.

Laying his brother on the hard rock floor of the temple, Ackerman examined the wound. It was in a bad spot. The bullet could very well have hit some vital part of Marcus's anatomy. It wasn't a fatal shot outright, but could turn into one if Marcus didn't receive medical attention soon.

Tearing off a piece of his brother's shirt, Ackerman made an emergency medical compress and told Marcus to hold the fabric in place over his wound and apply pressure.

Liana had followed them to cover and was now crouched down on the other side of Marcus. She asked, "How can I help?"

Ackerman was about to instruct her to come around and assist Marcus, while he found a way to dispatch whoever had shot his brother. But his machinations were cut short by a man's scream. The sound was strange in the cavernous space. It echoed and compounded upon itself. The cry of pain was cut short by a wet thwack, immediately followed by gunfire of another caliber. This time Ackerman estimated it to be a 9mm.

Back at the hotel, Ackerman had confiscated Yazzie's pearl-handled Peacemaker and gun belt and had decided to use them himself. Now, he pulled the forty-five long Colt revolver from its holster and cocked back the hammer.

When Ackerman heard the first shot and realized that Marcus had been hit by a sniper's bullet, he disregarded everyone else in the group and immediately went to his brothers aid. Looking back to the other side of the cavern, he saw where Reyna Canyon had found her own shelter in a similar cleft in the rock. But there was no sign of Xavier Yazzie, and Ackerman also noted that Marcus's MP5 was no longer beside the pit where his brother had dropped it.

He estimated that the attack had been carried out by two men operating under Yazzie's order. One man wielding an AK-47 and the other—the one who shot Marcus and would soon die by Ackerman's hand—had set up behind the scope of a .30-06 sniper rifle. Neither of these attackers were of much concern to him. But Yazzie, armed with a submachine gun, could definitely be a wrench in the gears.

Reyna Canyon looked to him with terror in her eyes from across the cavernous temple. He held up a hand to instruct her to stay where she was.

He heard someone stumbling down from the waterfall stalactite and stalagmite formation where he had estimated the gunfire to have originated. Not waiting for them to arrive, he rolled forward from his hiding spot, landed in a crouch, and took aim at the armed figure headed toward them. When he realized who it was, a strange warmth passed over him at seeing his little sister alive.

He rushed toward Maggie. She held a 9mm Beretta clutched tightly in her right fist. It was clear that Maggie, having somehow escaped the pit, had dispatched the men who had laid an ambush and shot Marcus. Grabbing his unsteady little sister beneath the shoulders, he carried her back to the rock formation where he had left Marcus and Liana.

Maggie, upon seeing the blood spreading across Marcus's shirt, pulled away from Ackerman and rushed to Marcus's side. They didn't bother checking each other's wounds. The couple merely embraced one another and kissed deeply, tears streaming down both their cheeks.

Feeling oddly voyeuristic, Ackerman focused his mind on other tasks. Namely, determining where Xavier Yazzie had wandered off to.

105

The joy Maggie felt overshadowed every bit of the hurt and pain. In that moment, when she embraced Marcus, she forgot about everything else. She forgot about the search for her brother and the whereabouts of the man who took him. She forgot about her days in the pit of the dead, her very soul being drained away by the spirits that Yazzie worshiped. In that moment, all she cared about was holding the man she loved, something that she never thought she would get to do again.

They held each other for what felt like an eternity. Maggie felt her tears streaming down and mixing with Marcus's as she held him cheek to cheek. He was the first to break the silence. He said, "I'm so sorry, Maggie. I should've been there for you. I should've realized how important it was to find your brother. Everything that's happened in the past few years should never have happened, because I should've dropped everything to help you. I love you, more than anything, and I'm sorry that it takes situations like this to make me realize that."

Marcus's statement was punctuated by a cough and a rattling sound in his chest that Maggie hoped wasn't blood. Pulling away only far enough so that they could talk, Maggie said, "None of that matters now. I'm sorry too. I should've never went off on my own. I should've trusted you. But we can talk about all that later."

Marcus squeezed her hand. He said, "There might not be a later. We always think that we'll have another chance to say what we need to say, but we never know when someone we love is going to be taken away. And I have something very important that I've been meaning to ask you."

A woman, who Maggie recognized as Reyna Canyon, appeared at her shoulder, interrupting Marcus and saying, "What happened to the people shooting at us?"

Maggie, hoping merely to placate the frightened woman, replied, "We're safe now."

"We need to find my brother or none of us will ever be safe. It may take him years, but Xavier always gets his revenge."

Marcus, still holding a compress to the bullet wound in his stomach, said, "Reyna was the one who sent you the photograph, Maggie."

Reluctantly tearing her eyes away from Marcus, Maggie looked for the first time at the wife of John Canyon and sister to Xavier Yazzie. All she could manage to say was, "Why?"

Reyna's cheeks were wet with tears. She replied, "I'm so sorry for the things that my brother and husband have done. I should've stood up sooner. But John recently discovered that Xavier had been sending his little care packages out to the families of the children we stole."

"You were involved? You, your husband, and your brother... All three of you were the Taker?"

"My brother had the idea, John had the connections, and I was along for the ride. We always took kids out of bad homes, but I suppose it doesn't really matter."

"No, it doesn't. You're every bit as bad as the others."

Reyna directed her gaze to the stone floor but continued, "There's nothing I can do but say that I'm sorry. I can't turn back time. I don't know what happened to all of the kids, but if it helps at all, I know that your brother was given a decent life. I made sure of that."

Grabbing the other woman by the shirt and pulling her close, she said, "Don't you dare lie to me. If you know my brother, then where is he now?"

Reyna quickly explained, "We couldn't sell him once they found out he was a half-blood. The client only wanted one hundred percent caucasians. My brother suggested taking the boy out into the desert and disposing of him, but I wouldn't have it. I insisted that we find a place for him, and my uncle Red agreed to take him in. We gave your brother a new name and a new life. It might not have been the life he was meant to have, but at least he got to live it. His name now is Jamie Ramirez. He works for my husband. We even got him good enough fake papers so that he could go to the military."

Maggie went silent as the pieces started to fall into place. Reyna said more, but Maggie was unable to hear. It was as if she had gone deaf or the entire rest of the world had gone silent.

Jamie Ramirez.

She thought back on the young Hispanic man who had pulled her from the pit. Recalling his facial features, she could see a bit of her mother in him.

Her whole body trembled. She felt like a porcelain doll in an earthquake, and she was slowly cracking apart.

Pushing the older woman aside and rushing back up the sloping floor of the cavern, Maggie thought back on the manner in which she had dispatched their two attackers. She had fully intended to kill both of the gunman, but when she had stumbled and fallen back, she found a rock that fit perfectly in her fist. At the time, she had merely figured that the rock would make for a quick and possibly silent knockout. Which hadn't worked like she intended. Ramirez had squeezed off a shot and required two blows for the knockout. With his partner alerted to the danger, she had been forced to shoot the skinny young man with the 9mm she pulled from the holster on Ramirez's hip. She didn't think she had hit Ramirez hard enough to kill him, but she couldn't be sure. At the time, her only concern had been disarming them and protecting herself and her family.

The joy she had felt only a moment earlier at seeing Marcus was forgotten now, replaced by an all-encompassing desire to find her brother, who had been closer than she could have possibly imagined. After everything she had been through, after all the years of wondering what had happened to him, all the years of searching, all the years pain, and now, she had nearly killed him with her own hands.

As she reached the rock formation from which they had set the ambush, Maggie felt a terrible weight lifted from her when she discovered that she hadn't killed her brother. Apparently, she hadn't even fully knocked him unconscious because the man named Ramirez—and his rifle—were gone.

106

Ackerman followed the stink of Yazzie's fear through the stone corridors, away from the natural rock formation of the temple, to a spot where he could see daylight in the distance. The passage opened upon a collection of Anasazi dwellings sheltered beneath a canopy of rock, all sandstone and amazingly preserved against the ravages of time within the massive alcove. The place was an archaeologist's dream, reminding Ackerman of the multi-storied ruins of the Cliff Palace found at Mesa Verde National Park.

The ancient settlement was built in stair-stepped tiers, likely adhering to the natural formations of the rock. The passageway leading down to the temple exited onto the highest tier of the necropolis. The air here was so hot that it almost smelled burnt. He supposed it was due to some sort of natural current of air traveling up from the canyon beyond. The Cliff Palace at Mesa Verde was built to receive the sun in the winter. Although these structures were completely hidden from the sun, he supposed that the warm air flow more than compensated.

Ackerman held the Peacemaker out in front of him, hoping for the opportunity to use it on its owner. The pistol was better suited for close quarters combat, but now that he was in the open, he unslung the AK-47 that he had retrieved from one of the dead gunmen. Yazzie was armed with a submachine gun and two magazines of thirty rounds where

Ackerman had six in the revolver, a dozen shells on Yazzie's gun belt, and thirty in the assault rifle.

Being outgunned wasn't a concern, but Yazzie was also relatively uninjured, while Ackerman's wounds had reopened after the battle at Canyon's blockade and the hike into the hills. Now, he was again at the mercy of his mortal coil and realized that his body would soon start to shut down from blood loss. He was already feeling woozy, and his eyes were having trouble adjusting to the faint glow that shining in upon the city of the Old Ones.

As he traversed the prehistoric pathways, Ackerman had wondered why Yazzie hadn't simply turned the MP5 on them at the site of the sacrificial pit. The answer was of course that Yazzie was a forward-thinking tactician. When the first shot rang out, Yazzie seized his opportunity and then let the pieces fall where they may. If his men succeeded in killing his adversaries, problem solved. But what if they didn't?

Ackerman surmised that the Yazzie had seen enough demonstrations to realize that he and his brother were specialists in the field of not dying. With that in mind, Yazzie likely had a backup plan and a secondary ambush already set. Ackerman then determined that the exit of the tunnel would be the most likely place for Yazzie to set up camp and wait for someone to step into the light. The submachine gun that he now had in his possession would certainly make quick work of whoever was on the receiving end.

Now, standing a few feet back inside the tunnel to avoid Yazzie's aim, Ackerman tried to guess from which direction the attack would come, but without knowing the full layout he was most definitely at a disadvantage, while Yazzie likely knew every inch of these ruins that he had been visiting since he was a boy.

Still, Ackerman needed to verify his theory. So, removing his dry fit long-sleeve shirt, he slipped the AK-47 through one arm hole to the other. Then, with his makeshift scarecrow in place, he held the rifle by the butt, extended the shirt out in front of him, and started walking forward.

Yazzie, being armed with a submachine gun and not a sniper rifle, would likely be ready to open fire on the first figure who walked out of the exit. Or at least anyone who wasn't dressed in a pink shirt like his sister Reyna.

It wasn't long before he was rewarded with a series of holes being stitched through his black shirt.

Ackerman immediately pulled back to cover, having learned Yazzie's location. With this information in mind, he was able to approach the end of the tunnel without fear of attack from the opposite direction. Moving toward the opening, he called out, "That was my favorite shirt, captain. I regret to inform you that I will now have to end your life. Well, because of the shirt, and the fact that you kidnapped my little sister and shot my brother."

From the left of the tunnel's exit Yazzie called out, "My recently-deceased friend John thought you were the Coyote from Diné mythology."

"And what do you think? Do you believe me to be some sort of trickster god?"

"No, Mr. Ackerman. I believe you're a man. Flesh and blood. A man who's about to meet his end."

A chuckle formed in Ackerman's throat, and he was about to respond when he felt a disturbance on the dirt floor of the tunnel beneath him. Then, feeling something snap and tighten around his feet, he was yanked forward over the edge of the third tier and straight out of the tunnel.

107

As he flew through the air, Ackerman knew that he had less than a second to react to Yazzie's latest trap. The snare around his foot had been constructed from some type of nylon rope, which was attached to a weight, that Yazzie had concealed in the dirt of the tunnel's entrance. When Ackerman was in the proper position, Yazzie must've activated his trap by pushing the weighted end into the canyon.

The first object Ackerman struck on his way down was the sandstone roof of an Anasazi dwelling. He felt something snap with the impact. Luckily, the break was in his left arm, and so he was still able to pull his bone-handled Bowie knife from its sheath with his right. Using the abdominal muscles that he had worked so hard to maintain for just such an instance, he jerked his torso forward and plunged the knife into the ground in front of his feet, severing the rope and releasing his foot from the weight Yazzie had attached. By the time he was able to cut the rope, however, he had been dragged down to the lowest tier of the ruins.

His feet still tangled in Yazzie's snare, Ackerman rolled away, leaving his bone-handled bowie knife in the ground. As the world spun, he noticed a large piece of rock where the dome ceiling had broken off and landed halfway between the city of the dead and a precipice of unknown depth beyond the sheltered alcove.

As he moved, he heard the sound of automatic gunfire and felt the explosions in the dirt close by, but he kept rolling toward cover. As soon as he reached the relative safety of the fallen rocks, Ackerman pulled Yazzie's pistol and fired two shots in the general direction of his opponent.

Yazzie drove Ackerman down with a volley of his own and then called out, "They say it's bad luck to try to kill a man with his own gun."

Ackerman was feeling the weight of his injuries in many unsettling and unpleasant ways, and he really wasn't in the mood for chit chat. But he couldn't resist. And tactically, it always made sense to keep your enemy talking while you prepared your next attack. Ackerman yelled, "Who are they? And what right do they have to tell me what to do?"

Yazzie's voice seemed to come from a completely different part of the necropolis when he replied, "I suppose they, in this instance, would be the kind of people likely to kill someone else with their own gun. Someone like me or like you, Mr. Ackerman."

He wondered if he had lost consciousness for a second between his question and Yazzie's reply. His left arm had gone completely numb, and he was unable to move it. Glancing down, he saw a strange bulge on his upper arm that might have been a bone ready to poke through the skin. Ackerman considered setting the broken or dislocated bone himself, but he felt that such a sharp strike would likely cause unconsciousness, which would allow his adversary to get the better of him. Still, he feared that unconsciousness would soon take him either way. And that unconsciousness would likely result in his death.

Calling out to his opponent, Ackerman asked, "Where do you think we go when we die, Yazzie?"

Replying from an entirely different part of the ruins, Yazzie said, "According to whose god? From what I know of your white man's God, I would say the two of us will end up in Hell. But my people don't believe that way, and my god is lord over death."

"My God is the Lord of Lords and King of Kings and my final destination will have nothing to do with the things I've done in this life, but rather my faith and trust in Him."

"Everything comes back around. Your God will make you pay for every life you've taken, but mine, He Who Devours the World will repay me tenfold for every drop of blood I spill in his name."

Ackerman couldn't help but chuckle, which caused a racking cough. Paraphrasing scripture, he called out, "Greater is the one who is in me than he who devours the world."

"Every debt has to be paid, Mr. Ackerman. The devil always gets his due, and he'll be coming to collect from you real soon."

Ackerman replied, "My debt is already paid, my friend. I tell you what…you put your gun down, and I'll tell you all about it."

Yazzie responded by firing another volley of 9mm rounds in his direction. Ackerman had lost count of how many shots Yazzie had fired, which was very uncharacteristic for him. But he did recall that, true to form, his brother had taped an extra magazine on to the MP5's current magazine, which meant that Yazzie had at least sixty rounds and had fired nowhere near that many. In response, Ackerman fired two shots of his own and then slipped four fresh shells into the Peacemaker. He wished that he had kept hold of the AK-47 and his shirt, but he had lost them somewhere between the first and second tiers of the ruins.

Yazzie said, "Out in the world, you probably could've taken me easily. You're much faster and stronger than me. But not here. Here among the screams of the dead and the spirits of the Old Ones, here in the temple of my god, under the watchful eye of He Who Devours The World, I'm invincible."

Ackerman chuckled. "You just caught me on a bad day, friend."

Ackerman examined the wound in his side and found it seeping blood. His left arm felt like it had been severed and lay useless in the dirt of his small spot of concealment.

Firing another few rounds, Yazzie said, "It's time to die, Coyote."

Ackerman replied, "I've always thought of myself as more of a wolf. Or perhaps a lion. Great white shark. Any of those would be fine."

He then heard another voice, one coming from a man standing behind him near the drop off into the canyon below. Thomas White, or at least Ackerman's mental projection of him, said, "I've always thought of you as more of a hyena. Or maybe some sort of snake. Always crawling on your belly in the dirt."

Ackerman whispered, "Don't you start too."

His father continued, "You're about to die, Francis. Your body is shutting down. How sure are you about that final destination? Maybe you should just let me take control and finish this whole thing. I'm sure I could wring the last reserves of strength from you and save your miserable little life."

It even hurt for Ackerman to roll his eyes, the inside of the lids feeling as harsh as the desert floor. Ignoring his father and trying to keep Yazzie talking, Ackerman said, "Your god—with a little G—sounds like a bit of a douchebag, Yaz. No offense."

"That's the way of your people. You mock what you do not understand."

"My God—with a big G—is the God of love and creation. Yours seems to the lord of hatred and destruction. From what I know of your people, that doesn't seem to fit at all."

Yazzie said, "One day, all people will be of one mind and will be remade into the image of He Who Devours."

"He's merely a god of your own making, isn't he? A spiritual explanation for your every carnal desire."

"He came to me in a vision and chose me to be his emissary. To prepare the way on this plane." This time, Yazzie's reply came the first tier, growing closer and closer.

Ackerman squeezed off a shot in Yazzie's direction, warning him to stay back.

Yazzie's voice changed position again, and Ackerman wondered if it was really the captain moving around the ruins with such great speed or if his own senses were playing tricks on him. And was that a different caliber weapon? He couldn't be sure of anything now. He could barely stave off unconsciousness.

Yazzie said, "My people are dead. They just don't know it yet. Your government caged us and slowly eroded our spirits, but that wasn't enough. So they also left us to wonder every day how much longer before the radioactive materials from their uranium mines will result in cancers overtaking our bodies. For most of us, it's really not a question of if but when. I'm actually at the upper edge of my life expectancy now. I wouldn't be surprised if there's some sort of stage four tumor gestating in me as we speak. But soon, many of your people will also know what it's like to live on borrowed time."

"We're all living on borrowed time, my friend. And I'm not a fan of the government either. In fact, I've never paid taxes in my life."

"But you work for them?"

"No, I work with them. I work for myself."

"Your people killed generations of mine. And now, with the help of your belegana greed, I've repaid the favor."

Ackerman wasn't sure as to what Yazzie was referring, but at the moment, he had more pressing concerns. One of those concerns was the fact that Yazzie kept getting closer and closer, which likely meant that he was using his knowledge of the landscape to perform some sort of flanking maneuver. Ackerman's second most pressing concern was that he really wanted to take a nap. In fact, he desired sleep more than he ever had in his life.

The latter won out, and Ackerman allowed his head to fall to the dirt floor of the cavern, unconsciousness taking him in less than a second.

108

The blood in her veins had become like lava. She felt dead inside and yet more alive than ever. She was a heatseeking missile. She was on fire and full of adrenaline, and yet, she was also somehow detached, as if standing outside herself. Nothing felt real. Everything was accelerated and yet so crystal clear. She wondered if any of the recent events had even taken place. Had she imagined Marcus and Ackerman as well? Perhaps she was still down in the pit suffering the effects of carbon dioxide poisoning or dehydration.

Either way, whether this was real or imagined, Maggie was sure of two things.

The first was that Jamie Ramirez was truly her baby brother. The more she thought of his facial features, the more she now saw a grown-up version of the brother for whom she had spent her life searching. He was alive but wounded, still waiting for her to find him.

The second thing was that Xavier Yazzie needed to die.

In her right hand, Maggie held the Beretta pistol. In her left, the sharpened splinter of bone, which she intended to drive into Yazzie's neck. The only thoughts that could fill her mind, the only treatment for the wounds on her soul, was to find her brother and take the life of the Taker.

She followed the ancient corridors until the point where she saw a dim light and heard voices ahead.

The Anasazi ruins reminded Maggie of an amphitheater

or coliseum with the tiny dwellings shaped in a semi-circle around a central area. As she reached the third tier of the ruins, she saw that the performers for the day were Ackerman and the object of her hate, Yazzie.

Ackerman appeared to be passed out behind a pile of stones, and Yazzie was bent over him, removing his gun belt. Maggie sighted in with the Beretta, but it wasn't a great weapon for distance, and her hands were shaking so badly that she wasn't sure if she could make the shot from only a few yards away. She needed to get closer.

Finding the stone stairs, she descended, hoping that Ackerman was merely unconscious and not dead. She had nearly lost one brother to Yazzie. She didn't intend to lose her adopted brother as well.

But either way, Yazzie had to die.

She was reminded suddenly of a line from *Moby Dick*, which she hadn't read since high school. She had taken it on as a project, in order to prove to everyone how smart she was, but had ended up regretting that she hadn't chosen something short and fun like all the other girls had for their reports. Now, she recalled the way Melville had described Ahab's hatred for the legendary whale. "…as if his chest had been a mortar, he burst his hot heart's shell upon it."

She felt like Ahab now and could definitely relate to his bloodlust. Just like the white whale, Yazzie had taken too much. He had to be stopped, at any cost.

As she bounded down the stone stairs to reach the first tier of the dwellings, Maggie slid the sharpened bone shiv into the back pocket of her jeans, for easy access. She merely needed to get close enough. Truth be told, she didn't want to use the gun. She wanted to drive the sharpened splinter of bone into Yazzie's neck and watch as he bled out. She wondered if she would actually get to witness the moment when Yazzie's own personal demons showed up to drag him down to hell to meet his god.

109

As Maggie reached the first tier of the ruins, she tried to stay out of sight until the very last moment. And apparently, she had succeeded because Yazzie showed no reaction to her approach, which seemed strange for a man so cunning.

The rage pulsing through her veins pushed her forward despite the growing presence of an almost childlike fear of confronting what was to her the equivalent of the boogeyman. There hadn't been a day where she hadn't thought of Tommy and the man who stole him. The man with the black eyes. The man who made her realize that there were monsters in this world. The man who'd stolen her childhood and destroyed her family.

And now, she suspected that he had intentionally attempted to manipulate her into killing her own brother.

Facing away from her and standing over Ackerman's unconscious form, Yazzie slipped the gun belt through the loops of his pants. He had just begun to slide the leather through the buckle when Maggie raised a shaking arm and aimed the Beretta at center mass.

She debated on simply shooting him in the back, but she needed him to see it coming. She needed him to die on his knees and know exactly who had taken his life.

In a voice that was half rage and half determination, she screamed, "Put your hands on your head and turn around! Just give me a reason to end you!"

His eyes still on Ackerman, the faux police captain slowly placed his hands upon his head and turned to face her. Only after following her directions did he redirect his gaze. His eyes were no longer black as they had been on that day—Maggie having learned that the black eyes were the result of colored contacts—but now, his eyes were just as terrifying. She knew that he suffered from ocular albinism in one eye, a condition that resulted in a lack of pigment. But it still gave him a sense of being supernatural and otherworldly and again reduced her to the same trembling child she had been all those years ago.

Yazzie smiled and said, "Hello, little girl."

All of her muscles tensed, one side of her fighting to maintain her aim and one side wanting to curl up into a ball and cry. Rage and determination won the day. Keeping her aim true, she said, "Was it your plan that I would end up killing my own brother? Is that why you sent him up here to set your little traps?"

Yazzie cocked an eyebrow and said, "I certainly had my hopes that something along these lines would come to pass. But I've learned that one can merely calculate and then set events into motion. The results are often very different than what one originally intends. You just have to start the dominoes tumbling, sit back, and hope for a favorable outcome. But yes, in a perfect world, that's exactly how I hoped things would turn out."

"Well, you failed. He's still alive, probably hiding in the ruins or one of the tunnels. I'm going to find him. Right after I kill you and make sure that you won't hurt us, or anyone else, ever again."

Yazzie smiled and, looking behind her, said, "Shoot her, nephew."

Maggie's breath caught in her throat, but her aim didn't waver. The "what's that behind you" ruse might very well have been the oldest trick in the book. She remained frozen until, a few seconds later, a quiet voice said, "Drop the piece, lady."

Immediately recognizing the speaker, Maggie raised her hands but kept hold of the Beretta. She slowly turned around and laid eyes upon Jamie Ramirez, the man she now knew to be her long-lost brother. He held the same .30-06 hunting rifle that he had used to shoot Marcus, and she knew that, if she wasn't careful, he would use it on her as well.

"I said to shoot her, Jamie!"

Tears streaming down her cheeks, she said, "Your name is Jamie Ramirez now, but you weren't born with that name."

She could see in his eyes that he knew, that perhaps he had always known. She supposed that being abducted from your family and nearly sold off like a piece of cattle wasn't something a person easily forgot.

"Shoot her, or I will!"

"Let her speak, Uncle," Ramirez whispered.

"Your real name is Tommy Carlisle. This man took you from your home when you were a child. You had a sister. Her name was—"

"Maggie..." Ramirez interrupted, his grip on the rifle loosening and his own tears falling.

From behind her, Yazzie chuckled and said, "Little girl, you haven't changed a bit."

She looked over her shoulder just in time to see Yazzie

snatch up his Peacemaker with a speed that she had never witnessed firsthand. The gun seemed to materialize in his fist from thin air. Then she heard the shots and watched her brother stumble back, his eyes going lifeless and the rifle flying from his grasp.

A scream of primal fury rising in her throat, Maggie spun toward their attacker, reacquiring her target with the Beretta. But before she could even lower her arm, she heard the Peacemaker spit fire once more and felt a terrible pain in her right shoulder.

110

The report of a .45 caliber pistol awakened Ackerman from a dream about the bloodbath that was the Roman Coliseum. It took him a moment to register he was awake. But when he did, he realized that he needed to act as soon as possible. He immediately recognized the necessity of action because he had heard Maggie scream. Unfortunately, he was unable to move his limbs. For a moment, all he could manage was the opening of his eyes, which were filled with sand and grit.

Standing above him somewhere, he heard the voice of Thomas White. His father said, "You need to get up, or you're going to die. Francis, get up!"

Ackerman mumbled aloud, "Don't call me, Francis. What's it to you anyway? You hate me."

With the shake of his head, his father replied, "I am you!" Then, he reached up, and grabbing his face as if it were a rubber mask, he ripped the skin away to reveal the sinew and bone beneath. Leaning down to Ackerman's ear, the spectral projection said, "I am you...Frank, if that's what you prefer. If you don't act now, Yazzie is going to win. He is going to kill Maggie, make you watch, and then he's going to kill you. So, if you're planning something brilliant, now would be the time."

Ackerman nodded to the hallucination and said, "I'm

right, of course. But we have no weapons, nor the means to wield them."

He no longer knew whether he was awake and speaking aloud or if he was dreaming and merely thinking the words in his head, or any combination of the two. However, he was still certain that action needed to be taken.

Ackerman forced himself to sit up enough to see the commotion near the edge of the small cliff leading away from the ruins. Yazzie, gun in hand, stood over Maggie's prone form. When Yazzie spoke, it sounded to Ackerman as if they were underwater, Yazzie said, "Are you talking to yourself over there, Frank, or were you speaking to me?"

He didn't waste the energy in replying.

Ghost eyes filled with madness and malice, Yazzie smiled over at him and said, "Don't you go dying on me. Not yet. Not until you watch what I do to your friend."

Yazzie then closed the gap between himself and Maggie and pulled her up by her hair. Maggie screamed and clutched her wounded shoulder. Ackerman had noted the Beretta in the dust behind her, but it was too far out of his reach. He needed to act, but he wasn't sure what he could do. There was the garrote concealed in his watch, the push daggers, the Beretta, and the Bowie knife that he had left embedded in the ground after severing Yazzie's trap. But, when he looked for the knife, he was unable to find the spot where it stuck out from the dirt.

He supposed it didn't really matter. He didn't have the strength to brandish any of the weapons at his disposal. He barely had the strength left to keep his eyelids from falling.

Yazzie said, "Stay with me a few more moments now,

Frank." Then he dragged Maggie to the edge of the canyon where the stone floor met open air. Yazzie placed his pearl-handled Peacemaker against the side of her head and asked, "Which would be more cruel? To shoot her in the head before tossing her over the edge, or let her enjoy the fall?"

Ackerman raised a shaking arm and proclaimed, "I have a few last words."

Yazzie pressed the muzzle of the gun deeper into Maggie's flesh. Tears streamed down her cheeks. Her right arm hung lifeless at her side. The right side of her shirt was soaked in blood.

Yazzie said, "I'm curious enough by nature to hear what you have to say, but you had better make it quick."

Ackerman barely had the strength to speak, and his reasoning was beginning to blur. A rather larger part of himself was still unsure whether he was dreaming or awake. He declared, "I know how to be brought low, and I know how to abound. In any and every circumstance, I have learned the secret of facing plenty and hunger, abundance and need. I can do all things through him who strengthens me."

Yazzie looked at him strangely for second and then said, "Is that a quote from your white man's Bible?"

Ackerman replied, "Yes, I'm having a bit of trouble focusing right now and that was the first thing that came to mind."

"Are you trying to stall me for some reason, Mr. Ackerman?"

"Well, yes, I suppose I am. I've always found it best to stall in situations like this."

"Why is that?"

Frank shrugged. "Because something always happens. Marcus will save the day, or a brilliant idea will come to me at the last moment. Trust me, it will work out just fine. It always does."

Yazzie laughed. "I'm afraid, my friend, that there is a time when all of our debts come due, and things aren't going to work out for you this time. But better luck in your next life." Yazzie cocked back the hammer of his single action revolver and added to Maggie, "What about you, my dear? I suppose I owe you a few last words."

Maggie seemed to consider this a moment and then locked gazes with Ackerman. She said, "Tell your brother that my answer is yes. One hundred percent, yes. In another life."

Yazzie laughed and said, "My dear, why are you telling him? He'll be following you in death a moment later and your boyfriend is probably already on the other side. Now, since I have taken your entire family away from you twice in your life, it's only fair that I give you the choice. Would you prefer me to shoot you first or would you like to enjoy the ride down? I imagine that the fall wouldn't be entirely unpleasant."

Maggie winked at Ackerman, and in her eyes, he saw a cold determination. He knew that she was about to make a move, and based on the finality of her earlier comment, he surmised that it was going to be something drastic.

Now was his time to act.

While they had been conversing, Ackerman had been building up his strength and positioning one of the push daggers in his hand, readying it for a toss directly at Xavier Yazzie's eye.

He silently prayed, Lord, give me strength for one more moment.

Then, expending his finals reserves, Ackerman launched the push dagger from his fist.

The small blade sliced through the air with speed and precision, and thankfully, enough force to hit its mark. Unfortunately, either his vision or his aim had been slightly off, and instead of puncturing Yazzie's eye as he had intended, the push dagger sliced a long gash into his adversary's forehead and fell away. Yazzie instinctively released Maggie's hair and brought his left hand to his bleeding head as he turned the pistol's aim toward Ackerman.

This gave Maggie an opening, and from a hiding place that to Ackerman seemed like magic, she produced his bone-handled Bowie knife. With the knife in her left hand, she sliced Yazzie's forearm to the bone, the razor-sharp knife doing its job well. Yazzie wailed in agony and released his gun.

Ackerman lacked the strength to further join the fight, but perhaps he could crawl to the Beretta.

Digging deep for more power, he rolled over, but the effort exhausted him and caused the world to slide out of focus. In his dizzied senses, he looked up to see Maggie pounce upon Yazzie with the ferocity of a feral animal. In her left hand, she had some sort of weapon resembling an ice pick. With a savage scream, she stabbed Yazzie in the neck and drove him back over the edge into the open air. Riding him down, stabbing all the way, Maggie disappeared from Ackerman's view.

He heard her screaming fade in volume and then abruptly stop.

Rolling over and looking up at a stone sky, Ackerman prayed that this had all been a dream, but a strange and overwhelming emotion that cut deep into his soul told him that what had just transpired had been very real. He wondered if this feeling was what the normals experienced when they spoke of pain.

111

Marcus dreamed that he was back in his father's pit in Leavenworth, Kansas, the one in which he had been held, mostly in darkness, for the better part of a year. When he woke up, he found that reality was a far more frightening prospect. At least in the dream, he knew Maggie was out there somewhere safe. As he came to consciousness and surveyed his surroundings, Marcus's first thought was that he hadn't had the chance to ask Maggie to marry him. Now, looking at his bedside and not seeing her there sent a cold chill through the core of his body. He heard the usual beeps and whirs of medical machinery around him, the type that measured heart rate and pumped vital fluids. Even if he had woken up and been unable to see, he would've known he was in a hospital purely from the sound and that terrible antiseptic smell, one which was completely unnatural to him and which Maggie adored. The curtains around him were drawn, and so he couldn't see into the hallway or any of the beds. But he could tell by the ceiling that he was in an average hospital room. As he looked around, he dismissed his earlier fear of Maggie not being there. Now that he remembered the pain and the feeling of being so near to death he had felt after being shot, he supposed that he might've been resting for at least a day or two. Which meant that the explanation of her absence could have been as simple as her stepping out for a bite to eat.

Marcus blinked himself awake and wondered how long

he had been out. He didn't intend to call the nurse and ask, at least not before he got his bearings. And there was still a part of him that expected Maggie to walk through that door at any second. Last he had seen of her, she was alive and well. He had no reason to believe that she was in any other state than that now, but he felt more than knew that something wrong. A quiet discomfort that he couldn't quite explain filled his soul. He pushed himself up a little in bed, which rattled the frame and caused some beeping from a few of the machines.

At the sound, the curtain flew back and his brother appeared wearing his usual long-sleeved skintight black shirt, but he didn't look himself. Ackerman was always the epitome of confidence. His brother had once told him that he simply assumed he would come out on top in any given situation, and he considered that belief to be the very reason for his success.

The man before him now was disheveled with a hollow look in his eyes. Judging from the beard growth on Ackerman's face, Marcus quickly deduced that he had been out longer than a couple of days

Ackerman rushed forward and embraced him. Marcus returned the hug. Ackerman said, "I thought I was going to lose you too."

The words and their implication felt like the cold tip of a dagger piercing Marcus's heart. He asked, "Where's Maggie, Frank?"

"You've been out for almost three weeks, Marcus. You were in surgery for hours and—"

"Where is she, Frank?"

He could see the answer in Frank's eyes, but Marcus still

wanted to hear it. Ackerman redirected his gaze toward the floor, his face streaked with tears, and said, "I failed you, brother. I failed Maggie. I couldn't protect her."

"Are you saying that she's—"

"She's gone, Marcus. I'm so sorry."

Marcus gripped the handrails of the hospital bed for support, although he still felt like he was falling. He had felt grief before. He had felt pain before. He had faced death. He'd experienced the loss of people he loved, people who were friends, family. But he had never felt pain like this. The loss was so crushing, so total and final, that he felt like his heart was in a vice and his brain was on fire. He couldn't breathe. He couldn't think. Nothing seemed real. He wanted to break something. He wanted to hurt someone, to hurt himself. He didn't know what he wanted. He didn't know what to feel. He wanted to be angry, and yet the despair kept the rage at bay. He felt himself cycling the stages of grief. Anger, denial, etc. etc. He felt like he was going through a stage with every thought, with every breath. With every moment, the cold dagger twisted deeper into his heart.

Ackerman started to say something more, but Marcus interrupted, "Can I have a minute, please?"

"That's what I'm trying to tell you, brother. I'm not sure how much time they'll give you. And if we want to stage a little escape, now would be the time while they still believe you to be in a coma."

"Escape? What are you talking about?"

Ackerman sighed and pulled up a chair. He said "Where to begin? A lot's changed while you've been sleeping, and I'm afraid that you and I are in a spot of trouble."

112

Ackerman barely had time to explain the most basic of details to Marcus before the nurses noticed that their coma patient had awakened and the room was flooded with hospital staff. By the time they were done, Andrew Garrison and his new friend from the FBI had joined them.

Garrison had once been a member of Marcus's team but had recently been groomed by the Director for management. He had also once been Marcus's best friend, but the pair had grown apart of late. Mainly because of the secrets that Garrison now kept from Ackerman's brother. Ackerman wasn't sure how he felt about Garrison. The man had certainly been a good friend to Marcus, and yet Ackerman couldn't help but be bored to death by the man. The other suit who had followed Garrison into the room was a different story. Ackerman found him intensely interesting. FBI Deputy Director Samuel Carter was a handsome black man, maybe sixty years old, and he carried himself with a quiet confidence that spoke of years of dealing with life and death situations.

As the medical staff did their work, checked their machines, and asked their questions, the first thing that Marcus did was turn to Garrison and ask, "Where the hell was our backup?"

Garrison merely shook his head and replied, "Don't you dare try to put any of this on me. You knew the risks of going off on your own."

"There was a time when you would've done anything for Maggie as well."

Ackerman watched as Garrison visibly restrained himself. The man seemed to be an expert at pushing his anger down and also in putting up with his brother. After a few seconds, Garrison said, "I may not have loved Maggie in the same way that you did, but I still loved her like a sister. And I've known her a hell of a lot longer than you have."

Ackerman cleared his throat and said, "If I may interject a moment. This bickering is pointless. Neither of you are to blame. And us cannibalizing each other is not what Maggie would've wanted."

The room was silent a moment, and Ackerman added, "Why don't you introduce Marcus to our new friend?"

Deputy Director Carter stepped forward and was about to speak when a doctor poked his head in, noticed Marcus's agitation, and protested the questioning so soon after the patient waking up. Carter motioned with his eyes for Garrison to handle the doctor.

Then Deputy Director Carter smiled at Marcus and said, "I could really go for a cup of coffee. How about you?"

Marcus maintained his typical scowl and replied, "Coming at a man through his addictions is bad form."

Carter stepped to the doorway, just beyond which Garrison and the doctor were still arguing, and said to the doctor, "Hey Doc, could you round up a couple coffees?" The doctor had a few choice words for Deputy Director Carter and then stormed off. Returning to Marcus's bedside, Carter pulled up a chair, had a seat, and put his feet up on the bed beside Marcus.

Ackerman noted that Carter didn't ask if he wanted a cup of coffee. The fact that Carter knew that he didn't often partake and the fact his brother was a caffeine addict unsettled Ackerman.

Carter sighed and said, "You boys are a regular two-man wrecking crew. Within the space of twenty-four hours, you've declared war on a sovereign nation that exists inside our borders, killed and injured several people, and burned up millions upon millions of dollars in property damage. That's not to mention the kidnapping and theft, which don't seem to be all that bad when looking at the big picture."

Garrison returned with four cups of coffee, and the gesture toward Ackerman did not go unnoticed. Although, he still declined a cup, his body being a temple he didn't like to desecrate with highly addictive substances like caffeine. Although, he wasn't above using the drug on occasion when the situation required, but it wasn't a habit that he intended to maintain on a regular basis.

Removing the lid from his coffee and blowing the steam from the top, Carter said, "And I suppose you should know that me calling you Agent Williams is a professional courtesy, since you are technically no longer employed by the Department of Justice."

Marcus closed his eyes and seemed to be slightly shaking, like a volcano before eruption. He said, "I just woke up from a coma and found out the love of my life is dead, and before I can even process that information, you're gonna come at me with all this?"

Carter, taking a sip of his coffee and gently cursing himself for trying to drink it while it was too hot, said, "I apologize for the abruptness of our questioning, but there is a lot of political heat around this incident."

Marcus leaned up in bed, and the machines began to beep and whir faster. He said, "I don't play games, and politics is the most crooked game in town."

Ackerman interjected, "Brother,"—he laid a hand on Marcus's shoulder—"let him speak. If you don't, you'll just sit in here and be asking yourself all the same questions anyway. You might as well get the answers and then get some rest."

Garrison came around the bed and tried to hand Marcus a cup of coffee. Marcus looked at the proffered item as if he wanted to throw it Andrew's face, but then he apparently decided that he really could use a coffee and accepted the cup, his addictions winning out as they often seemed to do in the end when it came to the whole of humanity.

Garrison said, "The moment the Director died, I became the acting head of the Shepherd Organization, and my first act was to shutter the entire program and call for an investigation into some of the Director's past dealings. But don't worry, that part of things won't be a problem for either you."

Marcus scowled at his former best friend and said, "That's easy for you to say. I'm sure you've secured yourself a nice position with the FBI or another agency. You're always looking out for number one, aren't you Drew?"

Garrison turned his head and bit his tongue. Probably realizing that it was pointless to argue with Marcus, something that Ackerman had learned early on in their relationship.

Carter intervened by leaning forward, placing his styrofoam cup on Marcus's food tray, and saying, "This coffee is terrible." And then—returning to his chair and once again reclining his feet—he said, "I hope you don't mind, I have some foot problems, and it helps to recline them."

Marcus said nothing

Carter continued, "Let's cut to the chase. The only reason that you're not sitting in a prison hospital chained to the bed is the fact that you took down a monster like Xavier Yazzie."

"We didn't take down anyone. It was Maggie. Maggie took down Yazzie and Canyon and his whole operation, which was funded on the sale of stolen children."

"Well, that's the thing. Canyon was politically connected. If you'd only been responsible for his downfall, your own would've been inevitable. But as it turns out, your friend Yazzie was even worse than a serial killer. Not only was he kidnapping and murdering people and complicit in Canyon's illegal activities as a representative of the law, but through his connection with the casino, Yazzie was able to make special modifications to the south tower of the casino's hotel. He would then choose which guests would be placed there. I won't go into all the details, but let's just say that the water that came out of the pipes in the south tower came directly from a water source of the Navajo which was tainted by uranium mining. He also creatively worked in uranium dust and other small particulates that will likely result in forming cancer in all of those people years down the road. The only reason we know any of this is the fact that Yazzie had it set up that upon his death they would all get a letter explaining their impending doom and the reasons for it."

Marcus closed his eyes and shook his head at this new revelation.

Carter continued, "You can imagine the political shit storm surrounding this whole debacle. The situation is further complicated by the fact that your brother, Mr. Ackerman, is a non-entity. He's not supposed to exist, so there's no way to offer him up as a sacrificial lamb."

The implications hung in the air. Ackerman already knew all of this. He was the one who had brokered the deal that Carter was about to explain.

Marcus replied, "So... I'm the scapegoat."

Carter shrugged. "It's not as bad as it sounds. Thanks to your brother."

Marcus quickly turned toward him, but Ackerman laid a hand on his brother's shoulder and said, "Please continue, Deputy Director."

The look in Marcus's eyes was that of a man sensing he had been betrayed, and it cut Ackerman to his core. But he had expected this. And he still knew that it was for the best.

The FBI Deputy Director said, "We worked out a deal for you to quietly accept some charges under the table. You'll do a year of house arrest. Then some probation. I mean, damn kid, you had to have been expecting some kind of consequences."

Marcus cocked an eyebrow and replied, "I don't have a home. How are you going to put me on house arrest? I sleep on a futon in my office when we're not on the road, but we're always on the road. I figured why even have an apartment back there. I've got plenty of room at our station house to keep everything that I have."

Carter merely smiled and nodded. "I'm aware of all this. I was a bit surprised that you had merely cleaned out a storage room to act as your son's bedroom, but to each his own. However, if you recall, at one time you inherited a ranch in Asherton, Texas."

Marcus shook his head then said, "But that was all part of one of the Director's insane dramas. It's the property of the Shepherd Organization, not my own."

Carter shrugged and retrieved his coffee. He took a massive gulp of the liquid and choked it down with a grimace. He said, "I'm also a caffeine addict, Mr. Williams. And as far as anyone's concerned, that property is still in your name. I think it'd be a great place to raise a son, and your brother agrees with me. He's the one that came up with the idea."

Ackerman watched as Marcus's jaw clenched and his head twisted to the side, cracking his neck in the typical fashion when he was readying himself for a fight. Ackerman said, "You told me how much you love it there. The quiet. And Dylan loves it there as well."

Marcus and Maggie had visited the ranch several times since Marcus's recruitment into the Shepherd Organization. He had shared with Ackerman tales of the picnics the couple had with Dylan beneath an old oak tree overlooking a meadow. In making the deal that would secure the future of his family, Ackerman had felt that the ranch would be the perfect place for his brother to recover from their ordeal. He knew that his brother would also realize that this was the best move, in time.

Marcus rubbed the bridge of his nose and said, "So, I'm out of a job, and I'm on a year of house arrest."

Carter interjected, "Technically, you will be laid off from the DOJ, so you should be able to apply for other work. Of course, the charges that you'll be pleading to are still felonies, so finding work… Well, we can discuss all those details at a later date. You need to rest, but it was necessary to discuss some of this before your brother has to go off to his new life."

Ackerman narrowed his eyes at the Deputy Director. It seemed to him that Carter was playing this a bit more adversarially than was necessary. Maintaining his calm, Ackerman said, "I think our associate is being a bit dramatic, Marcus. You and Dylan will go live on the ranch, and in the meantime, I've agreed—in order to mitigate your charges— to work on some unsavory project that the Deputy Director has in mind."

Carter smiled and downed the rest of the coffee, causing him to wince. "It will be nothing unsavory, Mr. Ackerman. In fact, it might even be something rather righteous. Regardless, that's the long and short of it, Mr. Williams. You have a new life, you have a home for you and your son, and you will also receive a generous severance package from the remainder of the SO's funds. You'll be perfectly set up to start a new life. Unfortunately, that life will be without your brother. The two of you will not be allowed contact, for the foreseeable future."

Ackerman leaned forward, gripped the edge of Marcus's bed, and snarled, "That was never part of our arrangement."

Carter winked at Marcus and patted him on the leg, then

looking to Ackerman, he said, "I'm altering the deal. Pray I don't alter it any further."

Ackerman felt his own rage rising. "Are you having a senior moment, Samuel? You seem to be confused. This is happening because I allowed it. I could just as easily snap your neck and exfiltrate my brother from this hospital."

Carter smiled and said, "Now who's being dramatic? Mr. Williams, your brother wants you to be safe and secure. You and your son. This is the way that happens. Maybe, if your marginally-reformed serial killer of a brother does well, then he'll be able to join you on your ranch. His performance could also encourage me to allow some communication between the two of you. However, it's become apparent that you feed off each other, and the powers that be—and I'm sorry to say that this was a decision above my pay grade—have deemed that the two of you are too volatile to be together."

Carter then stood and, after ordering Garrison to leave, said, "If you do well, Mr. Ackerman, then we'll see what happens. As of now, I suggest that you say your goodbyes. Our flight leaves in an hour."

With that, the FBI Deputy Director turned and left the room.

Silence hung in the air for several seconds. Ackerman could feel his brother seething, the heat almost palpable, the rage almost creating a humming in the air.

Marcus finally said, "How dare you decide what's best for me and my son."

Ackerman rolled his eyes. "Oh, come now, brother. You should know better than to lecture me. I did what was best in the moment in order to keep our family alive. Carter talks a good game, but I've been around him enough to know that he's a good man. He'll try to blackmail me using you as leverage, but as he said, all of this will be based on my performance. And I'm confident that my capabilities in whatever task he has for me will so outweigh his expectations, that this whole matter will be cleaned up in a few short months. Consider it a vacation. You have to understand, Marcus, you were in a coma during this time. I made the decisions that I felt were best, and I hope that we've been through enough together that you would trust me to make some of those decisions in your stead."

Marcus placed a hand over his face, holding it there for a moment, and then wiped it across his eyes, smearing tears down his cheeks. He said, "I've lost Maggie, and now I'm going to lose you too."

"Nonsense. We'll be together within a matter of—"

Marcus cut him off. "You don't know how these people work, Frank. These clandestine organizations and worlds within worlds and bureaucracies within the shadowy corners of Washington. They're going to try to use you up and throw you away. Probably get you killed in the process. Tell me that you at least won't be working for the CIA."

Ackerman shook his head. "No, the FBI actually. Technically, I think that I'll be handling some sort of outlandish cases encountered by the BAU. They want to use my expertise on serial killers. Honestly, I'm not even sure if they're wanting to send me out into the field, or if they're just wanting to ask me questions and show me files. They want me to be the monster in the basement of Quantico."

His brother's tears fell again. This time, Marcus didn't try to wipe them away. "You know, I'm supposed to be the stable one, the one protecting you. Not the other way around."

Ackerman squeezed his brother's shoulder. "We're supposed to protect each other. That's what I've done. The circumstances may be less than ideal, but we simply must— as you always say—roll with the punches. This latest blow is certainly a difficult one, but we will overcome. Don't worry, brother. They're going to love me so much at the FBI that I'm sure we'll be back together in the blink of an eye."

113

Marcus Williams poured two fingers of vodka into his oversized Brooklyn PD coffee mug before filling it with black liquid and stepping onto the front porch of his South Texas ranch house. He almost spilled the coffee as Dylan shot around him, running awkwardly in a pair of rubber boats that came up to his knees. Marcus yelled after him, "Stay out of that dry creek bed. It can be like quicksand. And Dylan...be nice to the animals, if you find any."

Dylan rolled his eyes and said, "I know the Golden Rule, Dad."

As his son ran off on some imaginary adventure, Marcus wondered if knowing the Golden Rule was anywhere close to enough. He had so much that he wanted to teach his son, and so much he wanted to say, but it always seemed like the wrong time. It always seemed like Dylan wasn't ready to hear it. And so instead, Marcus did his best to help the boy to crawl before he walked or ran.

Once his son was out of sight, Marcus hiked his way into the meadow, past a field of flowers, and up to Maggie's tree, which sat alone on the tallest point of the property. Upon reaching the large oak tree, he dropped into the grass beside Maggie's tombstone and rested his arm atop the granite. The air smelled sweet and pure, the uncorrupted aromas of soil and vegetation. He had once sat in this same spot and considered the fragility of life after his aunt's death. That felt like a lifetime ago now.

Taking a sip of his coffee and looking out across the meadow, he said, "I've been thinking about building a new house right here. That way I don't have to walk so far to come see you. I mean, I know you're not actually here, but I guess I'm sentimental. I was thinking something kinda rustic, like a log cabin or maybe a proper ranch house. I don't know, but I've got quite a bit more time to work on it until I get this thing off my ankle… I haven't seen Frank since your memorial service. It's been almost six months now, and the only update I've received was a call from Deputy Director Carter where I basically only found out that he's still alive and doing well. To be honest, I'm pretty worried about him, Maggie."

Marcus thought back to his last interaction with his brother. It'd been on the same hillside as he was walking down to where they had arranged the cars. Ackerman's FBI escort waited impatiently for him beside a black sedan.

Ackerman hugged him tightly and whispered, "This too shall pass, my brother."

Marcus squeezed him back and said, "You once told me that you were the epitome of darkness, that you were the night. But I've come to see that, although you may have traveled as far down that road as a person could possibly go, it's a testimony to the light inside of you that you've overcome the darkness of this world. I'm proud of you, Frank."

Ackerman pulled away but kept hold of Marcus's shoulders. "I'm the same person. Just a new purpose and a new spirit."

Tears formed in Marcus's eyes. He said, "Just be careful and remember everything that I've taught you."

This made Ackerman's grin grow wide. "You know what the funny thing is, dear brother. You still think that you're the one looking out for me. But from your big brother, here's a little bit of advice. Get some rest. Don't worry about anything else. Take care of our boy and get some rest."

Now, sitting beside Maggie's tombstone, Marcus sipped his spiked coffee and continued aloud, "Maybe I shouldn't be worried about him. He is my big brother, after all. And he's definitely the toughest kid on the playground. If Ackerman was here, he'd probably quote a Bible verse at me about not being anxious about anything, but I can't help but worry. He's my brother and I love him. It's funny that he's really only been in my life for the past few years. Feels like he's always been there. It was the same with you."

Marcus choked on his own tears and was unable to speak for a moment. He took one last gulp of the coffee, sucking down a mouthful of grounds in the process. He didn't mind.

Standing up and looking down at the grave, Marcus noticed a few spots where some grass or other debris clung to the monument. He brushed them away and said, "As I look back on everything now, I thought that I was the hero. Well, maybe not a hero, but at least one of the good guys. But now, I wonder if I've been just as lost as any of them. I wonder if it was really me who saved Frank from a life as a serial killer or if it was Frank who saved me. And then I wonder if I'm saved at all. The Director always loved to quote that line about police officers being like shepherds keeping the wolves away. But maybe it's Ackerman who's been looking after us. Maybe we really were the little brother and little sister. Maybe we would've been better off listening to him more. And even saying that out loud, makes me think of you looking at me like I should get my head examined."

After he finished brushing away the debris, Marcus wiped away the last of his tears and looked down to the meadow where he planned to build his cabin. He said, "Dylan's growing like a weed. I want him to have a nice place to live. I think it'd be kinda cool for him to one day inherit something I actually built with my own two hands. And I know what you're thinking... I'm a city boy, and the only time I swing a hammer is when it's at somebody's head. But I think I can find a way to manage. Especially since I'm not a luddite like my brother, and so I know how to use YouTube."

As he examined the inscription on the stone, he whispered, "I'll see you tomorrow morning, Mrs. Williams."

Although the tombstone displayed the last name of Carlisle, Marcus knew that they were married in their hearts, and to have had her heart, even for a short time, was more than enough for him and much more than he deserved.

Before heading back to check on Dylan, Marcus studied the last two lines of the epitaph that had been etched into the granite of Maggie's tombstone. The first read, "Killed in the Line of Duty." The second displayed the words, Psalm 23:1, "The Lord is my shepherd; I shall not want."

114

The elevator bounced to a stop, and the door slid open onto the lowest level of a clandestine facility near Quantico, VA that now housed the FBI's famed Behavioral Analysis Unit. The air was thick with the smell of drywall dust clinging to warm copper piping. The ceilings were exposed conduits. The floors were concrete. Ackerman had come to enjoy the smell. He had come to call this place home.

Deputy Director Samuel Carter gestured for him to exit and said, "After you, Mr. Stine."

Ackerman had yet to acclimate to his new name, even though he had chosen it himself. He had insisted that they now call him Franklin Stine. He remembered the way Carter had rolled his eyes, but the old man had also known better than to fight him on it and that Ackerman's little joke was harmless. Although Carter had drawn the line at allowing him to call himself Dr. Franklin Stine.

He said, "Age before beauty."

Carter shrugged. "I suppose you are beautiful, in a predatory sort of way."

Ackerman cocked an eyebrow. "Is there any other kind of beauty?"

Stepping out of the elevator, Carter said, "All of the work you requested on your office is complete."

Ackerman fell in beside the senior agent.

Carter continued, "I agreed to the requests on your office

and on your name change. And don't forget that I also agreed to allow you to keep your scars as long as they stay properly covered. But I'm not sure on your plans for living quarters, especially with you having a dog down here."

Ackerman looked up and down the half-finished, half-concrete, all-dreary tunnel through which they were walking and said, "Do you truly believe Theodore is the only so-called animal down here? Honestly, Samuel, what's the situation with the decor? Do you have real people down here or am I the only one?"

Carter didn't break step. "You're not the only one. It's under renovation. It will be quite nice once it's done. Don't change the subject. I can't have you living out of your office."

"My brother did."

"That was a different world."

Ackerman said, "You're a very attractive man, Samuel. Do you hit the gym often? You appear to be in the physical condition of a man half your age."

Deputy Director Carter replied, "Yes, I do. Thank you for noticing. Now, back to the matter of your quarters. I can't have you living, working, showering, taking a dog on walks, and I don't know what all situations are gonna come up…but I can't have you living down here, Frank."

"There are ample showers in the gym. There's a cafeteria and other eating establishments within walking distance. And you need not worry about my associate, Theodore. He's quite well behaved and trained," Ackerman said, referring to the Shih Tzu that Emily Morgan had given to him before her departure from the Shepherd Organization.

Gesturing to their surroundings, he added, "Has Theodore caused a problem of some sort? Has someone down here in the dungeon complained?"

Carter turned the corner without breaking stride. "Don't be a smartass, kid."

"I mean if some of your other agents or assets are complaining that I have it too cushy, perhaps we can—"

Carter stopped and interrupted with, "What about that American Indian girl that keeps flying across the country to see you? Don't you think she would like to be able to meet up at a nice apartment with a kitchen and dining room?"

"She stays at a hotel, and I'm afraid that—even if I were to be here long enough to require living quarters for entertaining guests—she would find them neither comfortable nor accommodating. The hotel works out just fine."

Carter shook his head and raised his hands in surrender. Then, continuing down the concrete hallway, they reached a nondescript door that had once been a large storage room. Ackerman had converted it into his perfect living and working quarters. He noticed a newly-installed gold name plaque beside the door. "Franklin Stine" it said in large black letters embossed into the gold. Below that there was an inscription that read, "Abandon all hope, ye who enter here."

Ackerman grinned broadly and said, "Good work on the plaque. The second line is a quote from Dante's *Inferno*. I have a feeling that I'll smile every time I see it."

Carter said, "I hope you like your new office. I worked hard on it. Well, not really. I just passed your requests on to some asswipe junior agent and he did the rest, but I worked hard for many years to get to the point of having asswipe junior agents to do things for me, so..."

Ackerman opened the door and was immediately greeted by Theodore. He leaned down and rubbed the dog's ears. Then he began whispering affirmative sayings to his small companion. After the obligatory greeting, he stood back up and surveyed his new domicile. The walls were completely black, a special paint that he had requested. The floor was concrete beneath, able to support more weight than he would be able to load into the room, even with its ample size. Not that he planned to fill the space with anything besides what was already there: a stack of files, a bed for Theodore, and a litter box in the corner.

Carter cocked an eyebrow and said, "You trained him to go in that?"

"That's correct. Theodore defecates into the box for easier waste disposal."

The black and white Shih Tzu barked up at them. Ackerman looked down and said, "Yes, I know. You do an excellent job, sir."

A self-satisfied smile that Marcus—had he been present—would've described as a shit-eating grin sat on Carter's face. With a chuckle, Carter said, "I don't understand the carpet. I thought you preferred concrete."

"It's for Theodore's benefit. The bare floor hurts his paws, but as I see, you followed my instructions and the padding doesn't reach all the way to the edges."

The entire carpeted area was one large section, separated from the wall by two feet on every side. This allowed the carpet to easily be rolled up, if he so desired.

Ackerman said, "Well, everything seems to be in order.

So, if you don't mind, I've been running on fumes over the past week's investigation, and I would love to get some rest."

"You don't get off that easy," Carter said. "What about Agent Klein?"

"He was an idiot. I'm not sure how else to describe him. Skittish, perhaps. He was overly skittish. And I told you, I don't need a babysitter."

"Your partner is not there to babysit you, Frank. He's mainly there to help deflect the local authorities and all those people whom you refer to as 'normals.'"

"I appreciate the concern, but I do just fine on my own."

"It was part of the terms of our agreement. It's non-negotiable. And now, I'm going to have to find another agent to tag-along with you."

"You will, of course, do as you wish, Deputy Director."

"What about your brother and his boy? It's been a long time since they've heard from you. You sure you don't want to reach out?"

Ackerman tried not to think too often of his brother and nephew. There was work to be done, and the work he did ensured their safety. Matching Carter's gaze, he said, "It's not time yet. My brother coming into my life has been such a benefit to me that I often forget how much of a burden I've been to him. He belongs on that ranch, and I derailed his life and sent him on a rollercoaster ride of pain and despair. I thought that I could protect them and be with them, but I was wrong. I no longer desire those kinds of attachments and responsibilities."

Carter nodded his head and looked to the floor. "I understand where you're coming from, and I appreciate the dedication to your work, but family makes us stronger, not the other way around. And I've seen a lot of agents burn themselves out over the years by having nothing in their lives but work."

"I'm not an agent, and you've never encountered anyone quite like me."

"Yes, I would have to agree with you on that. The Man Without Fear. Once the evil doctor's monster, and now, you're the monster in the basement of Quantico. Is the real reason that you want to live here so that you can haunt the halls and perhaps intimidate some of your former pursuers?"

Ackerman smiled. "I don't keep a record of transgressions, my friend, but the normals do find me rather intimidating. Now, if we're done here, I would like to spend a few moments inside my mind and then drift into REM sleep."

Carter reached into his briefcase and removed a file. He said, "One last thing, if you're up to it before you turn in, take a look at this."

Ackerman glanced down at the proffered item and, with a raised eyebrow, said, "A new case so soon? It seems that the whole world has gone mad."

Carter said, "You're not wrong." Then, holding the file out farther, he asked, "Not up for the challenge?"

Snatching the file and sticking it under his arm, Ackerman smiled back at his new zookeeper and said, "Oh, Samuel, you know how it is… A true player is always looking for a good game."

ACKNOWLEDGMENTS

First of all, I want to thank my beautiful wife—Gina—and my children—James, Madison, and Calissa—for their love and support (especially Gina who has to endure a lot craziness in the name of research and put up with me in general).

Next, I wish to thank my parents, Leroy and Emily, for taking me to countless movies as a child and instilling in me a deep love of stories. Also, thank you to my mother, Emily, for always being my first beta reader and my mother-in-law, Karen, for being my best saleswoman.

As always, none of this would be possible without the help of my wonderful agents, Danny Baror and Heather Baror-Shapiro, my mentor and friend, Lou Aronica, my amazing assistant, Allison Maretti, and my social media guru, Colby Applegate. In addition, I wouldn't be here without the guidance and friendship of all my fellow authors at the International Thriller Writers organization.

To all those who have helped me along the way and to my extraordinary readers, thank you so much. I couldn't be living my dream without your support.

ABOUT THE AUTHOR

ETHAN CROSS's Ackerman thrillers are international bestsellers. Before becoming a full time writer, he was a computer programmer, a Chief Technology Officer and a Marketing Director for a New York publisher. He lives in Illinois with his wife, three kids, and two Shih Tzus.

@EthanCrossBooks www.ethancross.com

THE ACKERMAN THRILLERS

Marcus Williams and Francis Ackerman Jr. become unwilling pawns in a US government conspiracy.

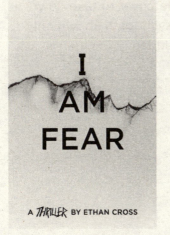

Francis Ackerman Jr. and special agent Marcus Williams confront 'the Anarchist', a killer who drugs and kidnaps victims before burning them alive.

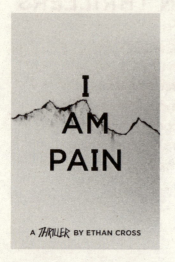

Special agent Marcus Williams and serial killer Francis Ackerman Jr. face their dark pasts as they hunt for 'the Coercion Killer'.

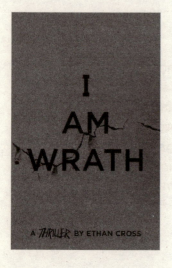

Francis Ackerman Jr. and Marcus Williams go undercover to take down a psychopath known only as 'Judas'.

I AM HATE

A *THRILLER* BY ETHAN CROSS

Marcus Williams and Francis Ackerman Jr. enter a modern-day coliseum and face a notorious contract killer called 'the Gladiator'.